taste of home
Mom's Best
made easy

luncheon pasta salad, page 102

26

99

130

taste of home

A TASTE OF HOME/READER'S DIGEST BOOK

© 2009 Reiman Media Group, Inc.
5400 S. 60th St., Greendale WI 53129
All rights reserved.

Taste of Home and Reader's Digest are registered trademarks of
The Reader's Digest Association, Inc.

"Timeless Recipes from Trusted Home Cooks" is a
registered trademark of Reiman Media Group, Inc.

Editor in Chief	Catherine Cassidy
Vice President, Executive Editor/Books	Heidi Reuter Lloyd
Creative Director	Ardyth Cope
Chief Marketing Officer	Lisa Karpinski
Food Director	Diane Werner RD
Senior Editor/Books	Mark Hagen
Art Director	Rudy Krochalk
Content Production Supervisor	Julie Wagner
Design Layout Artist	Emma Acevedo
Proofreaders	Linne Bruskewitz, Amy Glander
Recipe Asset System	Coleen Martin, Sue A. Jurack
Premedia Supervisor	Scott Berger
Recipe Testing & Editing	Taste of Home Test Kitchen
Food Photography	Taste of Home Photo Studio
Editorial Assistant	Barb Czysz
Editorial Intern	Danielle Calkins

THE READER'S DIGEST ASSOCIATION, INC.

President and Chief Executive Officer	Mary G. Berner
President, Food & Entertaining	Suzanne M. Grimes
SVP, Chief Marketing Officer	Amy J. Radin
President, Global Consumer Marketing	Dawn Zier

International Standard Book Number (10): 0-89821-768-7
International Standard Book Number (13): 978-0-89821-768-1
Library of Congress Control Number: 2009926639

For other Taste of Home books and products,
visit shoptasteofhome.com.

For more Reader's Digest products and information, visit
rd.com (in the United States)
or see rd.ca (in Canada).

COVER PHOTOGRAPHY

Photographer	Dan Roberts
Food Stylist	Kaitlyn Besasie
Senior Set Stylist	Jenny Bradley Vent

Pictured on front cover:
Country Fried Chicken (p. 71), Lemon-Pepper Green Beans (p. 116)
and Mashed Potatoes Supreme (p. 103).

Pictured on the back cover:
Italian Veggie Skillet (p. 101), Pizza in a Pot (p. 46) and
Peanut Butter 'n' Jelly Bars (p. 141).

Printed in China
1 3 5 7 9 10 8 6 4 2

mom's best made easy

table of contents

taste of home
Mom's Best
made easy

all of the comfort, **none of the fuss!**

Mom never had a problem setting a hot, hearty meal on the table. With today's busy weeknight schedules, however, few family cooks have time to prepare the favorite dishes their mothers created. But now, all that's about to change!

With *Mom's Best Made Easy*, re-creating those all-time classics is truly a breeze. Each of the 387 memory-making recipes found here comes together with less time, less work and less money than you'd expect.

Cheesy lasagnas, satisfying meat loaves, buttery breads, decadent desserts...you can prepare these specialties in a pinch. Just follow the effortless recipes in *Mom's Best Made Easy*.

You'll find that every dish relies on common kitchen staples you likely already have on hand. In addition, these traditional tastes take advantage of quick cooking methods and offer no-fuss, step-by-step directions.

Best of all, the recipes are shared by family cooks who know how to beat the kitchen clock. You can also take confidence in the fact that the dishes will turn out perfect every time because they've all been tested and approved by the Taste of Home Test Kitchen.

Mom's Best Made Easy is broken into nine chapters to help you quickly find the recipes you need.

MOM'S BEST BREAKFAST. Don't have time to make a breakfast like Mom? Think again! Thanks to convenience items and a few shortcuts, bringing eye-opening dishes to your table is simple.

MOM'S BEST SNACKS. With this collection of munchies and beverages, snack time couldn't be easier. Similarly, when you want a fast appetizer for guests or need a dish to pass at a party, this is the chapter to turn to.

MOM'S BEST MAIN COURSES. The timeless recipes found here make it simple to create cherished mealtime moments with your family. These memorable entrees have been simplified so you always have time to set a heartwarming main course on the table.

MOM'S BEST SIDE DISHES. With more than 50 dinner accompaniments to choose from, this chapter makes it a cinch to complete any supper-time lineup you have in mind. Turn here for vegetable dishes, soups, salads, breads and more.

MOM'S BEST DESSERTS. Wish you could bake like Mom but don't have the time? Check out this selection of effortless sweets. Whether you're craving a fruit pie, chocolate cake or crispy cookie, this chapter of no-fuss specialties has you covered.

MOM'S BEST 10-MINUTE DISHES. Beating the kitchen clock has never been as delightful as it is with these speedy bites. When you're tight on time, turn to these 28 recipes...each of which is table-ready in 10 minutes or less!

MOM'S BEST 30-MINUTE MEALS. Who says you can't serve a three-course meal in half an hour? Simply make any of the 16 complete suppers in this chapter. Each mouthwatering menu can be set on the table in a mere 30 minutes.

MOM'S BEST WEEKNIGHT MEALS. Don't let hurried weeknights stop you from enjoying dinner with loved ones; just peruse the ideas found here. Busy moms from coast to coast share the secrets behind 12 complete suppers they rely on during the hectic workweek.

MOM'S BEST HOLIDAY MENUS. Celebrating in style is easier than you might think. Whether you're hosting Christmas or Memorial Day, Easter Sunday or New Year's Eve, you can serve unforgettable holiday meals with only a fraction of the work but all of the flavor.

With *Mom's Best Made Easy*, you can satisfy your hungry bunch with all of the sensational tastes you remember enjoying at your mother's table. Bring those memories back to life with this handy cookbook, which makes it a snap to create a satisfying dinner...just like Mom's.

multigrain pancakes, page 14

breakfast

mom's best
breakfast

Nothing had the gang running to the kitchen like one of Mom's morning eye-openers. Now it's easier than ever to bring all of those glorious day-break dishes to your table...whether serving up breakfast before school or hosting a fun weekend brunch.

pear cooler, page 13

jack cheese oven omelet, page 8

ham 'n' cheese brunch strips, page 11

golden pancakes

golden pancakes

6	eggs
1	cup (8 ounces) cream-style cottage cheese
1/2	cup all-purpose flour
1/4	cup milk
1/4	cup canola oil
1/2	teaspoon vanilla extract
1/4	teaspoon salt

My mother made these delicious pancakes during the Depression. She beat the batter by hand, but I use my blender. It does a great job of breaking down the cottage cheese for a smoother batter.

—Ann Thomas, Telford, Pennsylvania

In a blender, combine all the ingredients; cover and process for 1 minute. Pour batter by 1/4 cupfuls onto a greased hot griddle; turn when bubbles form on top of pancakes. Cook until second side is golden brown. **YIELD: about 14 pancakes.**

jack cheese oven omelet

8	bacon strips, diced
4	green onions, sliced
8	eggs
1	cup milk
1/2	teaspoon seasoned salt
2-1/2	cups (10 ounces) shredded Monterey Jack cheese, *divided*

In a large skillet, cook bacon over medium heat until crisp. Using a slotted spoon, remove bacon to paper towels. Drain, reserving 1 tablespoon drippings. Saute onions in reserved drippings until tender; set aside.

In a large bowl, beat eggs. Add milk, seasoned salt, 2 cups cheese, bacon and sauteed onions. Transfer to a greased shallow 2-qt. baking dish. Bake, uncovered, at 350° for 35-40 minutes or until set. Sprinkle with remaining cheese. **YIELD: 6 servings.**

jack cheese oven omelet

Although it's easy, this omelet looks like you fussed. Sometimes I toss in mushrooms and cheddar cheese for a different flavor.

—Laurel Roberts, Vancouver, Washington

breakfast burritos

I steer clear of morning hunger without hitting the brakes at the drive-thru—I simply zap one of these frozen morning morsels in the microwave. This is my family's favorite combination, but try replacing the bacon with cooked breakfast sausage if you like.

—Audra Niederman, Aberdeen, South Dakota

breakfast burritos

12	bacon strips, diced
12	eggs, lightly beaten
Salt and pepper to taste	
10	flour tortillas (8 inches)

1-1/2	cups (6 ounces) shredded cheddar cheese
1/2	cup thinly sliced green onions

In a large skillet, cook bacon until crisp; remove to paper towels. Drain, reserving 1-2 tablespoons drippings. Add eggs, salt and pepper to drippings; cook and stir over medium heat until the eggs are completely set.

Spoon about 1/4 cup of egg mixture down the center of each tortilla; sprinkle with cheese, onions and reserved bacon. Fold bottom and sides of each tortilla over filling. Wrap each in waxed paper and aluminum foil. Freeze for up to 1 month.

To use frozen burritos: Remove foil. Place waxed paper-wrapped burritos on a microwave-safe plate. Microwave at 60% power for 1 to 1-1/2 minutes or until heated through. Let stand for 20 seconds. **YIELD: 10 burritos.**

editor's note: This recipe was tested in a 1,100-watt microwave.

breakfast pizza skillet

four-berry smoothies

This smoothie tastes even more scrumptious when I think of how much money I save by whipping up my own at home. As a breakfast, it keeps me satisfied and full of energy all morning. My husband and I appreciate the fact that it's nutritious, refreshing and fast.

—*Krista Johnson, Crosslake, Minnesota*

1-1/2	cups fat-free milk
1/2	cup frozen blackberries
1/2	cup frozen blueberries
1/2	cup frozen unsweetened raspberries
1/2	cup frozen unsweetened strawberries
2	tablespoons lemonade concentrate
1	tablespoon sugar
1/2	teaspoon vanilla extract

In a blender, combine all the ingredients. Cover and process until smooth. Pour into chilled glasses; serve immediately. **YIELD: 2 servings.**

breakfast pizza skillet

I found the recipe for this hearty stovetop dish several years ago and changed it to fit my family's tastes. When I served it at a Christmas brunch, it was an instant hit.

—*Marilyn Hash, Enumclaw, Washington*

1	pound bulk Italian sausage
5	cups frozen shredded hash brown potatoes
1/2	cup chopped onion
1/2	cup chopped green pepper
1/4	to 1/2 teaspoon salt
Pepper to taste	
1/2	cup sliced mushrooms
4	eggs, lightly beaten
1	medium tomato, thinly sliced
1	cup (4 ounces) shredded cheddar cheese
Sour cream and salsa, optional	

In a large skillet, cook sausage until no longer pink. Add the potatoes, onion, green pepper, salt and pepper. Cook over medium-high heat for 18-20 minutes or until the potatoes are browned.

Stir in mushrooms. Pour eggs over potato mixture. Arrange tomato slices on top. Sprinkle with cheese.

Cover and cook over medium-low heat for 10-15 minutes or until eggs are completely set (do not stir). Serve with sour cream and salsa if desired. **YIELD: 6 servings.**

four-berry smoothies

Spread mustard over four slices of bread. Layer each with a slice of cheese, ham and another cheese slice. Top with remaining bread.

Butter the outside of the sandwiches. In a large skillet over medium heat, toast sandwiches for 3-4 minutes on each side or until bread is lightly browned and cheese is melted. Remove to a cutting board; cut each sandwich lengthwise into thirds. **YIELD: 4 servings.**

baked oatmeal

My mom liked this recipe because it was quick and easy and made enough to fill up all seven of us hungry kids. Now I prepare it for my own family.

—Kathy Smith, Butler, Indiana

12	cups quick-cooking oats
2	cups sugar
2	cups packed brown sugar
4	teaspoons salt
2	teaspoons baking powder
4	cups milk
2	cups canola oil
8	eggs, lightly beaten

Additional milk

In a large bowl, combine the first eight ingredients. Pour into two greased 13-in. x 9-in. baking dishes. Bake, uncovered, at 350° for 30-35 minutes or until set. Serve with additional milk. **YIELD: 18 servings.**

ham 'n' cheese brunch strips

ham 'n' cheese brunch strips

These handheld sandwich strips pair well with scrambled eggs. Our home economists suggest substituting slices of cooked chicken or even turkey for the ham. Try them for a change-of-pace eye-opener.

2	tablespoons Dijon mustard
8	slices white bread, crusts removed
8	slices Swiss cheese
4	thin slices deli ham
2	tablespoons butter, softened

Kitchen Tip

Today's moms have to think quick when it comes to setting a breakfast on the table. After all, between getting little ones ready for school or day care and preparing themselves for work, there's little time left to fix breakfast. A bit of preparation, however, goes a long way when it comes to the most important meal of the day.

A batch of Ham 'n' Cheese Brunch Strips can be prepared ahead, individually wrapped and stored in the freezer. The tasty strips reheat well in the microwave for breakfast-on-the-go. Similarly, Baked Oatmeal can be made on the weekend, stored in the fridge and scooped into microwave-safe bowls for weekday breakfasts.

ham 'n' egg breakfast wrap

We raise chickens, so we always have lots of eggs to use up. I came up with this recipe for something different that can be served for breakfast or even dinner.

—Kathryn Martin, Quarryville, Pennsylvania

1-1/2	teaspoons butter
1	egg, lightly beaten
2	ounces thinly sliced deli ham, chopped
1	tablespoon chopped green pepper
1	tablespoon chopped onion
1	tablespoon salsa
1	tablespoon sour cream
1	flour tortilla (8 inches), warmed
2	tablespoons shredded cheddar cheese

In a small skillet, melt butter. Add egg; cook and stir over medium heat until completely set. Add the ham, green pepper, onion and salsa; cook until heated through. Spread sour cream over tortilla. Spoon filling over sour cream and sprinkle with cheese. Fold ends and sides over filling and roll up. YIELD: 1 serving.

ham 'n' egg breakfast wrap

cheddar french toast with dried fruit syrup

cheddar french toast with dried fruit syrup

My family loves this warm French toast on cold mornings in the North Carolina mountains where we take our yearly holiday. Each year, I alter the recipe slightly by experimenting with different dried fruits.

—Jackie Lintz, Cocoa Beach, Florida

1-1/2	cups maple syrup
1	package (8 ounces) dried fruit, diced
1/4	cup chopped walnuts
12	slices Italian *or* French bread (cut diagonally 1 inch thick)
1-1/3	cups shredded sharp cheddar cheese
4	eggs
2	cups milk
1/4	teaspoon salt

In a large bowl, combine the syrup, fruit and walnuts; cover and let stand overnight.

Cut a slit in the crust of each slice of bread to form a pocket. Stuff each pocket with 2 tablespoons cheese. In a large bowl, whisk the eggs, milk and salt; soak bread for 2 minutes per side. Cook on a greased hot griddle until golden brown on both sides. Serve with dried fruit syrup. YIELD: 6 servings.

country-style scrambled eggs

I added a little color and flavor to ordinary scrambled eggs with some green pepper, onion and red potatoes.

—Joyce Platfoot, Wapakoneta, Ohio

8	bacon strips, diced
2	cups diced red potatoes
1/2	cup chopped onion
1/2	cup chopped green pepper
8	eggs
1/4	cup milk
1	teaspoon salt
1/4	teaspoon pepper
1	cup (4 ounces) shredded cheddar cheese

In a large skillet, cook bacon over medium heat until crisp. Using a slotted spoon, remove to paper towels to drain. Cook and stir potatoes in drippings over medium heat for 12 minutes or until tender. Add onion and green pepper. Cook and stir for 3-4 minutes or until crisp-tender; drain. Stir in the reserved bacon.

In a large bowl, whisk the eggs, milk, salt and pepper; add to skillet. Cook and stir until eggs are completely set. Sprinkle with cheese and let stand until melted. **YIELD: 4 servings.**

country-style scrambled eggs

pear cooler

pear cooler

My daughter and I had eaten a cold fruit soup while on vacation. When we got home, we tried to create our own version—and wound up with this yummy smoothie. Everyone who tries it, enjoys it.

—Jeri Clayton, Sandy, Utah

1	can (15-1/4 ounces) sliced pears, undrained
2	cups ice cubes
1	envelope whipped topping mix
1/4	to 1/2 teaspoon vanilla *or* almond extract, optional

In a blender, combine all the ingredients; cover and process until smooth. Pour into chilled glasses; serve immediately. **YIELD: 3 servings.**

multigrain pancakes

My husband and I love foods prepared with whole grains, but our children prefer items such as white bread. So, I created this recipe to appeal to their love of pancakes while giving them a delicious taste of whole grain cooking.

—Ann Harris, Lancaster, California

multigrain pancakes

1/2 cup all-purpose flour	1/2 teaspoon salt
1/4 cup whole wheat flour	1 egg
1/4 cup cornmeal	1 cup buttermilk
2 tablespoons sugar	2 tablespoons butter, melted
1/2 teaspoon baking soda	Maple syrup

In a large bowl, combine the first six ingredients. In a small bowl, whisk the egg, buttermilk and butter. Stir into dry ingredients just until moistened.

Pour batter by 1/4 cupfuls onto a greased hot griddle; turn when bubbles form on top. Cook until the second side is golden brown. Serve with syrup. **YIELD: 8 pancakes.**

peach breakfast slush

> 1 can (15-1/4 ounces) sliced peaches, drained
> 1 can (6 ounces) frozen orange juice concentrate
> 1-1/2 cups apricot nectar
> 2 cups lemon-lime soda, chilled

In a blender, combine the peaches, orange juice concentrate and nectar; cover and process until smooth.

Pour into a freezer container; cover and freeze until firm. To serve, scoop 2/3 cup frozen mixture into a glass; add 1/3 cup soda. **YIELD: 6 servings.**

peach breakfast slush

This refreshing beverage is a favorite of mine to serve at our many brunch get-togethers. Because it's made ahead of time, I can avoid the last-minute rush before the guests arrive.

—Karen Hamilton, Ludington, Michigan

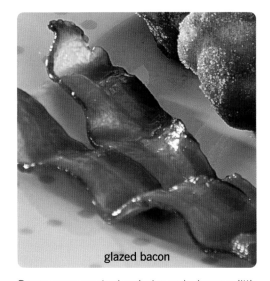

glazed bacon

Brown sugar, mustard and wine make bacon a little more special in this recipe. It's easy to prepare while working on the rest of the meal.

—Judith Dobson, Burlington, Wisconsin

glazed bacon

> 1 pound sliced bacon
> 1 cup packed brown sugar
> 1/4 cup white wine *or* unsweetened apple juice
> 2 tablespoons Dijon mustard

Place bacon on a rack in an ungreased 15-in. x 10-in. x 1-in. baking pan. Bake at 350° for 10 minutes; drain.

Combine the brown sugar, wine and mustard; drizzle half over bacon. Bake for 10 minutes. Turn bacon and drizzle with remaining glaze. Bake 10 minutes longer or until golden brown. Place bacon on waxed paper until set. Serve warm. **YIELD: 8 servings.**

deluxe ham omelet

Ham, vegetables and two cheeses are what makes this omelet deluxe. It's a hearty meal for one or two.

—Iola Egle, Bella Vista, Arkansas

1	tablespoon olive oil
3	eggs
2	tablespoons half-and-half cream
2	tablespoons minced chives
1/2	teaspoon garlic salt
1/4	teaspoon pepper
1/2	cup finely chopped fully cooked ham
2	tablespoons chopped green pepper
2	tablespoons chopped tomato
2	fresh mushrooms, sliced
2	tablespoons shredded cheddar cheese
2	tablespoons shredded part-skim mozzarella cheese

In a large nonstick skillet, heat oil over medium-high heat. Whisk the eggs, cream, chives, garlic salt and pepper. Add egg mixture to skillet (mixture should set immediately at edges).

As eggs set, push cooked edges toward the center, letting uncooked portion flow underneath. When the eggs are set, spoon the ham, green pepper, tomato and mushrooms over one side and sprinkle with cheeses; fold other side over filling. Invert omelet onto a plate to serve. **YIELD: 1-2 servings.**

bacon hash brown bake

About 15 years ago, a co-worker brought these rich potatoes to a potluck, and they were an instant hit. I've been bringing them to gatherings ever since. I usually start with frozen hash browns and bake the casserole for 40 to 50 minutes. Afterwards, I transfer the potatoes to a slow cooker to keep them warm while serving.

—Patricia Monahan, Smithfield, Rhode Island

1	package (3 ounces) crumbled cooked bacon
6	cups cooked shredded hash brown potatoes
1	cup mayonnaise
1/2	cup process cheese sauce

Set aside 1/4 cup bacon for topping. In a large bowl, combine the hash browns, mayonnaise, cheese sauce and remaining bacon.

Transfer to a greased 11-in. x 7-in. baking dish. Sprinkle with the reserved bacon. Bake, uncovered, at 350° for 20-25 minutes or until heated through. **YIELD: 6-8 servings.**

editor's note: Reduced-fat or fat-free mayonnaise is not recommended for this recipe.

Kitchen Tip

Get creative with Bacon Hash Brown Bake. Mix in some diced onion or green pepper, a can of chopped jalapenos or even cooked ground beef or pork sausage.

deluxe ham omelet

country brunch skillet

egg biscuit bake

Convenient refrigerated biscuits create a golden border around this all-in-one brunch dish. It's a variation of a simple egg-cheese combination my mother used to make. It's become our favorite comfort food.

—Alice Le Duc, Cedarburg, Wisconsin

1	can (5 ounces) evaporated milk
8	ounces process cheese (Velveeta), cubed
1	teaspoon prepared mustard
3/4	cup cubed fully cooked ham
1/2	cup frozen peas
2	tablespoons butter
10	eggs, lightly beaten
1	tube (12 ounces) refrigerated buttermilk biscuits

In a large saucepan, combine the milk, cheese and mustard; cook over low heat until smooth, stirring constantly. Stir in ham and peas.

Melt butter in a large skillet, heat butter until hot. Add eggs; cook and stir over medium heat until eggs are completely set. Add cheese sauce and stir gently.

Spoon into an ungreased shallow 2-qt. baking dish. Separate the biscuits and cut in half. Place with cut side down around outer edge of dish.

Bake, uncovered, at 375° for 15-20 minutes or until a knife inserted near the center comes out clean and the biscuits are golden brown. **YIELD: 4-6 servings.**

country brunch skillet

Frozen hash browns and packaged shredded cheese shave minutes off preparation of this skillet breakfast. It's an appealing meal-in-one that you can prepare in about 30 minutes flat.

—Elvira Brunnquell, Port Washington, Wisconsin

6	bacon strips
6	cups frozen cubed hash brown potatoes
3/4	cup chopped green pepper
1/2	cup chopped onion
1	teaspoon salt
1/4	teaspoon pepper
6	eggs
1/2	cup shredded cheddar cheese

In a large skillet, cook bacon over medium heat until crisp. Remove bacon; crumble and set aside. Drain, reserving 2 tablespoons of drippings. Add the potatoes, green pepper, onion, salt and pepper to drippings; cook and stir for 2 minutes. Cover and cook for about 15 minutes or until potatoes are browned and tender, stirring occasionally.

Make six wells in the potato mixture; break one egg into each well. Cover and cook on low heat for 8-10 minutes or until eggs are completely set. Sprinkle with cheese and bacon. **YIELD: 6 servings.**

egg biscuit bake

baked eggs and ham

overnight caramel french toast

Because this recipe can be prepared the night before, it's perfect to serve overnight guests. So it gives you extra time to visit over morning coffee.

—Denise Goedeken, Platte Center, Nebraska

1	cup packed brown sugar
1/2	cup butter
2	tablespoons light corn syrup
12	slices bread
1/4	cup sugar
1	teaspoon ground cinnamon, *divided*
6	eggs
1-1/2	cups milk
1	teaspoon vanilla extract

In a small saucepan, bring the brown sugar, butter and corn syrup to a boil over medium heat, stirring constantly. Remove from the heat. Pour into a greased 13-in. x 9-in. baking dish. Top with six slices of bread. Combine sugar and 1/2 teaspoon cinnamon; sprinkle half over the bread. Place remaining bread on top. Sprinkle with remaining cinnamon-sugar; set aside.

In a large bowl, whisk the eggs, milk, vanilla and remaining cinnamon. Pour over bread. Cover and refrigerate for 8 hours or overnight.

Remove from the refrigerator 30 minutes before baking. Bake, uncovered, at 350° for 30-35 minutes. YIELD: 6 servings.

baked eggs and ham

I give this single-serving dish Southwestern flair and zip by using cheese flavored with jalapeno peppers, but regular cheddar cheese also produces tasty results.

—Carolyn Crump, Center, Texas

1/4	cup seasoned croutons
2	tablespoons chopped fully cooked ham
1	tablespoon butter, melted
2	eggs
1	tablespoon shredded cheddar cheese

Fresh fruit, optional

In a greased shallow 2-cup baking dish, toss the croutons, ham and butter. Break the eggs carefully on top. Sprinkle with cheese. Bake, uncovered, at 350° for 15 to 18 minutes or until eggs reach desired doneness. Serve with fresh fruit if desired. YIELD: 1 serving.

Kitchen Tip

Mom likely added vanilla or almond extract to her French toast, but you can skip that step by replacing some of the milk called for in your recipe with flavored coffee creamer. Or, during the holidays, replace half of the milk with eggnog.

berry cream pancakes

The fresh strawberry filling adds a special touch to this classic buttermilk pancake recipe from our Test Kitchen. If you like, use your family's favorite berries for the strawberries. It's a wonderful dish for Mother's Day.

> 1 cup all-purpose flour
> 1 teaspoon sugar
> 3/4 teaspoon baking powder
> 1/2 teaspoon salt
> 1 egg
> 1 cup buttermilk
> 1 tablespoon butter, melted

CREAM FILLING:

> 1 package (8 ounces) cream cheese, softened
> 3/4 cup confectioners' sugar
> 1/2 teaspoon vanilla extract
> 3 cups sliced fresh strawberries

In a large bowl, combine the flour, sugar, baking powder and salt. In another bowl, whisk the egg, buttermilk and butter. Stir into the dry ingredients just until moistened.

Pour batter by 1/3 cupfuls onto a greased hot griddle; turn when bubbles form on top of pancakes. Cook until second side is golden brown.

Meanwhile, in a small bowl, beat the cream cheese, confectioners' sugar and vanilla until smooth. Spread down the center of each pancake; top with strawberries. Fold pancake over filling. **YIELD: 8-10 filled pancakes.**

berry cream pancakes

basic crepes

Our home economists suggest making this batter at least 30 minutes ahead so the flavor can absorb all the moisture before you start cooking the crepes.

> 1-1/2 cups milk
> 4 eggs
> 1 cup all-purpose flour
> 1-1/2 teaspoons sugar
> 1/8 teaspoon salt
> Butter

In a small bowl, combine the milk and eggs. Combine the flour, sugar and salt; add to the milk mixture and mix well. Cover and refrigerate for 1 hour.

Melt 1 teaspoon butter in an 8-in. nonstick skillet; pour 2 tablespoons batter into center of skillet. Lift and tilt pan to evenly coat bottom. Cook until top appears dry; turn and cook 15-20 seconds longer. Remove to a wire rack. Repeat with remaining batter, adding butter to skillet as needed. When cool, stack crepes with waxed paper or paper towels in between. **YIELD: 16 crepes.**

ham 'n' cheese omelet roll

This brunch dish has wonderful ingredients and an impressive look all rolled into one! I like hosting brunch, and this special omelet roll is one of my favorite items to prepare and share. A platter of these pretty swirled slices always disappears in no time.

—Nancy Daugherty, Cortland, Ohio

ham 'n' cheese omelet roll

4	ounces cream cheese, softened
3/4	cup milk
2	tablespoons all-purpose flour
1/4	teaspoon salt
12	eggs

2	tablespoons Dijon mustard
2-1/4	cups shredded cheddar cheese, *divided*
2	cups finely chopped fully cooked ham
1/2	cup thinly sliced green onions

Line the bottom and sides of a greased 15-in. x 10-in. x 1-in. baking pan with parchment paper; grease the paper and set aside.

In a small bowl, beat cream cheese and milk until smooth. Add flour and salt; mix until combined. In a large bowl, beat the eggs until blended. Add cream cheese mixture; mix well. Pour into prepared pan.

Bake at 375° for 30-35 minutes or until eggs are puffed and set. Remove from the oven. Immediately spread with mustard and sprinkle with 1 cup cheese. Sprinkle with ham, onions and 1 cup cheese.

Roll up from a short side, peeling parchment paper away while rolling. Sprinkle top of roll with the remaining cheese; bake 3-4 minutes longer or until cheese is melted. **YIELD: 12 servings.**

creamy orange drink

creamy orange drink

6   cups orange juice, *divided*
1/2 teaspoon vanilla extract
1   package (3.4 ounces) instant vanilla
    pudding mix
1   envelope whipped topping mix

In a small bowl, combine 3 cups orange juice, vanilla, and the pudding and whipped topping mixes; beat until smooth. Stir in remaining orange juice. Pour into chilled glasses; serve immediately. **YIELD: about 6 cups.**

This frothy orange sipper is a real treat as a snack or to quench your thirst on warm summer days. I love its combination of orange and cream.
—Julie Curfman, Chehalis, Washington

maple french toast bake

12 slices bread, cubed
1   package (8 ounces) cream cheese, cubed
8   eggs
1   cup milk
1/2 cup maple syrup
Additional maple syrup

Arrange half of the bread cubes in a greased shallow 2-qt. baking dish. Top with cream cheese and remaining bread. In a large bowl, whisk the eggs, milk and syrup; pour over bread. Cover and refrigerate overnight. Remove from the refrigerator 30 minutes before baking.

Cover and bake at 350° for 30 minutes. Uncover; bake 20-25 minutes longer or until golden brown. Serve with additional syrup. **YIELD: 8 servings.**

maple french toast bake

This yummy French toast casserole is ideal for busy mornings. Just whip it up the night before and bake the next morning. My family enjoys the richness it gets from the cream cheese and maple syrup.
—Cindy Steffen, Cedarburg, Wisconsin

sausage-stuffed mushrooms, page 39

snacks

mom's best snacks

Whether hosting a party or simply serving up after-school bites, Mom always had the best snack ideas at her fingertips. Take a look at this comforting collection of nibbles, munchies and beverages, and you'll see just how easy snack time can be!

creamy green onion spread, page 38

glazed meatballs, page 27

festive ham 'n' cheese spread, page 36

cinnamon raisin bread

cinnamon raisin bread

Slices of warm cinnamon bread and a cup of hot tea work wonders for visitors to our home. My mother received this recipe from a friend in West Virginia.

—Joan Ort, Milford, New Jersey

2	packages (1/4 ounce *each*) active dry yeast
2	cups warm water (110° to 115°)
1	cup sugar, *divided*
1/4	cup canola oil
3	teaspoons salt
2	eggs
6	to 6-1/2 cups all-purpose flour
1	cup raisins

Additional canola oil

3	teaspoons ground cinnamon

In a large bowl, dissolve yeast in warm water. Add 1/2 cup sugar, oil, salt, eggs and 4 cups flour. Beat until smooth. Stir in enough remaining flour to form a soft dough.

Turn onto a floured surface; knead until smooth and elastic, about 6-8 minutes. Place in a greased bowl, turning once to grease top. Cover and let rise in a warm place until doubled, about 1 hour.

Punch dough down. Turn onto a lightly floured surface; divide in half. Knead 1/2 cup raisins into each; roll each portion into a 15-in. x 9-in. rectangle. Brush with additional oil. Combine cinnamon and remaining sugar; sprinkle to within 1/2 in. of edges.

Tightly roll up, jelly-roll style, starting with a short side; pinch seam to seal. Place, seam side down, in two greased 9-in. x 5-in. loaf pans. Cover and let rise until doubled, about 30 minutes.

Brush with oil. Bake at 375° for 45-50 minutes or until golden brown. Remove from pans to wire racks to cool. **YIELD: 2 loaves (16 slices each).**

baked cheddar bacon spread

Parties at work just aren't the same without this deliciously rich spread.

—Kathy Fehr, Fairbury, Illinois

2	packages (8 ounces *each*) cream cheese, softened
2	cups (16 ounces) sour cream
1	medium onion, chopped
2	tablespoons mayonnaise
1	pound sliced bacon, cooked and crumbled
4	cups (16 ounces) shredded cheddar cheese, *divided*

Assorted crackers

In a large bowl, beat the cream cheese, sour cream, onion and mayonnaise until blended. Fold in bacon and 3 cups of cheddar cheese.

Transfer to a 2-qt. baking dish. Sprinkle with the remaining cheese. Bake, uncovered, at 375° for 30 minutes or until lightly browned. Serve with crackers. **YIELD: 7 cups.**

editor's note: Reduced-fat or fat-free mayonnaise is not recommended for this recipe.

peppery hush puppies

For our family, a good fish dinner just isn't complete without these zesty hush puppies. You can also serve them alone as a satisfying snack or as a side dish.

—Carolyn Griffin, Macon, Georgia

peppery hush puppies

2 cups cornmeal	2/3 cup water
1 cup plus 3 tablespoons all-purpose flour	1/2 cup buttermilk
2 teaspoons baking powder	1/2 cup butter, melted
1-1/2 teaspoons sugar	1 cup grated onion
1 teaspoon salt	2 jalapeno peppers, seeded and chopped
1/2 teaspoon baking soda	1 small green pepper, chopped
1 egg	Oil for deep-fat frying

In a large bowl, combine the cornmeal, flour, baking powder, sugar, salt and baking soda. In another bowl, whisk the egg, water, buttermilk and butter. Stir in the onion, jalapenos and green pepper. Stir into dry ingredients just until moistened.

In an electric skillet or deep-fat fryer, heat oil to 375°. Drop batter by teaspoonfuls, a few at a time, into hot oil. Fry until golden brown on both sides. Drain on paper towels. Serve warm. **YIELD: 6 dozen.**

editor's note: When cutting hot peppers, disposable gloves are recommended. Avoid touching your face.

ham and cheese calzones

This sort of inside-out pizza is something I concocted one evening when I had leftover baked ham and needed to fix a quick snack. My husband loved it—so did all his friends when he took some to work for lunch.

—Shelby Marino, Neptune Beach, Florida

2	**tubes (13.8 ounces** *each***) refrigerated pizza crust**
1	**cup ricotta cheese**
4	**to 6 ounces sliced pepperoni**
2	**cups diced fully cooked ham**
2	**cups (8 ounces) shredded part-skim mozzarella cheese**

Shredded Parmesan cheese, optional

Dried basil, optional

Meatless spaghetti sauce, warmed

Unroll one pizza crust on a greased baking sheet; roll out into a 14-in. x 11-in. rectangle. Spread half of ricotta lengthwise on half of the dough to within 1 in. of the edges.

Sprinkle with half of the pepperoni, ham and mozzarella. Fold dough over filling; press edges firmly to seal. Repeat with the remaining crust and the filling ingredients.

Bake at 400° for 20-25 minutes or until golden brown. Sprinkle with Parmesan and basil if desired. Cut into slices. Serve with spaghetti sauce. **YIELD: 2 calzones (7 servings each).**

ham and cheese calzones

chicken nuggets

With a crisp golden coating, these moist and tender bite-size pieces of chicken are greeted with enthusiasm whenever I serve them as a hearty snack or party appetizer.

—Cathryn White, Newark, Delaware

1	**cup dry bread crumbs**
1/2	**cup grated Parmesan cheese**
2	**teaspoons dried basil**
2	**teaspoons dried thyme**
2	**teaspoons paprika**
1	**teaspoon salt**
1	**teaspoon pepper**
3/4	**cup butter, melted**
2-1/2	**pounds boneless skinless chicken breasts, cut into 1-inch cubes**

In a shallow bowl, combine the bread crumbs, Parmesan cheese and seasonings. Place butter in another shallow bowl. Dip chicken in butter, then roll in bread crumb mixture.

Place in a greased 15-in. x 10-in. x 1-in. baking pan. Bake, uncovered, at 400° for 15-20 minutes or until chicken is no longer pink. **YIELD: 8 servings.**

glazed meatballs

glazed meatballs

Allspice adds a bit of a tasty twist to typical barbecue meatballs in this easy recipe.

—Nancy Horsburgh, Everett, Ontario

2	eggs
2/3	cup milk
1-1/4	cups soft bread crumbs
1	tablespoon prepared horseradish
1-1/2	pounds ground beef
1	cup water
1/2	cup chili sauce
1/2	cup ketchup
1/4	cup maple syrup
1/4	cup soy sauce
1-1/2	teaspoons ground allspice
1/2	teaspoon ground mustard

In a large bowl, beat eggs and milk. Stir in bread crumbs and horseradish. Crumble beef over mixture and mix well. Shape into 1-1/2-in. balls.

Place meatballs on a greased rack in a shallow baking pan. Bake at 375° for 15-20 minutes or until meat is no longer pink; drain.

In a large saucepan, combine the remaining ingredients. Bring to a boil; add the meatballs. Reduce heat; cover and simmer for 15 minutes or until heated through, stirring occasionally. **YIELD: about 3-1/2 dozen.**

lemon raspberry jumbo muffins

These are my favorite muffins because they can be made with blueberries instead of raspberries with the same delicious results.

—Carol Thoreson, Rockford, Illinois

2	cups all-purpose flour
1	cup sugar
3	teaspoons baking powder
1/2	teaspoon salt
2	eggs
1	cup half-and-half cream
1/2	cup canola oil
1	teaspoon lemon extract
1	cup fresh *or* frozen unsweetened raspberries

In a large bowl, combine the flour, sugar, baking powder and salt. In another bowl, whisk the eggs, cream, oil and extract. Stir into dry ingredients just until moistened. Fold in raspberries.

Fill greased jumbo muffin cups two-thirds full. Bake at 400° for 22-25 minutes or until a toothpick comes out clean. Cool for 5 min. before removing from pan to a wire rack. Serve warm. **YIELD: 8 jumbo muffins.**

editor's note: Sixteen regular-size muffin cups may be used; bake for 18-20 minutes If using frozen raspberries, do not thaw before adding to batter.

lemon raspberry jumbo muffins

apricot banana bread

1/3 cup butter, softened
2/3 cup sugar
2 eggs
1 cup mashed ripe bananas (2 to 3 medium)
1/4 cup buttermilk
1-1/4 cups all-purpose flour
1 teaspoon baking powder
1/2 teaspoon baking soda
1/2 teaspoon salt
1 cup 100% bran cereal (not flakes)
3/4 cup chopped dried apricots (about 6 ounces)
1/2 cup chopped walnuts

In a large bowl, cream butter and sugar until light and fluffy. Beat in eggs. Combine bananas and buttermilk. Combine the flour, baking powder, baking soda and salt; add to creamed mixture alternately with banana, beating well after each addition. Stir in bran, apricots and nuts.

Pour into a greased 9-in. x 5-in. loaf pan. Bake at 350° for 55-60 minutes or until a toothpick inserted near center comes out clean. Cool 10 minutes before removing from pan to a wire rack. **YIELD: 1 loaf (16 slices).**

apricot banana bread

This recipe gives a delightfully different twist to traditional banana bread. It tastes absolutely delicious spread with cream cheese or butter. When I take this bread to bake sales, it really goes fast. I also make it in small loaf pans to give as gifts.

—Betty Hull, Stoughton, Wisconsin

deviled eggs

6 hard-cooked eggs
2 tablespoons mayonnaise
1 teaspoon sugar
1 teaspoon white vinegar
1 teaspoon prepared mustard
1/2 teaspoon salt
Paprika

Slice eggs in half lengthwise; remove yolks and set whites aside. In a small bowl, mash yolks with a fork. Add the mayonnaise, sugar, vinegar, mustard and salt; mix well. Stuff or pipe into egg whites. Sprinkle with the paprika. Refrigerate until serving. **YIELD: 1 dozen.**

deviled eggs

For variety, you can use different ingredients in the filling in these creamy deviled eggs. Try green onions, a dash of hot sauce or make your own creation.

—Margaret Sanders, Indianapolis, Indiana

vegetable appetizer pizza

We love to serve this recipe from my sister at family get-togethers, and everyone just loves it. We're often asked to bring it to potlucks.

—Marcia Tiernan, Madrid, New York

---

4 tubes (8 ounces *each*) refrigerated crescent rolls

2 packages (8 ounces *each*) cream cheese, softened

2/3 cup mayonnaise

1 tablespoon dill weed

4 medium tomatoes, seeded and chopped

2 cups chopped fresh broccoli

3 green onions, thinly sliced

2 cups sliced fresh mushrooms

1/3 cup *each* chopped green pepper and chopped sweet red pepper

1 can (2-1/4 ounces) sliced ripe olives, drained

2 cups (8 ounces) shredded cheddar cheese

Unroll two tubes of crescent dough and press into each of two ungreased 15-in. x 10-in. x 1-in. baking pans; seal seams and perforations. Bake at 375° for 8-10 minutes or until lightly browned. Cool completely on a wire rack.

In a small bowl, beat the cream cheese, mayonnaise and dill until smooth. Spread over crusts.

vegetable appetizer pizza

Sprinkle with vegetables, olives and cheese. Cover and refrigerate for at least 1 hour. Cut into squares. Refrigerate leftovers. **YIELD: 4 dozen.**

trail mix snack

The salty peanuts and sweet raisins work well together in this tasty treat. It's a nice change from popcorn.

—Chris Kohler, Nelson, Wisconsin

---

1 jar (12 ounces) dry roasted peanuts

2 cups (12 ounces) semisweet chocolate chips

1-3/4 cups salted sunflower kernels

1-1/2 cups raisins

Combine all the ingredients in a large bowl. Store in an airtight container. **YIELD: 8 cups.**

sugared pecans

For a number of years, our neighbor gave us these wonderful treats at Christmas. I finally obtained the recipe and make them for others, too.

—Suzanne Brown, Blue Jay, California

---

1 egg white

1 tablespoon orange juice

3 cups pecan halves

1/2 cup sugar

1/2 teaspoon salt

1 teaspoon ground cinnamon

1/2 teaspoon ground nutmeg

1/2 teaspoon ground cloves

In a large bowl, beat egg white and orange juice until frothy. Add nuts; stir gently to coat. Combine the remaining ingredients. Add to nut mixture and stir gently to coat.

Spread onto a greased 15-in. x 10-in. x 1-in. baking pan. Bake, uncovered, at 300° for 30 minutes or until lightly browned, stirring every 10 minutes. Cool. Store in an airtight container. **YIELD: 3 cups.**

zesty marinated shrimp

These easy shrimp look impressive on a buffet table and taste even better! The zesty sauce has a wonderful spicy citrus flavor. I especially like this recipe because I can prepare it ahead of time.

—Mary Jane Guest, Alamosa, Colorado

zesty marinated shrimp

1/2 cup canola oil	1/2 teaspoon salt
1/2 cup lime juice	1/2 teaspoon dill weed
1/2 cup thinly sliced red onion	1/8 teaspoon hot pepper sauce
12 lemon slices	2 pounds medium shrimp, cooked, peeled and deveined
1 tablespoon minced fresh parsley	

In a large bowl, combine the first eight ingredients. Stir in shrimp. Cover and refrigerate for 4 hours, stirring occasionally. Drain before serving. **YIELD: 12 servings.**

salsa strips

1 tube (8 ounces) refrigerated crescent rolls
2 tablespoons Dijon mustard
3/4 cup salsa
1 cup (4 ounces) shredded part-skim
mozzarella cheese
Minced fresh cilantro

Unroll crescent roll dough and separate into four rectangles. Place on greased baking sheets. Spread mustard and salsa on each rectangle.

Bake at 350° for 10 minutes. Sprinkle with cheese; bake 8-10 minutes longer or until golden brown. Cool for 10 minutes. Cut each into four strips; sprinkle with cilantro. **YIELD: 16 appetizers.**

salsa strips

Refrigerated crescent rolls are the base to these crisp Southwestern appetizers. Choose mild, medium or hot salsa to suit your taste.

—Joann Woloszyn, Fredonia, New York

cucumber party sandwiches

cucumber party sandwiches

1 package (8 ounces) cream cheese, softened
2 tablespoons mayonnaise
2 teaspoons Italian salad dressing mix
30 slices snack rye bread
30 thin slices cucumber
Fresh dill sprigs and chive blossoms

In a large bowl, beat the cream cheese, mayonnaise and dressing mix until blended. Let stand for 30 minutes.

Spread on rye bread. Top each with a slice of cucumber, dill sprig and chive blossom. Cover and refrigerate until serving. **YIELD: 2-1/2 dozen.**

This is one of my favorite appetizers. We have lots of pig roasts here in Kentucky, and these small sandwiches are perfect to serve while the pig is roasting.

—Rebecca Rose, Mt. Washington, Kentucky

bacon cheddar muffins

bacon cheddar muffins

Cheddar cheese and bacon add hearty breakfast flavor to these tasty muffins. Calling for just six ingredients, they're quick to stir up and handy to eat on the run.

—*Suzanne Mckinley, Lyons, Georgia*

2	cups biscuit/baking mix
2/3	cup milk
1/4	cup canola oil
1	egg
1	cup (4 ounces) finely shredded sharp cheddar cheese
8	bacon strips, cooked and crumbled

In a large bowl, combine the biscuit mix, milk, oil and egg just until moistened. Fold in cheese and bacon. Fill greased muffin cups three-fourths full.

Bake at 375° for 20 minutes or until golden brown. Cool for 10 minutes; remove from pan to a wire rack. Refrigerate leftovers. **YIELD: about 1 dozen.**

easy egg rolls

I've always loved egg rolls, but every recipe I found seemed too complicated. So I decided to start with a packaged coleslaw mix. Now I can make these yummy treats at a moment's notice.

—*Samantha Dunn, Leesville, Louisiana*

1	pound ground beef, cooked and drained
1	package (16 ounces) coleslaw mix
2	tablespoons soy sauce
1/2	teaspoon garlic powder
1/4	teaspoon ground ginger

Onion powder to taste

40	egg roll wrappers
1	tablespoon all-purpose flour

Oil for frying

In a small bowl, combine the first six ingredients. Place a heaping tablespoonful of beef mixture in the center of one egg roll wrapper. (Keep remaining wrappers covered with a damp paper towel until ready to use.) Fold bottom corner over filling. Fold sides toward center over filling.

In a small bowl, combine flour and enough water to make a paste. Moisten top corner with paste; roll up tightly to seal. Repeat. In an electric skillet, heat 1 in. of oil to 375°. Fry egg rolls for 3-5 minutes or until golden brown. **YIELD: 40 egg rolls.**

triple cheese spread

Carrots add color and crunch, while a combination of cheeses gives great flavor to this spread. Best of all, it's lighter than other spreads.

—*Debbie Smith, Crossett, Arkansas*

1	cup (8 ounces) fat-free cottage cheese
1/2	cup shredded reduced-fat Swiss cheese
1/4	cup grated Parmesan cheese
2	tablespoons fat-free milk
1/2	teaspoon dill weed
1/8	teaspoon pepper
1/4	cup shredded carrot
1/4	cup unsalted sunflower kernels, optional

In a blender, combine the cheeses, milk, dill and pepper; cover and process until smooth. Transfer to a small bowl. Stir in carrot. Cover and refrigerate until chilled. Just before serving, stir in the sunflower kernels if desired. **YIELD: 1-3/4 cups.**

popcorn caramel crunch

For munching or gift-giving, this popcorn snack is chock-full of goodies. I like to store it in airtight containers to keep the popcorn crisp.

—Lucille Hermsmeyer, Scotia, Nebraska

4	cups popped popcorn
1	cup dry roasted peanuts
1	cup chow mein noodles
1/2	cup raisins
1	cup sugar
3/4	cup butter, cubed
1/2	cup light corn syrup
2	tablespoon water
1	teaspoon ground cinnamon

In a large greased bowl, combine the popcorn, peanuts, noodles and raisins; set aside.

In a large saucepan, combine the sugar, butter, corn syrup and water. Cook over medium heat, stirring occasionally, until mixture reaches soft-crack stage (270°-290°) with a candy thermometer. Remove from the heat. Stir in cinnamon.

Pour over the popcorn mixture; stir until evenly coated. Immediately pour onto a greased 15-in. x 10-in. x 1-in. pan.

popcorn caramel crunch

When cool enough to handle, break into pieces. Store in airtight containers. **YIELD: about 8 cups.**

editor's note: We recommend that you test your candy thermometer before each use by bringing water to a boil; the thermometer should read 212°. Adjust your recipe temperature up or down based on your test.

hot crab dip

This is great for a party because you can make it a day ahead and refrigerate it. Feel free to experiment with different cheeses to suit your tastes. You can also use nonfat ingredients for those watching their diets.

—Cammy Brittingham, Cambridge, Maryland

1	package (8 ounces) cream cheese
1/2	cup sour cream
2	tablespoons mayonnaise
1	teaspoon Worcestershire sauce
1/2	teaspoon seafood seasoning
1/2	teaspoon spicy brown mustard
1/2	teaspoon soy sauce
1/8	teaspoon garlic salt
2	cans (6 ounces *each*) crabmeat, drained, flaked and cartilage removed *or* 1/2 pound imitation crabmeat, flaked
1/3	cup plus 2 tablespoons shredded reduced-fat cheddar cheese, *divided*
1/3	cup plus 2 tablespoons shredded part-skim mozzarella cheese, *divided*

Melba rounds *or* crackers

In a large bowl, beat the cream cheese until smooth. Add the sour cream, mayonnaise, Worcestershire sauce, seafood seasoning, mustard, soy sauce and garlic salt; mix well. Stir in crab, 1/3 cup cheddar cheese and 1/3 cup mozzarella cheese.

Transfer to a greased shallow 1-qt. baking dish. Sprinkle with the remaining cheeses. Bake at 350° for 25-30 minutes or until bubbly around the edges. Serve warm with melba rounds or crackers. **YIELD: 2-1/2 cups.**

pumpkin bread

pumpkin bread

This is definitely a deliciously spicy, pumpkin-rich quick bread. I keep my freezer stocked with home-baked goodies like this winner.

—Joyce Jackson, Bridgetown, Nova Scotia

1-2/3	cups all-purpose flour
1-1/2	cups sugar
1	teaspoon baking soda
1	teaspoon ground cinnamon
3/4	teaspoon salt
1/2	teaspoon baking powder
1/2	teaspoon ground nutmeg
1/4	teaspoon ground cloves
2	eggs
1	cup canned pumpkin
1/2	cup canola oil
1/2	cup water
1/2	cup chopped walnuts
1/2	cup raisins, optional

In a large small bowl, combine flour, sugar, baking soda, cinnamon, salt, baking powder, nutmeg and cloves. In a small bowl, whisk the eggs, pumpkin, oil and water. Stir into dry ingredients just until moistened. Fold in walnuts and raisins if desired.

Pour into a greased 9-in. x 5-in. loaf pan. Bake at 350° for 65-70 minutes or until a toothpick inserted in the center comes out clean. Cool in the pan for 10 minutes before removing to a wire rack. YIELD: 1 loaf (16 slices).

sour cream blueberry muffins

When we were growing up, my mom made these warm, delicious muffins on chilly mornings. I'm now in college and enjoy baking them for friends.

—Tory Ross, Cincinnati, Ohio

2	cups biscuit/baking mix
3/4	cup plus 2 tablespoons sugar, *divided*
2	eggs
1	cup (8 ounces) sour cream
1	cup fresh *or* frozen blueberries

In a large bowl, combine biscuit mix and 3/4 cup sugar. In a small bowl, combine the eggs and sour cream; stir into the dry ingredients just until combined. Fold in blueberries.

Fill the greased muffin cups three-fourths full. Sprinkle with the remaining sugar. Bake at 375° for 20-25 minutes or until a toothpick inserted near the center comes out clean. Cool for 5 minutes before removing from pan to a wire rack. YIELD: 1 dozen.

editor's note: If using frozen blueberries, do not thaw before adding to batter.

sour cream blueberry muffins

easy stromboli

My family prefers this stromboli instead of ordinary pizza. Experiment with different filling ingredients to suit your family's tastes.

—Katie Troyer, Meadville, Pennsylvania

1	tablespoon active dry yeast
1	cup warm water (110° to 115°)
3	tablespoons vegetable oil
1/2	teaspoon salt
2-3/4	to 3-1/4 cups all-purpose flour
1	cup pizza sauce
1	pound bulk pork sausage, cooked and drained
1	can (4 ounces) mushroom stems and pieces, drained
1	package (3-1/2 ounces) sliced pepperoni
1	cup (4 ounces) shredded part-skim mozzarella cheese

In a large bowl, dissolve yeast in warm water. Add the oil, salt and 2 cups flour. Beat until smooth. Stir in enough remaining flour to form a soft dough.

Turn onto a floured surface; knead until smooth and elastic, about 6-8 minutes. Cover and let rest for 10 minutes. Turn onto a lightly floured surface; roll into a 14-in. x 12-in. rectangle.

Transfer to a greased 15-in. x 10-in. x 1-in. baking pan. Spoon pizza sauce to within 1/2 in. of edges. Top with the sausage, mushrooms, pepperoni and cheese. Roll up jelly-roll style, starting with a long side; pinch seam to seal and tuck ends under.

Bake stromboli at 400° for 30-35 minutes or until golden brown. Serve warm. Refrigerate leftovers. YIELD: 1 loaf.

cinnamon bread rolls

My aunt shared this recipe, which my children and I make assembly-line style. The kids love to help, and they now sure love to eat these creamy snacks.

—Cathy Stanfield, Bernie, Missouri

24	slices soft white sandwich bread, crusts removed
2	packages (8 ounces *each*) cream cheese, softened
1-1/2	cups sugar, *divided*
2	egg yolks
2	teaspoons ground cinnamon
1	cup butter, melted

Flatten bread with a rolling pin. In a large bowl, beat the cream cheese, 1/2 cup sugar and yolks. Spread on bread; roll up jelly-roll style.

Combine the cinnamon and remaining sugar. Lightly dip rolls in butter, then in cinnamon-sugar. Place on ungreased baking sheets. Bake at 350° for 20 minutes. YIELD: 2 dozen.

crunchy combo

My husband and our sons enjoy this mix any time of year. I love to munch on it at night. What's more, the snack carries well to gatherings and makes a nice present when packaged in pretty tins.

—Gloria Schmitz, Elkhart, Indiana

6	cups toasted oat cereal
1-1/2	cups miniature pretzels
1-1/2	cups Cheetos
1/2	cup butter, melted
1/4	cup grated Parmesan cheese
1/2	teaspoon garlic salt
1/2	teaspoon onion salt
1/2	teaspoon Italian seasoning, optional

In a large bowl, combine the cereal, pretzels and Cheetos. Combine the remaining ingredients; pour over cereal mixture and stir to coat. Spread into an ungreased 15-in. x 10-in. x 1-in. baking pan.

Bake at 275° for 30 minutes, stirring every 10 minutes. Cool. Store in an airtight container. YIELD: about 9 cups.

editor's note: This recipe was tested with Quaker Toasted Oatmeal Squares.

mexican pizza

mexican pizza

1 tube (8 ounces) refrigerated crescent rolls
2 cups thick, prepared chili
1/2 cup sliced ripe olives
1/4 cup chopped onion
3/4 cup shredded cheddar cheese
1/2 cup crushed corn chips
Avocado slices, shredded lettuce, chopped tomatoes *and/or* sour cream, optional

Unroll crescent roll dough; press onto the bottom and up the sides of an ungreased 13-in. x 9-in. baking pan. Press seams and perforations to seal. Bake at 400° for 10 minutes.

In a large bowl, combine the chili, olives and onion. Spread over crust. Sprinkle with cheese and corn chips. Bake 8-10 minutes longer or until bubbly. Garnish with avocado, lettuce, tomatoes and/or sour cream if desired. **YIELD: 6-8 servings.**

This quick and easy pizza will be the star of your appetizer buffet. It's packed with everyone's favorite Mexican food ingredients and finishes up leftover chili.

—Gail Reino, Franklinville, New York

festive ham 'n' cheese spread

2 packages (8 ounces *each*) cream cheese, softened
1/2 cup sour cream
2 tablespoons onion soup mix
1 cup chopped fully cooked ham
1 cup (4 ounces) shredded Swiss *or* cheddar cheese
1/4 cup minced fresh parsley
Assorted crackers

In a small bowl, beat the cream cheese, sour cream and soup mix until blended. Stir in ham and cheese. Form into a ball or spoon into a plastic wrap-lined mold. Roll in parsley. Refrigerate until serving. Serve with crackers. **YIELD: about 4 cups.**

festive ham 'n' cheese spread

My family goes wild over this mild-tasting, hearty cheese spread. Now they refuse to eat any store-bought varieties.

—Cara Flora, Olathe, Colorado

crispy chicken wing appetizers

If I can make these chicken wings, anybody can! The recipe came from a co-worker at the hospital where I am a nurse's aide. I make savory wings for holidays, picnics, softball parties...you name it. They're always a hit.

—Nancy Lesky, La Crosse, Wisconsin

crispy chicken wings appetizers

2	pounds chicken wings	2	tablespoons minced fresh parsley	
1/2	cup butter, melted			
1/4	teaspoon garlic powder	1/2	teaspoon salt	
1	cup dry bread crumbs	1/4	teaspoon pepper	
1/2	cup grated Parmesan cheese			

Cut chicken wings into three sections; discard wing tip sections.

In a small shallow bowl, combine butter and garlic powder. In another bowl, combine the remaining ingredients. Dip chicken into butter mixture, then into crumb mixture.

Place on greased baking sheet; bake at 350° for 50-60 minutes or until chicken juices run clear. **YIELD: 20 appetizers.**

editor's note: Uncooked chicken wing sections (wingettes) may be substituted for the whole chicken wings.

munchable snack mix

My family loves to take along individual bags of this colorful, fast-to-fix mixture when we go on long car trips. The sweet and salty flavors really work well together.

—Lisa Keylor, Louisville, Kentucky

1	package (16 ounces) M&M's
1	can (12 ounces) salted peanuts
1	package (11 ounces) butterscotch chips
2	cups raisins
1	cup cashews

In a large bowl, combine all the ingredients. Place in resealable plastic bags. **YIELD: about 10 cups.**

tropical fruit dip

This fruity dip is easy to prepare and so refreshing for summer get-togethers or brunches. The secret ingredient is the lemon-lime soda. It adds a little extra zing. Crushed pineapple and coconut extract bring a hint of the tropics to the smooth dip. Serve it with strawberries, grapes and bite-size melon pieces.

—Linda Venema, Fulton, Illinois

3/4	cup cold fat-free milk
2	tablespoons diet lemon-lime soda
1	can (8 ounces) crushed unsweetened pineapple, undrained
1/2	cup reduced-fat sour cream
2	drops coconut extract
1	package (1 ounce) sugar-free instant vanilla pudding mix

Assorted fruit

In a blender, combine the milk, soda, pineapple, sour cream, coconut extract and the pudding mix; cover and process until smooth. Cover and refrigerate for at least 1 hour. Serve with fruit. **YIELD: 2 cups.**

creamy green onion spread

creamy green onion spread

Pineapple is a delicious surprise in this simple spread, which is great on crackers. You can make it without pineapple for a more traditional flavor, but once you've tried it with the fruit, you won't go back.

—Sue Seymour, Valatie, New York

1	package (8 ounces) cream cheese, softened
2	tablespoons milk
2	green onions with tops, chopped
1/4	cup crushed pineapple, drained, optional

Crackers

In a small bowl, beat cream cheese and milk until smooth. Stir in onions and pineapple if desired. Serve with crackers. **YIELD: 1 cup.**

sausage-stuffed mushrooms

A few years back, I was looking for a snack that would suit my family's tastes. I combined three different recipes and came up with this one. We love the rich Parmesan.

—Kathy Deezik, Hartstown, Pennsylvania

20	to 24 large fresh mushrooms
2	tablespoons finely chopped onion
2	to 3 garlic cloves, minced
1	tablespoon butter
1/4	pound bulk pork sausage, cooked, crumbled and drained
3	tablespoons seasoned bread crumbs
3	tablespoons grated Parmesan cheese
1	tablespoon dried parsley flakes
1	egg white

Remove mushroom stems from caps. Set caps aside (discard stems or save for another use). In a small skillet, saute onion and garlic in butter until tender.

In a bowl, combine the sausage, bread crumbs, Parmesan, parsley and egg white. Stir in onion mixture. Fill the mushroom caps; place in a lightly greased 15-in. x 10-in. x 1-in. baking pan.

Bake at 350° for 10-15 minutes or until the mushrooms are tender and tops are browned. **YIELD: about 2 dozen.**

sausage-stuffed mushrooms

zucchini chip bread

zucchini chip bread

Mild orange-flavored loaves packed with chocolate chips, nuts and spices make for a super treat. This bread is quick to stir up, yet it looks like you spent hours in the kitchen.

—Edie DeSpain, Logan, Utah

3	cups all-purpose flour
2	cups sugar
1	teaspoon *each* baking soda and salt
1	teaspoon ground nutmeg
1/2	teaspoon ground cinnamon
1/4	teaspoon baking powder
3	eggs
1/2	cup unsweetened applesauce
1/2	cup canola oil
1	tablespoon grated orange peel
2	teaspoons vanilla extract
2	cups shredded zucchini
1	cup chopped walnuts
1	cup (6 ounces) semisweet chocolate chips

In a large bowl, combine flour, sugar, baking soda, salt, nutmeg, cinnamon and baking powder. In another bowl, whisk the eggs, applesauce, oil, orange peel and vanilla. Stir into dry ingredients just until moistened. Fold in zucchini, nuts and chocolate chips. Transfer to two greased 8-in. x 4-in. loaf pans.

Bake at 350° for 55-60 minutes or until a toothpick inserted near the center comes out clean. Cool for 10 minutes before removing from pans to wire racks to cool completely. **YIELD: 2 loaves (16 slices each).**

cucumber dill spread

For a delightfully different way to serve refreshing cucumbers, try this recipe. The creamy spread is so good on a hot summer day served with an assortment of fresh vegetables or reduced-fat crackers.

—Doris Heath, Franklin, North Carolina

- 2 **packages (8 ounces *each*) cream cheese, softened**
- 2 **teaspoons lemon juice**
- 2 **teaspoons finely chopped onion**
- 1/2 **teaspoon dill weed**
- 1/4 **teaspoon prepared horseradish**

Dash hot pepper sauce

- 3/4 **cup finely diced seeded cucumber**

Assorted crackers *or* assorted fresh vegetables

In a large bowl, beat cream cheese until smooth. Add the lemon juice, onion, dill, horseradish and pepper sauce. Fold in cucumber. Cover and chill for at least 1 hour. Serve with crackers or fresh vegetables. **YIELD: 2-1/3 cups.**

cucumber dill spread

old-fashioned popcorn balls

Popcorn always make a crowd-pleasing snack...but you can make it into a chewy, sweet treat with this classic recipe. It's so easy.

—American Pop Corn Co., Sioux City, Iowa

- 2 **quarts popped popcorn**
- 1 **cup sugar**
- 1/3 **cup light *or* dark corn syrup**
- 1/3 **cup water**
- 1/4 **cup butter**
- 1/2 **teaspoon salt**
- 1 **teaspoon vanilla extract**

Place popcorn in a baking pan and keep warm in a 200° oven. Meanwhile, in a large saucepan, stir together the sugar, corn syrup, water, butter and salt. Cook over medium heat, stirring constantly, until mixture comes to a boil.

Continue cooking without stirring until the temperature reaches 270° on a candy thermometer. Remove from the heat. Add vanilla; stir just enough to mix. Slowly pour over the popcorn. Cool just enough to handle. Shape with buttered hands. **YIELD: 1 dozen.**

editor's note: We recommend that you test your candy thermometer before each use by bringing water to a boil; the thermometer should read 212°. Adjust your recipe temperature up or down based on your test.

Kitchen Tip

Candy thermometers may seem a bit intimidating at first, but the simple devices are a cinch to use...and save time in the end. Pick one up at a kitchen supply shop, and be sure it features a clip that secures it to the side of the pan.

beef 'n' cheese tortillas

1/2 cup garlic-herb cheese spread
4 flour tortillas (10 inches)
3/4 pound thinly sliced cooked roast beef
20 to 25 whole spinach leaves
11 to 12 sweet banana peppers

Spread about 2 tablespoons of the cheese spread over each tortilla. Layer with the roast beef and spinach. Remove the seeds from peppers and slice into thin strips; arrange over spinach. Roll up each tortilla tightly; wrap in plastic wrap. Refrigerate until ready to serve. **YIELD: 4 servings.**

beef 'n' cheese tortillas

I like to take these hearty snacks along on our many outings. They can be made in advance and don't get soggy. You'll appreciate the convenience...your family and friends will love the great taste!

—Myra Innes, Auburn, Kansas

lemon poppy seed bread

lemon poppy seed bread

1 package (18-1/4 ounces) white cake mix
1 package (3.4 ounces) instant lemon pudding mix
1 cup warm water
4 eggs
1/2 cup canola oil
4 teaspoons poppy seeds

In a large bowl, combine the cake mix, pudding mix, water, eggs and oil; beat on low speed for 30 seconds. Beat on medium for 2 minutes. Fold in poppy seeds.

Pour into two greased 9-in. x 5-in. loaf pans. Bake at 350° for 35-40 minutes or until a toothpick inserted near the center comes out clean. Cool in the pans for 10 minutes before removing to a wire rack. **YIELD: 2 loaves (16 slices each).**

If the days that you have time for baking are few and far between, try this extra-quick bread. You'll love the ease of preparation and the delicious flavor.

—Karen Dougherty, Freeport, Illinois

chicken noodle casserole, page 47

main courses

mom's best
main courses

Nothing brings back memories like the aroma of an entree that Mom lovingly prepared. Now you can re-create those favorites for your family. The classics in this chapter have been simplified so you always have time to set a heartwarming dish on the table.

chicken potpie, page 60

quick tater tot bake, page 75

meatball sub sandwiches, page 77

fillets with mushroom sauce

Grilled tenderloin steaks get an extra special treatment with the onion, mushroom and tomato sauce in this recipe. The sauce can be whipped up while the meat is on the grill for a quick main dish.

—Carolyn Brinkmeyer, Aurora, Colorado

fillets with mushroom sauce

4	beef tenderloin fillets (4 ounces *each*)
1	large onion, cut into 1/2-inch slices
1/2	pound fresh mushrooms, thickly sliced
2	tablespoons butter
1	can (14-1/2 ounces) diced tomatoes, undrained
1/4	cup water
1/2	teaspoon dried basil
1/2	teaspoon beef bouillon granules
1/8	teaspoon pepper

Grill fillets, covered, over medium heat for 6-9 minutes on each side or until meat reaches desired doneness (for medium-rare, a meat thermometer should read 145°; medium, 160°; well-done, 170°).

Meanwhile, in a large skillet, saute onion and mushrooms in butter until tender. Stir in the tomatoes, water, basil, bouillon and pepper. Bring to a boil; cook and stir over medium heat for 5 minutes or until thickened. Serve with beef. **YIELD: 4 servings.**

slow 'n' easy chili

1/2	pound ground beef, cooked and drained
1/2	pound bulk pork sausage, cooked and drained
1	can (28 ounces) crushed tomatoes
1	can (15 ounces) chili beans, undrained
1	can (10-3/4 ounces) condensed tomato soup, undiluted
1	large onion, chopped
2	envelopes chili seasoning

Shredded cheddar cheese, optional

In a 3-qt. slow cooker, combine the first seven ingredients. Cover and cook on low for 6-8 hours or until thickened and heated through, stirring occasionally. Garnish with cheese if desired. **YIELD: 6-8 servings.**

slow 'n' easy chili

What's nice about this recipe is that you can add any extras (such as chopped bell peppers or sliced fresh mushrooms) to make your own specialty. I only get the best reviews when I serve it.

—Ginny Puckett, Lutz, Florida

sauerkraut casserole

Mom brewed her own sauerkraut and, of course, the cabbage was from our big farm garden! Blending the kraut with spicy sausage and apples was Mom's favorite way to fix it. I still love this country dish. —Rosemary Pryor, Pasadena, Maryland

sauerkraut casserole

1 **pound mild Italian sausage links, cut into 1-inch slices**

1 **large onion, chopped**

2 **medium apples, peeled and quartered**

1 **can (27 ounces) sauerkraut, rinsed and well drained**

1 **cup water**

1/2 **cup packed brown sugar**

2 **teaspoons caraway seeds**

In a large skillet, cook sausage and onion over medium heat until sausage is no longer pink and onion is tender; drain. Stir in the apples, sauerkraut, water, brown sugar and caraway seeds.

Transfer to a 2-1/2-qt. baking dish. Cover and bake at 350° for 1 hour. **YIELD: 6-8 servings.**

pizza in a pot

With warm breadsticks or garlic toast on the side, this is one dinner I know my family will always enjoy. If you'd like, substitute 1/2 pound bulk Italian sausage for the pepperoni. Simply cook it along with the ground beef, green pepper and onion.

—Dianna Cline, Philippi, West Virginia

1-1/2	pounds ground beef
1	medium green pepper, chopped
1	medium onion, chopped
1	can (15 ounces) tomato sauce
1	jar (14 ounces) pizza sauce
2	tablespoons tomato paste
3	cups spiral pasta, cooked and drained
2	packages (3-1/2 ounces *each*) sliced pepperoni
2	cups (8 ounces) shredded part-skim mozzarella cheese

In a large skillet, cook the beef, green pepper and onion over medium heat until meat is no longer pink; drain. Stir in the tomato sauce, pizza sauce and tomato paste.

In a 5-qt. slow cooker, layer the pasta, beef mixture, pepperoni and cheese. Cover and cook on low for 3-4 hours or until heated through. **YIELD: 8 servings.**

pizza in a pot

salmon in lime sauce

salmon in lime sauce

I marinate salmon and vegetables in a pleasant lime mixture, then tuck individual portions into foil packets. I like to serve them with grilled skewers of corn-on-the-cob rounds, mushrooms and cherry tomatoes.

—Helen Vail, Glenside, Pennsylvania

1-1/3	cups lime juice
1/4	cup canola oil
1	teaspoon grated lime peel
1/2	teaspoon cayenne pepper
4	salmon fillets (6 ounces *each*)
1	small tomato, chopped
1	small sweet red pepper, chopped
2	green onions, thinly sliced

In a small bowl, combine the first four ingredients. Pour half of the marinade into a large resealable plastic bag; add the salmon. Seal bag and turn to coat. Add the tomato, pepper and onions to remaining marinade; refrigerate fish and vegetables for 30 minutes.

Drain and discard marinade from fish and vegetables. Place each salmon fillet and about 1/3 cup vegetable mixture on a double thickness of heavy-duty foil (about 18 in. square). Fold foil around mixture and seal tightly.

Grill, covered, over medium heat for 15-20 minutes or until fish flakes easily with a fork. Open carefully to allow steam to escape. **YIELD: 4 servings.**

chicken noodle casserole

This tasty dish gets even better after it's been refrigerated a day or two, so the leftovers are always great. We eat it hot in the winter and cold in the summer.

—Cheryl Watts, Natural Bridge, Virginia

1	package (16 ounces) egg noodles
1	medium sweet red pepper, chopped
1	large onion, chopped
1	celery rib, chopped
2	garlic cloves, minced
1/4	cup butter, cubed
1-1/2	cups sliced fresh mushrooms
3	tablespoons all-purpose flour
3	cups chicken broth
3	cups half-and-half cream
2	packages (8 ounces *each*) cream cheese, cubed
12	cups cubed cooked chicken
1	to 1-1/2 teaspoons salt

TOPPING:

1	cup finely crushed cornflakes
2	tablespoons butter, melted
1	tablespoon vegetable oil
3	tablespoons minced fresh parsley
1/2	teaspoon paprika

chicken noodle casserole

Cook noodles according to package directions; drain. In a large skillet, saute the red pepper, onion, celery and garlic in butter until tender. Add mushrooms; cook 1-2 minutes longer or until tender. Remove vegetables with a slotted spoon; set aside.

Add flour to the skillet; stir until blended. Gradually add broth. Bring to a boil; cook and stir for 2 minutes or until thickened. Reduce heat. Gradually stir in cream. Add the cream cheese; cook and stir until cheese is melted. Remove from the heat.

In a large bowl, combine the chicken, salt, noodles, vegetables and cheese sauce. Transfer to two ungreased shallow 3-qt. baking dishes.

Combine topping ingredients. Sprinkle over top. Cover and bake at 350° for 20 minutes. Uncover; bake 15-20 minutes longer or until hot and bubbly. **YIELD: 2 casseroles (8-10 servings each).**

simple sloppy joes

My mom and I had fun creating this recipe together. My daughter could eat these sandwiches every day. It's a good thing the recipe makes a big batch!

—Ona Allen, Huber Heights, Ohio

2	pounds ground beef
1	large onion, chopped
2	garlic cloves, minced
1	can (8 ounces) tomato sauce
1	can (6 ounces) tomato paste
1/2	cup ketchup
1/3	cup packed brown sugar
3	tablespoons soy sauce
12	hamburger buns, split and toasted

In a large skillet, cook the beef, onion and garlic over medium heat until meat is no longer pink; drain. Stir in the tomato sauce and paste, ketchup, brown sugar and soy sauce.

Bring to a boil. Reduce heat; cover and simmer for 15-20 minutes, stirring occasionally. Spoon about 1/2 cup meat mixture onto each bun. **YIELD: 12 servings.**

busy day beef stew

busy day beef stew

Here's a classic, old-fashioned beef stew that simmers for hours in the slow cooker. I call it my "lazy" stew because it's so easy to make on busy days.

—Beth Wyatt, Paris, Kentucky

1   boneless beef chuck roast (1 to 1-1/2 pounds)
1   envelope onion soup mix
2   teaspoons browning sauce, optional
1/2 teaspoon salt
1/2 teaspoon pepper
6   cups water
2   cups cubed peeled potatoes (1/2-inch pieces)
6   to 8 medium carrots, cut into chunks
1   medium onion, chopped
1   cup frozen peas, thawed
1   cup frozen corn, thawed, optional
5   tablespoons cornstarch
6   tablespoons cold water

Place roast in a 5-qt. slow cooker; sprinkle with soup mix, browning sauce if desired, salt and pepper. Pour water over meat. Cover and cook on low for 8 hours.

Remove roast to a cutting board; let stand for 5 minutes. Add vegetables to slow cooker. Cube beef and return to slow cooker. Cover and cook on low for 1-1/2 hours or until vegetables are tender.

Combine cornstarch and cold water until smooth; stir into stew. Cover and cook on high for 30-45 minutes or until thickened. **YIELD: 8-10 servings.**

grilled salmon fillet

Growing up on a family-owned resort, I was expected to help around the kitchen. Grilling salmon became my specialty.
      —Paul Noetzel, Grafton, Wisconsin

1   salmon fillet (about 1 pound)
2   tablespoons lemon juice
2   tablespoons red wine vinegar
2   teaspoons grated lemon peel
1-1/2 teaspoons dried basil
1   teaspoon garlic powder
1   teaspoon soy sauce
4-1/2 teaspoons grated Parmesan cheese
Dash pepper

Place fish, skin side down, in disposable foil pan. Combine the lemon juice, vinegar, lemon peel, basil, garlic powder and soy sauce; pour over fish. Sprinkle with Parmesan cheese and pepper.

Place pan on grill. Cover grill and cook over medium heat for 15-20 minutes or until fish flakes easily with a fork. **YIELD: 4 servings.**

grilled salmon fillet

hearty burritos

hearty burritos

These beyond-compare burritos are chock-full of tasty in-gredients and frozen individually, so you can bake only as many as needed.

—Janelle McEachern, Riverside, California

1/2	pound ground beef
1	large green pepper, chopped
1	medium onion, chopped
1	package (16 ounces) frozen cubed hash brown potatoes, thawed
1	can (15 ounces) black beans, rinsed and drained
1	can (14-1/2 ounces) Mexican diced tomatoes, undrained
1	cup frozen corn, thawed
1/2	cup salsa
1/2	cup cooked rice
2	teaspoons chili powder
1/2	teaspoon salt
2	cups (8 ounces) shredded cheddar cheese
8	flour tortillas (10 inches), warmed

Sour cream, chopped tomatoes, guacamole, additional shredded cheddar cheese and salsa, optional

In a large skillet, cook the beef, green pepper and onion over medium heat until meat is no longer pink; drain. Add the potatoes, beans, tomatoes, corn, salsa, rice, chili powder and salt. Sprinkle 1/4 cup cheese off-center on each tortilla; top with about 1 cup beef mixture. Fold sides and ends over filling.

Wrap burritos individually in foil and freeze for up to 3 months. Or place burritos seam side down on a baking sheet.

Bake at 350° for 25 minutes or until heated through. Serve with sour cream, tomatoes, gua-camole, additional cheese and salsa if desired.

To use frozen burritos: Thaw in the refrigerator overnight. Bake and serve as directed. **YIELD: 8 burritos.**

breaded pork chops

These traditional pork chops have a wonderful home-cooked flavor like the ones Mom used to make. The breading makes them crispy outside and tender and juicy inside. Why not treat your family to them tonight?

—Deborah Amrine, Grand Haven, Michigan

1	egg, lightly beaten
1/2	cup milk
1-1/2	cups crushed saltines
6	boneless pork loin chops (1 inch thick and 4 ounces *each*)
1/4	cup canola oil

In a shallow bowl, combine egg and milk. Place cracker crumbs in another shallow bowl. Dip each pork chop in egg mixture, then coat with cracker crumbs, patting to make a thick coating.

In a large skillet, cook chops in oil for 8-10 minutes on each side or until meat is no longer pink. **YIELD: 6 servings.**

breaded pork chops

chicken tetrazzini

This is my revised version of a recipe a friend shared with me more than 35 years ago. It's nice to give to friends who don't cook much. —Helen McPhee, Savoy, Illinois

chicken tetrazzini

1   package (12 ounces) spaghetti

1/3   cup butter, cubed

1/3   cup all-purpose flour

3/4   teaspoon salt

1/4   teaspoon white pepper

1   can (14-1/2 ounces) chicken broth

1-1/2   cups half-and-half cream

1   cup heavy whipping cream

4   cups cubed cooked chicken

3   cans (4 ounces *each*) mushroom stems and pieces, drained

1   jar (4 ounces) sliced pimientos, drained

1/2   cup grated Parmesan cheese

Cook spaghetti according to package directions. Meanwhile, in a Dutch oven, melt butter. Stir in the flour, salt and pepper until smooth. Gradually add the broth, half-and-half and whipping cream. Bring to a boil; cook and stir for 2 minutes or until thickened.

Remove from the heat. Stir in the chicken, mushrooms and pimientos. Drain spaghetti; add to the chicken mixture and toss to coat.

Transfer to two greased 11-in. x 7-in. baking dishes. Sprinkle with Parmesan cheese. Cover and freeze one casserole for up to 2 months. Bake the second casserole, uncovered, at 350° for 20-25 minutes or until heated through.

To use frozen casserole: Thaw in the refrigerator overnight. Cover and bake at 350° for 30 minutes. Uncover; bake 15-20 minutes longer or until heated through. Stir before serving. **YIELD: 2 casseroles (3-4 servings each).**

grilled pork roast

2/3 cup canola oil
1/3 cup soy sauce
1/4 cup red wine vinegar
2 tablespoons lemon juice
2 tablespoons Worcestershire sauce
2 garlic cloves, minced
1 to 2 tablespoons ground mustard
1 to 2 teaspoons pepper
1 teaspoon salt
1 boneless pork loin roast (2-1/2 to 3 pounds)

grilled pork roast

In a large resealable plastic bag, combine the first nine ingredients; add pork. Seal bag and turn to coat. Refrigerate overnight.

Prepare grill for indirect heat. Drain and discard marinade. Grill roast, covered, over indirect heat for 1-1/2 hours or until a meat thermometer reads 160°. Let stand for 10 minutes before slicing. **YIELD: 8 servings.**

We enjoy the mild mustard flavor of this juicy, tender pork roast. With a little advance preparation, this roast is simple since it creates no dirty dishes, and I get the rest of the meal ready while it cooks.

—Myra Innes, Auburn, Kansas

honey lemon schnitzel

honey lemon schnitzel

2 tablespoons all-purpose flour
1/2 teaspoon salt
1/2 teaspoon pepper
4 pork sirloin cutlets (4 ounces *each*)
2 tablespoons butter
1/4 cup lemon juice
1/4 cup honey

In a large resealable plastic bag, combine the flour, salt and pepper. Add pork, two pieces at a time, and shake to coat. In a large skillet, cook pork in butter over medium heat for 3-4 minutes on each side or until juices run clear. Remove and keep warm.

Add lemon juice and honey to the skillet; cook and stir for 3 minutes or until thickened. Return pork to pan; cook 2-3 minutes longer or until heated through. **YIELD: 4 servings.**

These pork cutlets are coated in a sweet sauce with honey, lemon juice and butter. They're certainly good enough for company, but perfect for a quick, weeknight meal, too. Very seldom are there any leftovers.

—Carole Fraser, North York, Ontario

italian spaghetti and meatballs

This is an authentic Italian recipe. It was given to me by my cousin's wife, who is from Italy. It's so hearty, everyone's eyes light up when I tell my family that we're having this for supper!

—Etta Winter, Pavillion, New York

2	cans (28 ounces *each*) diced tomatoes, undrained
1	can (12 ounces) tomato paste
1-1/2	cups water, *divided*
1	tablespoon sugar
3	tablespoons grated onion
2-1/2	teaspoons salt, *divided*
1-1/2	teaspoons dried oregano
1	teaspoon minced garlic, *divided*
3/4	teaspoon pepper, *divided*
1	bay leaf
6	slices day-old bread, torn into pieces
2	eggs, lightly beaten
1/2	cup grated Parmesan cheese
2	tablespoons minced fresh parsley
1	pound ground beef

Hot cooked spaghetti
Additional Parmesan cheese, optional

italian spaghetti and meatballs

In a Dutch oven, combine the tomatoes, tomato paste, 1 cup water, sugar, onion, 1-1/2 teaspoons salt, oregano, 1/2 teaspoon garlic, 1/2 teaspoon pepper and bay leaf. Bring to a boil. Reduce heat and simmer, uncovered, for 1-1/4 hours.

Meanwhile, soak the bread in remaining water. Squeeze out excess moisture. In a large bowl, combine the bread, eggs, Parmesan cheese, parsley and remaining salt, garlic and pepper. Crumble beef over mixture and mix well. Shape into thirty-six 1-1/2-in. meatballs.

Place meatballs on a rack in a shallow baking pan. Bake, uncovered, at 400° for 20 minutes or until no longer pink; drain. Transfer to spaghetti sauce. Simmer, uncovered, until heated through, stirring occasionally. Discard the bay leaf. Serve with spaghetti and additional Parmesan if desired. **YIELD: 6 servings.**

hot turkey sandwiches

My mom made these turkey sandwiches as far back as I can remember...and I still make them often today. You'll love their fast-to-fix convenience.

—Elaine Cooley, Louisville, Kentucky

4	slices bread, toasted
4	teaspoons butter, softened
4	slices cooked turkey
1/2	cup shredded cheddar *or* processed American cheese
8	bacon strips, cooked and drained
4	slices tomato, optional
1/4	cup grated Parmesan cheese

Spread each slice of toast with 1 teaspoon butter. Place toast in a shallow baking pan. Top with the turkey, cheddar cheese, two bacon strips and tomato if desired. Sprinkle with Parmesan cheese.

Broil 5 in. from the heat for 3-4 minutes or until cheddar cheese is melted. **YIELD: 4 servings.**

ranch mac 'n' cheese

ranch mac 'n' cheese

I came up with the recipe for this creamy and satisfying macaroni and cheese, which has a special twist. My husband requests it often.

—Michelle Rotunno, Independence, Missouri

1	cup milk
1/4	cup butter, cubed
2	envelopes ranch salad dressing mix
1	teaspoon lemon-pepper seasoning
1	teaspoon garlic pepper blend
1	teaspoon garlic salt
1	cup cubed Colby cheese
1	cup cubed Monterey Jack cheese
1	cup (8 ounces) sour cream
1	package (16 ounces) elbow macaroni, cooked and drained
1/2	cup crushed saltines

Grated Parmesan cheese

In a Dutch oven, combine the first eight ingredients. Cook and stir over medium heat until cheese is melted and mixture begins to thicken.

Fold in the sour cream. Add macaroni and crackers. Cook until heated through, stirring frequently. Sprinkle with the Parmesan cheese. **YIELD: 6-8 servings.**

quick chicken cordon bleu

The moist chicken and flavorful cheese sauce make this entree perfect for a special occasion.

—Shirley Jackson, Elkton, Virginia

4	boneless skinless chicken breast halves
2	teaspoons Dijon mustard
1/2	teaspoon paprika
4	thin slices fully cooked ham
1	cup soft bread crumbs
1/4	cup grated Parmesan cheese
1/4	teaspoon pepper
3	to 4 tablespoons mayonnaise

SAUCE:

1	tablespoon butter
1	tablespoon all-purpose flour
1	cup milk
1/4	teaspoon salt
1/2	cup shredded Swiss cheese
2	tablespoons white wine

Flatten the chicken to 1/2-in. thickness. Spread mustard on one side; sprinkle with paprika. Top each with a ham slice. Roll up tightly; secure with toothpicks.

In a small bowl, combine the bread crumbs, Parmesan cheese and pepper. Brush chicken with mayonnaise; roll in crumb mixture.

Place in a shallow 2-qt. microwave-safe dish; cover loosely. Microwave on high for 7 minutes; turn chicken. Cook 5-1/2 minutes more or until meat is no longer pink; keep warm.

In a 1-qt. microwave-safe dish, heat butter on high for 20 seconds; stir in flour until smooth. Cook, uncovered, on high for 20 seconds. Add milk and salt. Cook 2-3 minutes longer or until thickened. Stir in cheese until smooth. Add wine. Discard toothpicks from chicken; serve with sauce. **YIELD: 4 servings.**

editor's note: This recipe was tested in a 1,100-watt microwave.

potato chicken packets

potato chicken packets

I season chicken breasts with a delightful combination of herbs before topping each with veggies. Servings are individually wrapped in foil, so I can enjoy nature's beauty in my backyard while the packets cook on the grill.

—Pam Hall, Elizabeth City, North Carolina

4	boneless skinless chicken breast halves (4 ounces *each*)
1/4	cup olive oil
3	teaspoons dried rosemary, crushed
1	teaspoon dried thyme
1/2	teaspoon dried basil
1	garlic clove, minced
8	to 10 small red potatoes, quartered
2	medium yellow summer squash, cut into 1/4-inch slices
1	large onion, chopped
2	tablespoons butter, cubed

Salt and pepper to taste

Place each chicken breast on a double thickness of heavy-duty foil (about 12 in. square). Combine the oil, rosemary, thyme, basil and garlic; drizzle over chicken. Top with potatoes, squash, onion and butter. Sprinkle with salt and pepper. Fold foil over mixture and seal tightly.

Grill, covered, over medium heat for 30 minutes or until a meat thermometer reads 160°. Open foil carefully to allow steam to escape. **YIELD: 4 servings.**

tuna noodle hot dish

This is an old recipe that I tweaked to suit my family's tastes. I like to serve it with breadsticks and a veggie tray.

—Sheila Sjolund, Deer River, Minnesota

12	ounces uncooked egg noodles
2	cans (10-3/4 ounces *each*) condensed cream of chicken soup, undiluted
1	cup (8 ounces) sour cream
1/3	cup milk
1	can (12 ounces) tuna, drained and flaked
1	cup shredded process cheese (Velveeta)
1	medium onion, chopped
1	jar (2 ounces) diced pimientos, drained
1	can (2-1/4 ounces) sliced ripe olives, drained
1	cup crushed potato chips

Paprika

Cook noodles according to package directions; drain. In a large bowl, combine the soup, sour cream and milk. Stir in the noodles, tuna, cheese, onion, pimientos and olives.

Pour into a greased 3-qt. baking dish. Sprinkle with potato chips and paprika. Bake, uncovered, at 375° for 30-35 minutes or until heated through. **YIELD: 6-8 servings.**

tuna noodle hot dish

sunday chicken stew

I love this recipe because I can prepare the veggies the night before and, in the morning, brown the chicken and assemble everything in the slow cooker before I go to church. I can spend time with my family while Sunday dinner cooks.

—Diane Halferty, Corpus Christi, Texas

1/2	cup all-purpose flour
1	teaspoon salt
1/2	teaspoon white pepper
1	broiler/fryer chicken (3 pounds), cut up and skin removed
2	tablespoons canola oil
3	cups chicken broth
6	large carrots, cut into 1-inch pieces
2	celery ribs, cut into 1/2-inch pieces
1	large sweet onion, thinly sliced
1	teaspoon dried rosemary, crushed
1-1/2	cups frozen peas

DUMPLINGS:

1	cup all-purpose flour
2	teaspoons baking powder
1/2	teaspoon salt
1/2	teaspoon dried rosemary, crushed
1	egg, lightly beaten
1/2	cup milk

In a large resealable plastic bag, combine the flour, salt and pepper; add chicken, a few pieces at a time, and shake to coat. In a large skillet, brown chicken in oil; remove and keep warm. Gradually add broth to the skillet; bring to a boil.

In a 5-qt. slow cooker, layer the carrots, celery and onion; sprinkle with rosemary. Add the chicken and hot broth. Cover and cook on low for 6-7 hours or until chicken juices run clear, vegetables are tender and stew is bubbling. Stir in peas.

For dumplings, in a small bowl, combine the flour, baking powder, salt and rosemary. Combine the egg and milk; stir into dry ingredients. Drop by heaping teaspoonfuls onto simmering chicken mixture. Cover and cook on high for 25-30 minutes or until a toothpick inserted in a dumpling comes out clean (do not lift the cover while simmering). **YIELD: 6 servings.**

simple shepherd's pie

simple shepherd's pie

Our son, Charlie, loves to help in the kitchen. When we have leftover mashed potatoes, he fixes this dish. It's a great meal with a green salad.

—Lera Joe Bayer, Wirtz, Virginia

1	pound ground beef
2	cans (10-3/4 ounces *each*) condensed cream of potato soup, undiluted
1-1/2	cups frozen peas, thawed
1-1/2	cups frozen sliced carrots, thawed
4	cups mashed potatoes (with added milk and butter)

In a large skillet, cook beef over medium heat until no longer pink; drain. Add the soup, peas and carrots. Pour into a greased 11-in. x 7-in. baking dish. Top with potatoes.

Bake, uncovered, at 350° for 30-40 minutes or until heated through. **YIELD: 4 servings.**

garlic pot roast

garlic pot roast

- 1 boneless beef chuck roast (3 pounds)
- 4 garlic cloves, peeled and halved
- 3 teaspoons garlic powder
- 3 teaspoons Italian salad dressing mix
- 1/2 teaspoon pepper
- 1 tablespoon canola oil
- 3 cups water
- 1 envelope onion soup mix
- 1 teaspoon reduced-sodium beef bouillon granules
- 5 medium potatoes, peeled and quartered
- 1 pound fresh baby carrots
- 1 large onion, cut into 1-inch pieces

Using the point of a sharp knife, make eight slits in the roast. Insert garlic into slits. Combine the garlic powder, salad dressing mix and pepper; rub over roast. In a Dutch oven, brown roast in oil on all sides; drain.

Combine the water, onion soup mix and bouillon; pour over roast. Cover and bake at 325° for 1-1/2 hours.

Add the potatoes, carrots and onion. Cover and bake 1 hour longer or until meat and vegetables are tender. Thicken pan juices if desired. **YIELD: 8 servings.**

My family loves garlic, the more the better. So, one day, I came up with this recipe...yum, yum good! Now, my family requests my mouthwatering roast for Sunday dinner every other week.

—Rhonda Hampton, Cookeville, Tennessee

old-fashioned egg salad

- 1/4 cup mayonnaise
- 2 teaspoons lemon juice
- 1 teaspoon dried minced onion
- 1/4 teaspoon salt
- 1/4 teaspoon pepper
- 6 hard-cooked eggs, chopped
- 1/2 cup finely chopped celery

old-fashioned egg salad

In a large bowl, combine the mayonnaise, lemon juice, onion, salt and pepper. Stir in eggs and celery. Cover and refrigerate. **YIELD: 3 servings.**

Here's a quick version of a long-time staple. You can also add a little cream cheese to the recipe for an extra-creamy sandwich if you'd like.

—Linda Braun, Park Ridge, Illinois

chicken cacciatore

My husband and I milk 125 cows, and there are days when there's just no time left for cooking! It's nice to be able to come in from the barn at night and smell this meal simmering—dinner is a simple matter of dishing it up. I've used this recipe for many years, and everyone who tries it likes it. It's very easy to make, but it's also special enough to serve company.

—Aggie Arnold-Norman, Liberty, Pennsylvania

chicken cacciatore

2	medium onions, thinly sliced
1	broiler/fryer chicken (3 to 4 pounds), cut up and skin removed
2	garlic cloves, minced
1	to 2 teaspoons dried oregano
1	teaspoon salt
1/2	teaspoon dried basil
1/4	teaspoon pepper

1	bay leaf
1	can (14-1/2 ounces) diced tomatoes, undrained
1	can (8 ounces) tomato sauce
1	can (4 ounces) mushroom stems and pieces, drained *or* 1 cup sliced fresh mushrooms
1/4	cup white wine *or* water
	Hot cooked pasta

Place sliced onions in a 5-qt. slow cooker. Add the chicken, seasonings, tomatoes, tomato sauce, mushrooms and wine or water. Cover and cook on low for 6-8 hours or until chicken juices run clear. Discard bay leaf. Serve chicken with sauce over pasta. YIELD: 6 servings.

oregano roasting chicken

This is a fantastic five-ingredient recipe that comes from our Test Kitchen. It takes almost no time to prep for the oven.

- 1/4 **cup butter, melted**
- 1 **envelope Italian salad dressing mix**
- 2 **tablespoons lemon juice**
- 1 **roasting chicken (6 to 7 pounds)**
- 2 **teaspoons dried oregano**

In a small bowl, combine the butter, salad dressing mix and lemon juice. Place chicken on a rack in an ungreased roasting pan. Spoon butter mixture over chicken.

Cover and bake at 350° for 45 minutes. Uncover; sprinkle with oregano. Bake, uncovered, for 1-1/2 to 1-3/4 hours or until a meat thermometer reads 180°.

Remove chicken from roasting pan; let stand for 5 minutes. Strain drippings. Cut one chicken breast half into 1-in. cubes. Cover and refrigerate cubed chicken breast and 1/4 cup drippings; save for another use. Transfer remaining chicken to serving platter. **YIELD: 4 servings plus 2 cups cubed cooked chicken breast and 1/4 cup drippings.**

oregano roasting chicken

saucy turkey

saucy turkey

This speedy stovetop dish uses cooked turkey. The spicy sauce is fast to stir together because it uses convenience foods such as mustard, ketchup and hot pepper sauce. What could be easier?

—Mrs. Johnye Masteres, Rayville, Louisiana

- 1/2 **cup chopped green pepper**
- 1/3 **cup chopped onion**
- 2 **tablespoons butter**
- 1-1/2 **cups ketchup**
- 1/2 **cup chicken broth**
- 1-1/2 **teaspoons Worcestershire sauce**
- 1 **teaspoon prepared mustard**
- 1/4 **to 1/2 teaspoon hot pepper sauce**
- 1/4 **teaspoon pepper**
- 3 **cups cubed cooked turkey**
- 4 **sandwich buns, split, optional**

In a large saucepan, saute green pepper and onion in butter until tender. Stir in the ketchup, broth, Worcestershire sauce, mustard, hot pepper sauce and pepper. Add turkey. Simmer, uncovered, for 20 minutes or until heated through. Serve on buns if desired. **YIELD: 4 servings.**

beef and tomato mac

For a quick dinner, this one is at the top. It has only a handful of ingredients. To turn up the heat, use two 10-ounce cans of diced tomatoes and green chilies instead of plain tomatoes.

—Daria Wicinski, Round Lake, Illinois

- 3 cups uncooked elbow macaroni
- 1 pound ground beef
- 1 medium onion, chopped
- 2 cans (14-1/2 ounces *each*) diced tomatoes, undrained
- 1 can (15-1/4 ounces) whole kernel corn, drained

Salt and pepper to taste

Cook macaroni according to package directions. Meanwhile, in a large skillet, cook beef and onion over medium heat until meat is no longer pink; drain. Stir in tomatoes and corn. Drain macaroni; stir into beef mixture.

Cook, uncovered, for 12-15 minutes or until heated through; season with salt and pepper. **YIELD: 4-6 servings.**

beef and tomato mac

chicken 'n' corn bread bake

chicken 'n' corn bread bake

Here's Southern comfort food at its best! This casserole is delicious made with chicken or turkey. It's often on the menu when I cook for my husband, our four children, their spouses and our 10 grandkids.

—Ann Hillmeyer, Sandia Park, New Mexico

- 2-1/2 cups reduced-sodium chicken broth
- 1 small onion, chopped
- 1 celery rib, chopped
- 1/8 teaspoon pepper
- 4-1/2 cups corn bread stuffing mix, *divided*
- 4 cups cubed cooked chicken
- 1-1/2 cups (12 ounces) sour cream
- 1 can (10-3/4 ounces) condensed cream of chicken soup, undiluted
- 3 green onions, thinly sliced
- 1/4 cup butter, cubed

In a large saucepan, combine the broth, onion, celery and pepper. Bring to a boil. Reduce heat; cover and simmer for 5-6 minutes or until vegetables are tender. Stir in 4 cups stuffing mix.

Transfer to a greased 13-in. x 9-in. baking dish. Top with chicken. In a small bowl, combine the sour cream, soup and green onions. Spread over chicken. Sprinkle with remaining stuffing mix; dot with butter.

Bake, uncovered, at 325° for 25-30 minutes or until heated through. **YIELD: 8 servings.**

chicken potpie

chicken potpie

Few dishes are as comforting as potpie. This version is loaded with veggies and chunks of chicken, and it comes together easily with a packaged pastry crust.

—Lucille Terry, Frankfort, Kentucky

3	medium carrots, sliced
2	medium red potatoes, cut into 1/2-inch pieces
1	medium turnip, peeled and cut into 1/2-inch pieces
1/4	cup butter, cubed
1/4	cup all-purpose flour
2	cups chicken broth
1	teaspoon dried thyme
1/2	teaspoon salt
1/2	teaspoon pepper
2	cups cubed cooked chicken
1	cup frozen peas, thawed
1	jar (4-1/2 ounces) sliced mushrooms, drained
4	green onions, sliced

Pastry for single-crust pie (9 inches)

Place the carrots, potatoes and turnip in a large saucepan; cover with water. Bring to a boil. Reduce heat; cover and cook for 10-15 minutes or until vegetables are tender.

Meanwhile, in a small saucepan, melt butter over medium heat. Stir in flour until smooth. Gradually add the broth, thyme, salt and pepper. Bring to a boil; cook and stir for 2 minutes or until white sauce is slightly thickened.

Drain vegetables and place in a large bowl; stir in the white sauce, chicken, peas, mushrooms and onions. Transfer mixture to a greased 2-qt. round baking dish.

Place pastry over filling; trim, seal and flute edges. Cut slits in top. Bake at 375° for 25-30 minutes or until crust is golden brown and filling is bubbly. **YIELD: 4 servings.**

tortellini alfredo

I jazz up refrigerated tortellini with ham, mushrooms, peas and my homemade Alfredo sauce for a fast supper. When we're having company, I prepare the dinner shortly before guests arrive, put it in a casserole dish and keep it warm in the oven.

—Chris Snyder, Boulder, Colorado

2	packages (9 ounces *each*) refrigerated cheese tortellini
1/2	cup chopped onion
1/3	cup butter, cubed
1-1/2	cups frozen peas, thawed
1	cup thinly sliced fresh mushrooms
1	cup cubed fully cooked ham
1-3/4	cups heavy whipping cream
1/4	teaspoon coarsely ground pepper
3/4	cup grated Parmesan cheese

Shredded Parmesan cheese, optional

Cook tortellini according to package directions. Meanwhile, in a large skillet, saute onion in butter until tender. Add the peas, mushrooms and ham; cook until mushrooms are tender. Stir in cream and pepper; heat through. Stir in the grated Parmesan cheese until melted.

Drain tortellini and place in a serving dish; add the sauce and toss to coat. Sprinkle with shredded Parmesan cheese if desired. **YIELD: 4-6 servings.**

dilled pot roast

It is hard to believe that this mouthwatering pot roast comes together so easily. I rely on dill weed, cider vinegar and a simple sour cream sauce to flavor the entree.

—Amy Lingren, Jacksonville, Florida

2	teaspoons dill weed, *divided*
1	teaspoon salt
1/4	teaspoon pepper
1	boneless beef chuck roast (2-1/2 pounds)
1/4	cup water
1	tablespoon cider vinegar
3	tablespoons all-purpose flour
1/4	cup cold water
1	cup (8 ounces) sour cream
1/2	teaspoon browning sauce, optional

Hot cooked rice

In a small bowl, combine 1 teaspoon dill, salt and pepper. Sprinkle over both sides of roast. Place in a 3-qt. slow cooker. Add water and vinegar. Cover and cook on low for 7-8 hours or until the meat is tender.

Remove meat and keep warm. In a small bowl, combine flour and remaining dill; stir in cold water until smooth. Gradually stir into slow cooker.

Cover and cook on high for 30 minutes or until thickened. Stir in sour cream and browning sauce if desired; heat through. Slice meat. Serve with sour cream sauce and rice. **YIELD: 6-8 servings.**

dilled pot roast

bacon-topped grilled cheese

bacon-topped grilled cheese

Sourdough bread adds a delicious twist to an all-American lunch classic. This robust version gets its heartiness from bacon and extra flavor from the onion, sour cream and oregano. Two types of cheese make it special.

—Nita Crosby, St. George, Utah

4	slices part-skim mozzarella cheese
8	slices sourdough bread
2	large tomatoes, thinly sliced
8	bacon strips, cooked
4	tablespoons sour cream
4	tablespoons finely chopped onion
1/4	teaspoon dried oregano
4	slices cheddar cheese
2	tablespoons butter, softened

Place mozzarella cheese on four bread slices; layer each with a fourth of the tomato slices, two bacon strips, 1 tablespoon sour cream, 1 tablespoon onion, a pinch of oregano, one slice of cheddar cheese. Top with remaining bread.

Butter outsides of sandwiches. In a small skillet over medium heat, toast sandwiches for 3-4 minutes on each side or until cheese is melted. **YIELD: 4 servings.**

corned beef 'n' cabbage

I've been making this meal for more than 40 years. It is so easy and delicious. It's especially good served with a salad of peaches and cottage cheese.

—Ruth Warner, Wheat Ridge, Colorado

corned beef 'n' cabbage

4 cups water

1 corned beef brisket with spice packet (2 pounds)

1 medium head cabbage, cut into 8 wedges

2 large red potatoes, cut into 2-inch chunks

1 can (14-1/2 ounces) chicken broth

4 large carrots, cut into 2-inch chunks

1 medium onion, cut into 2-inch pieces

In a 6-qt. pressure cooker, combine water and contents of corned beef seasoning packet; add beef. Close cover securely; place pressure regulator on vent pipe. Bring cooker to full pressure over high heat. Reduce heat to medium-high and cook for 45 minutes. (Pressure regulator should maintain a slow steady rocking motion; adjust heat if needed.)

Meanwhile, in a large saucepan, combine the cabbage, potatoes and broth. Bring to a boil. Reduce heat; cover and simmer for 10 minutes. Add carrots and onion. Cover and simmer 20-25 minutes longer or until vegetables are tender; drain.

Remove pressure cooker from the heat; allow pressure to drop on its own. Remove beef to a serving platter. Discard cooking liquid. Serve beef with cabbage, potatoes, carrots and onion. **YIELD: 4-6 servings.**

hot dogs with the works

1-1/2   **cups (6 ounces) shredded pepper Jack cheese**
3/4   **cup chopped seeded tomato**
3   **tablespoons chopped onion**
2   **tablespoons sweet pickle relish**
8   **hot dogs**
8   **hot dog buns**

hot dogs with the works

In a small bowl, combine the cheese, tomato, onion and relish. Place hot dogs in buns; top with cheese mixture.

Wrap each hot dog in a double thickness of heavy-duty foil (about 12 in. x 10 in.). Grill, covered, over medium-hot heat for 8-10 minutes or until heated through. Open foil carefully to allow steam to escape. **YIELD: 8 servings.**

What screams summer more than grilled hot dogs? I place hot dogs in buns before topping them with a zesty cheese sauce and grilling them in a double layer of foil.

—Maria Regakis, Somerville, Massachusetts

crunchy beef bake

crunchy beef bake

2   **cups uncooked spiral pasta**
1   **pound ground beef**
3/4   **cup chopped green pepper**
1   **garlic clove, minced**
1   **can (14-1/2 ounces) diced tomatoes, undrained**
1   **can (10-3/4 ounces) condensed cream of mushroom soup, undiluted**
3/4   **cup shredded cheddar cheese**
3/4   **teaspoon seasoned salt**
1   **can (2.8 ounces) french-fried onions**

Cook pasta according to package directions. Meanwhile, in a Dutch oven, cook the beef, green pepper and garlic over medium heat until meat is no longer pink and green pepper is tender; drain.

Drain pasta; add to the beef mixture with the tomatoes, soup, cheese and salt.

Transfer to a greased 2-qt. baking dish. Cover and bake at 350° for 30-40 minutes. Uncover; sprinkle with onions and bake 5 minutes longer. **YIELD: 4-6 servings.**

I always use corkscrew noodles when preparing this, because the sauce seems to cling to them better than it does to flat noodles—ensuring plenty of good taste in every bite!

—Janie Moore, Marion, Ohio

Double the Barbecued Beef Sandwiches recipe, and freeze the extras for later. Just line a baking sheet with parchment paper; set 1-cup mounds of the meat mixture on the sheet. Cover and freeze. Heated in the microwave, the mounds make great no-fuss sandwiches when time is tight.

crumb-topped haddock

barbecued beef sandwiches

With only three ingredients, you can assemble these sandwiches in short order, our food staff confirms. Store-bought barbecue sauce flavors leftover beef for sandwiches just as savory and juicy as Mom used to make.

2 **cups shredded cooked roast beef**
1 **bottle (18 ounces) barbecue sauce**
5 **kaiser rolls, split**

In a large saucepan, combine beef and barbecue sauce; heat through. Serve on rolls. **YIELD: 5 servings.**

editor's note: *This recipe works fine with deli roast beef as well.*

crumb-topped haddock

Featuring just a handful of items, this creamy dish with a crispy topping is a breeze to prepare.

—*Debbie Solt, Lewistown, Pennsylvania*

2 **pounds haddock *or* cod fillets**
1 **can (10-3/4 ounces) condensed cream of shrimp soup, undiluted**
1 **teaspoon grated onion**
1 **teaspoon Worcestershire sauce**
1 **cup crushed butter-flavored crackers (about 25 crackers)**

Arrange fillets in a greased 13-in. x 9-in. baking dish. Combine the soup, onion and Worcestershire sauce; pour over fish.

Bake, uncovered, at 375° for 20 minutes. Sprinkle with cracker crumbs. Bake 15 minutes longer or until fish flakes easily with a fork. **YIELD: 6-8 servings.**

barbecued beef sandwiches

fast chicken divan

Frozen broccoli and leftover chicken get an easy—but elegant—treatment in this dish. I dress them up with a saucy blend of cream soup and mayonnaise, then cover it all with a golden, cheesy crumb topping.

—Bertille Cooper, California, Maryland

8   **cups frozen broccoli florets *or* chopped broccoli**

3   **cups cubed cooked chicken**

2   **cans (10-3/4 ounces *each*) condensed cream of chicken soup, undiluted**

1   **cup mayonnaise**

1   **teaspoon lemon juice**

1   **cup (4 ounces) shredded sharp cheddar cheese**

3/4   **cup dry bread crumbs**

3   **tablespoons butter, melted**

1   **tablespoon sliced pimientos, optional**

In a large saucepan, cook the broccoli in boiling water for 1 minute; drain. Transfer to a greased 11-in. x 7-in. baking dish; top with chicken. Combine the soup, mayonnaise and lemon juice; spread over chicken. Sprinkle with cheese. Combine bread crumbs and butter; sprinkle over top.

Bake, uncovered, at 325° for 30 minutes or until bubbly and golden brown. Let stand for 10 minutes before serving. Garnish with pimientos if desired. YIELD: 4-6 servings.

editor's note: Reduced-fat or fat-free mayonnaise is not recommended for this recipe.

artichoke chicken

This recipe has evolved through generations to satisfy my family's fondness for artichokes. I enjoy preparing this for casual suppers as well as special-occasion dinners.

—Roberta Green, Hemet, California

2   **cans (14 ounces *each*) water-packed artichoke hearts, rinsed, drained and quartered**

2   **tablespoons olive oil**

3   **garlic cloves, minced**

2-2/3   **cups cubed cooked chicken**

2   **cans (10-3/4 ounces *each*) condensed cream of chicken soup, undiluted**

1   **cup mayonnaise**

1   **teaspoon lemon juice**

1/2   **teaspoon curry powder**

1-1/2   **cups (6 ounces) shredded cheddar cheese**

1   **cup seasoned bread crumbs**

1/4   **cup grated Parmesan cheese**

2   **tablespoons butter, melted**

In a bowl, combine the artichokes, oil and garlic. Place in a greased 2-1/2-qt. baking dish. Top with chicken. Combine the soup, mayonnaise, lemon juice and curry; pour over the chicken. Sprinkle with cheddar cheese. Combine the bread crumbs, Parmesan cheese and butter; sprinkle over top.

Bake, uncovered, at 350° for 30-35 minutes or until bubbly. YIELD: 6-8 servings.

editor's note: Reduced-fat or fat-free mayonnaise is not recommended for this recipe.

artichoke chicken

broccoli chicken casserole

broccoli chicken casserole

All ages really seem to go for this comforting, scrumptious meal-in-one. It takes just a few ingredients and minutes to put together. I've found that adding dried cranberries to the stuffing mix also adds flavor and color!
—Jenn Schlachter, Big Rock, Illinois

1-1/2	cups water
1	package (6 ounces) chicken stuffing mix
2	cups cubed cooked chicken
1	cup frozen broccoli florets, thawed
1	can (10-3/4 ounces) condensed broccoli cheese soup, undiluted
1	cup (4 ounces) shredded cheddar cheese

In a small saucepan, bring water to a boil. Stir in stuffing mix. Remove from the heat; cover and let stand for 5 minutes.

Meanwhile, layer chicken and broccoli in a greased 11-in. x 7-in. baking dish. Top with soup. Fluff stuffing with a fork; spoon over soup. Sprinkle with the cheese.

Bake, uncovered, at 350° for 30-35 minutes or until heated through. **YIELD: 6 servings.**

beef brisket in gravy

This tender roast has remained our favorite family dish over many years. Often, I make it ahead and reheat the beef in the gravy. It's delicious served with hot cooked noodles or mashed potatoes.
—Erlene Cornelius, Spring City, Tennessee

1	fresh beef brisket (about 2 pounds)
2	tablespoons canola oil
1	cup hot water
1	envelope beefy onion soup mix
2	tablespoons cornstarch
1/2	cup cold water

In a Dutch oven, brown brisket in oil on both sides over medium-high heat; drain. Combine hot water and soup mix; pour over brisket. Cover and bake at 325° for 2 to 2-1/2 hours or until meat is tender.

Remove brisket to a serving platter. Let stand for 10-15 minutes. Meanwhile, combine cornstarch and cold water until smooth; gradually stir into pan juices. Bring to a boil; cook and stir for 2 minutes or until thickened. Thinly slice meat across the grain; serve with the gravy. **YIELD: 6-8 servings.**

editor's note: This is fresh beef brisket, not corned beef.

beef brisket in gravy

homemade
fish fingers

Once you've tried these morsels, you'll never buy fish sticks again! Our Test Kitchen staff coated pieces of cod in a tasty Parmesan, herb and bread crumb mixture that is sure to have folks asking for seconds.

1	pound cod fillet
1/2	cup seasoned bread crumbs
2	tablespoons grated Parmesan cheese
1	tablespoon minced fresh parsley
1	teaspoon grated lemon peel
1/2	teaspoon paprika
1/2	teaspoon dried thyme
1/4	teaspoon garlic salt
1/2	cup buttermilk
1/4	cup plus 2 tablespoons all-purpose flour

Cut fillets into 3/4-in. strips; set aside. In a shallow bowl, combine the bread crumbs, Parmesan cheese, parsley, lemon peel, paprika, thyme and garlic salt. Place buttermilk and flour in separate shallow bowls. Coat fish strips with flour; dip into buttermilk, then coat with crumb mixture.

Place on a baking sheet coated with cooking spray. Refrigerate for 20 minutes.

Bake at 425° for 15-20 minutes or until fish flakes easily with a fork. Let stand for 2 minutes before removing from baking sheets. **YIELD: 4 servings.**

deluxe cheeseburgers

deluxe
cheeseburgers

I perk up ground beef with tomato paste, Worcestershire sauce, chopped onion and Parmesan and cheddar cheeses. We love to grill these flavorful burgers in the summer and broil them in the winter.

—Kathleen Vashro, Corcoran, Minnesota

1	egg
1	can (6 ounces) tomato paste
1	tablespoon Worcestershire sauce
1	medium onion, chopped
1/2	cup grated Parmesan cheese
1/2	teaspoon seasoned salt
1/2	teaspoon salt
1/8	teaspoon pepper
2	pounds ground beef
8	slices cheddar cheese
8	hamburger buns, split

In a large bowl, combine the first eight ingredients. Crumble beef over mixture and mix well. Shape into eight 3/4-in.-thick patties.

Grill, covered, over medium heat for 5 minutes on each side or until a meat thermometer reads 160° and meat is no longer pink. Top each burger with a cheese slice. Grill 1-2 minutes longer or until the cheese begins to melt. Serve on buns. **YIELD: 8 servings.**

homemade fish fingers

reuben burgers

A Reuben sandwich was always my first choice when eating out—until I found this recipe in a local newspaper. After that, my family could eat Reubens anytime. Our daughters used to make these when they were in charge of preparing a meal. I usually had all the ingredients on hand, so it didn't take long to get everything on the table.

—Betty Ruenholl, Syracuse, Nebraska

1/4	cup sauerkraut
1/4	teaspoon caraway seeds
1/2	pound ground pork
2	slices Swiss cheese (3/4 ounce *each*)
2	hamburger buns, split and toasted

In a small saucepan, heat sauerkraut and caraway seeds; keep warm. Shape pork into two patties. Grill, uncovered, over medium heat or broil 4-6 in. from heat for 6-8 minutes on each side or until a meat thermometer reads 160°.

Top each patty with cheese; continue cooking until cheese is melted. Drain sauerkraut. Place patties on buns; top with sauerkraut. Replace bun tops. **YIELD: 2 servings.**

beef pasties

Our Test Kitchen staff created this recipe for pasties as a way to put leftover pot roast to good use. Just tuck the cooked beef, carrots, potatoes and onion into pie pastry...your family will be amazed at the tender and flaky results!

beef pasties

2	cups cubed cooked roast beef (1/4-inch pieces)
1-1/2	cups diced cooked potatoes
1	cup beef gravy
1/2	cup diced cooked carrots
1/2	cup diced cooked onion
1	tablespoon chopped fresh parsley
1/4	teaspoon dried thyme
1/2	teaspoon salt
1/8	to 1/4 teaspoon pepper

Pastry for double-crust pie (9 inches)
Half-and-half cream

In a large bowl, combine the first nine ingredients; set aside. On a lightly floured surface, roll out a fourth of the pastry into an 8-in. circle. Mound 1 cup filling on half of circle. Moisten edges with water; fold dough over filling and press the edges with a fork to seal.

Place on an ungreased baking sheet. Repeat with remaining pastry and filling. Cut slits in top of each; brush with cream. Bake at 450° for 20-25 minutes or until golden brown. **YIELD: 4 servings.**

editor's note: If using purchased pre-rolled pastry, cut each circle in half. Mound filling on half of the pastry; fold over, forming a wedge.

no-fuss swiss steak

I received the recipe for this dish from my cousin. I make it regularly because our children love the savory steak, tangy gravy and fork-tender veggies.

—Sharon Morrell, Parker, South Dakota

no-fuss swiss steak

3	pounds boneless beef round steak, cut into serving-size pieces	1-3/4	cups water
2	tablespoons canola oil	1	can (11 ounces) condensed tomato rice soup, undiluted
2	medium carrots, cut into 1/2-inch slices	1	can (10-1/2 ounces) condensed French onion soup, undiluted
2	celery ribs, cut into 1/2-inch slices	1/2	teaspoon pepper
		1	bay leaf

In a large skillet, brown beef in oil over medium-high heat; drain. Transfer to a 5-qt. slow cooker. Add carrots and celery. Combine the remaining ingredients; pour over meat and vegetables. Cover and cook on low for 6-8 hours or until meat is tender.

Discard the bay leaf before serving. Thicken the cooking juices if desired. **YIELD: 8-10 servings.**

creamy lasagna casserole

Satisfy your gang easily with this casserole. I can whip up the rich combination of cream cheese, sour cream and cheddar cheese, layered with lasagna noodles and a beefy sauce in absolutely no time.

—Shelly Korell, Eaton, Colorado

2	pounds ground beef
1	can (29 ounces) tomato sauce
1	teaspoon salt
1/2	teaspoon pepper
1/2	teaspoon garlic powder
2	packages (3 ounces *each*) cream cheese, softened
2	cups (16 ounces) sour cream
2	cups (8 ounces) shredded cheddar cheese, *divided*
4	green onions, chopped
12	to 14 lasagna noodles, cooked and drained

In a Dutch oven, cook beef over medium heat until no longer pink; drain. Add the tomato sauce, salt, pepper and garlic powder. Bring to a boil. Reduce heat; simmer, uncovered, for 15 minutes. In a bowl, beat cream cheese until smooth. Add sour cream, 1 cup cheddar cheese and onions; mix well.

Spread about 1/2 cup meat sauce into two greased 8-in. square baking dishes. Place two to three noodles in each dish, trimming to fit if necessary. Top each with about 1/2 cup cream cheese mixture and about 2/3 cup meat sauce. Repeat layers twice. Sprinkle 1/2 cup cheddar cheese over each.

Cover and freeze one casserole for up to 1 month. Bake remaining casserole, uncovered, at 350° for 25-30 minutes or until bubbly and heated through. Let stand for 15 minutes before cutting.

To use frozen casserole: Thaw in the refrigerator for 18 hours. Remove casserole from the refrigerator 30 minutes before baking. Bake, uncovered, at 350° for 40-50 minutes or until heated through. YIELD: 2 casseroles (4-6 servings each).

creamy lasagna casserole

speedy steak sandwiches

Steak sauce, mustard and seasonings give these ground beef sandwiches great flavor. The recipe is sized for two people but could easily be doubled or tripled.

—Ruth Page, Hillsborough, North Carolina

4	slices French bread (3/4 inch thick)
	Butter, softened
	Prepared mustard
1/2	pound uncooked lean ground beef
1/4	cup milk
1	tablespoon dried minced onion
1	tablespoon steak sauce
1/2	teaspoon garlic salt
1/4	teaspoon pepper

In a broiler, toast one side of the bread. Spread untoasted sides with butter and mustard.

In a small bowl, combine remaining ingredients; spread over buttered side of bread. Broil 6 in. from the heat for 5-7 minutes or until meat is no longer pink. **YIELD: 2 servings.**

fast baked fish

fast baked fish

We always have a good supply of fresh fish, so I make this dish often. It's moist, tender and flavorful.

—Judie Anglen, Riverton, Wyoming

1-1/4	pounds fish fillets
1	teaspoon seasoned salt

Pepper to taste

Paprika, optional

| 3 | tablespoons butter, melted |

Place fish in a greased 11-in. x 7-in. baking dish. Sprinkle with seasoned salt, pepper and paprika if desired. Drizzle with butter.

Cover and bake at 400° for 15-20 minutes or until fish flakes easily with a fork. **YIELD: 4 servings.**

editor's note: *Orange roughy, haddock, trout or walleye may be used in this recipe.*

Kitchen Tip

Fresh fish should never have a fishy odor. Fillets and steaks should have a firm flesh with a moist look. Whole fish should have a firm body that's springy to the touch.

country fried chicken

This is one of our favorite recipes to take along on a picnic. We like to eat the chicken cold, with a salad and watermelon. It's a real treat!

—Rebekah Miller, Rocky Mountain, Virginia

1	cup all-purpose flour
2	teaspoons garlic salt
2	teaspoons pepper
1	teaspoon paprika
1/2	teaspoon poultry seasoning
1	egg
1/2	cup milk
1	broiler/fryer chicken (3 to 3-1/2 pounds), cut up

Oil for frying

In a large resealable plastic bag, combine the flour and seasonings. In a shallow bowl, beat egg and milk. Dip chicken pieces into egg mixture, then add to bag, a few pieces at a time, and shake to coat.

In a large skillet, heat 1/4 in. of oil; fry chicken in oil until browned on all sides. Cover and simmer for 35-40 minutes or until juices run clear and chicken is tender, turning occasionally. Uncover and cook 5 minutes longer. Drain on paper towels. **YIELD: 4 servings.**

country fried chicken

sweet 'n' sour chicken

sweet 'n' sour chicken

This entree was served at a special dinner hosted by my Sunday school teacher. The ingredients are simple, but the chicken is tender and delicious. I serve it to company and am often asked for the recipe.

—Christine McDonald, Riverdale, Utah

4	boneless skinless chicken breast halves (4 ounces *each*)
2/3	cup water
1/3	cup sugar
1/4	cup cider vinegar
1/4	cup reduced-sodium soy sauce
1	medium sweet red pepper, cut into 1-inch pieces
1	medium green pepper, cut into 1-inch pieces
2	tablespoons cornstarch
3	tablespoons cold water

Hot cooked rice

Place chicken in a 9-in. square baking dish; set aside. In a saucepan, bring the water, sugar, vinegar and soy sauce to a boil, stirring constantly. Add peppers; return to a boil. Combine cornstarch and cold water until smooth; gradually stir into pepper mixture. Bring to a boil; cook and stir for 1-2 minutes or until thickened. Pour over chicken.

Bake, uncovered, at 350° for 10-13 minutes on each side or until a meat thermometer reaches 170°. Serve with rice. **YIELD: 4 servings.**

beef in mushroom gravy

This is one of the best meals I've ever made. It has only five ingredients, and they all go into the pot at once. The meat is nicely seasoned and makes its own gravy that tastes wonderful when you serve it over a helping of mashed potatoes.

—Margery Bryan, Moses Lake, Washington

2	to 2-1/2 pounds boneless beef round steak
1	to 2 envelopes onion soup mix
1	can (10-3/4 ounces) condensed cream of mushroom soup, undiluted
1/2	cup water

Mashed potatoes, optional

Cut steak into six serving-size pieces; place in a 3-qt. slow cooker. Combine the soup mix, soup and water; pour over beef. Cover and cook on low for 7-8 hours or until meat is tender. Serve with mashed potatoes if desired. **YIELD: 6 servings.**

beef in mushroom gravy

mostaccioli bake

Layer half of the pasta mixture in a greased 11-in. x 7-in. baking dish coated with cooking spray. Top with spinach mixture, remaining pasta mixture and remaining spaghetti sauce.

Cover and bake at 350° for 35-40 minutes or until bubbly. Uncover; sprinkle with remaining mozzarella and Parmesan cheeses. Bake 5 minutes longer or until cheese is melted. **YIELD: 8 servings.**

mostaccioli bake

This homey lasagna-style casserole will appeal to the whole family. There's plenty of prepared spaghetti sauce to keep the dish easy and the layers of tender pasta and spinach-cheese mixture moist.

—Dorothy Bateman, Carver, Massachusetts

8	ounces uncooked mostaccioli
1	egg
1	egg white
2	cups (16 ounces) 1% cottage cheese
1	package (10 ounces) frozen chopped spinach, thawed and squeezed dry
1	cup (4 ounces) shredded part-skim mozzarella cheese, *divided*
2/3	cup shredded Parmesan cheese, *divided*
1/3	cup minced fresh parsley
1/4	teaspoon salt
1/4	teaspoon pepper
2-1/2	cups meatless spaghetti sauce, *divided*

Cook pasta according to package directions. Meanwhile, in a large bowl, combine the egg, egg white, cottage cheese, spinach, 2/3 cup mozzarella cheese, 1/3 cup Parmesan cheese, parsley, salt and pepper; set aside. Drain pasta; stir in 2 cups spaghetti sauce.

hot chicken salad

This rich and creamy chicken salad would be a welcome addition to any buffet table. This salad is among my family's favorite casseroles. It's great for potlucks.

—Eleanor Hein, Kirkland, Illinois

3/4	cup mayonnaise
3/4	cup sour cream
2	tablespoons lemon juice
2	teaspoons grated onion
1/2	teaspoon salt
3	cups cubed cooked chicken breast
1	cup chopped celery
1	can (8 ounces) sliced water chestnuts, drained and coarsely chopped
1	cup seasoned salad croutons
1/2	cup slivered almonds
1	cup soft bread crumbs
1	tablespoon butter, melted
1	cup (4 ounces) shredded cheddar cheese

In a large bowl, whisk the mayonnaise, sour cream, lemon juice, onion and salt until smooth. Stir in the cubed chicken, celery, water chestnuts, croutons and almonds.

Spoon into a greased 11-in. x 7-in. baking dish. Cover and bake at 350° for 25 minutes.

Combine bread crumbs and butter; stir in cheese. Sprinkle over casserole. Bake, uncovered, 5-10 minutes longer or until heated through and cheese is melted. **YIELD: 6 servings.**

ham 'n' cheese pasta

Kids and adults alike will love this dressed-up version of creamy macaroni and cheese from our Test Kitchen. It's loaded with the comforting flavor you'd expect from Mom's house.

ham 'n' cheese pasta

3	cups uncooked bow tie pasta		1/4	teaspoon pepper
3/4	pound fresh asparagus, trimmed and cut into 1-inch pieces		1/8	to 1/4 teaspoon dried thyme
2	tablespoons butter		2	cups milk
1	teaspoon minced garlic		2	cups (8 ounces) shredded cheddar cheese
2	tablespoons all-purpose flour		1/2	cup grated Parmesan cheese
1/4	teaspoon onion powder		1/2	pound sliced deli ham, chopped

Cook the pasta according to the package directions, adding the asparagus during the last 3 minutes.

Meanwhile, in a large saucepan, melt butter; add garlic. Stir in the flour, onion powder, pepper and thyme until blended; gradually add milk. Bring to a boil; cook and stir for 2 minutes or until thickened.

Reduce heat. Add cheeses; stir until melted. Stir in ham; heat through. Drain pasta and asparagus; toss with cheese mixture. **YIELD: 4 servings.**

the ultimate grilled cheese

1 package (3 ounces) cream cheese, softened
3/4 cup mayonnaise
1 cup (4 ounces) shredded part-skim mozzarella cheese
1 cup (4 ounces) shredded cheddar cheese
1/2 teaspoon garlic powder
1/8 teaspoon seasoned salt
10 slices Italian bread (1/2 inch thick)
2 tablespoons butter, softened

the ultimate grilled cheese

In a large bowl, beat cream cheese and mayonnaise until smooth. Stir in the cheeses, garlic powder and seasoned salt. Spread the five slices of bread with the cheese mixture, about 1/3 cup on each. Top with the remaining bread.

Butter the outsides of sandwiches. In a skillet over medium heat, toast sandwiches for 4-5 minutes on each side or until bread is lightly browned and cheese is melted. **YIELD: 5 servings.**

These gooey grilled cheese sandwiches, subtly seasoned with garlic, taste great for lunch with sliced apples. And they're really fast to whip up, too. To save seconds, I soften the cream cheese in the microwave, then blend it with the rest of the ingredients in the same bowl, making cleanup a breeze.

—Kathy Norris, Streator, Illinois

quick tater tot bake

quick tater tot bake

3/4 to 1 pound ground beef *or* turkey
1 small onion, chopped
Salt and pepper to taste
1 package (16 ounces) frozen Tator Tot potatoes
1 can (10-3/4 ounces) condensed cream of mushroom soup, undiluted
2/3 cup milk *or* water
1 cup (4 ounces) shredded cheddar cheese

I enjoy preparing this dish when time before supper is short. It serves two to three people, but if we have unexpected company, I double the ingredients and use a 9-in. x 13-in. pan. I like to call it my "Please Stay Casserole!"

—Jean Ferguson, Elverta, California

In a large skillet, cook beef and onion over medium heat until no longer pink; drain. Season with salt and pepper.

Transfer to a greased 2-qt. baking dish. Top with Tator Tot potatoes. Combine the soup and milk; pour over the potatoes. Sprinkle with cheese. Bake, uncovered, at 350° for 30-40 minutes or until heated through. **YIELD: 2-3 servings.**

ham and broccoli supper

I found this recipe in an old Amish cookbook a while back. It combines lots of my family's favorite foods, like ham, broccoli and rice, and it makes a very tasty meal.

—Angela Liette, Piqua, Ohio

1-1/2	cups chopped fresh broccoli
1/2	cup finely chopped onion
1-1/2	cups cooked rice
1-1/2	cups diced fully cooked ham
1	can (10-3/4 ounces) condensed cream of mushroom soup, undiluted
1-1/2	cups (6 ounces) shredded cheddar cheese
1/4	cup milk
2	slices bread, crusts removed
2	tablespoons butter

In a large saucepan, bring 1 in. water, broccoli and onion to a boil. Reduce heat; cover and simmer for 5-8 minutes or until the vegetables are crisp-tender; drain.

In a greased 1-1/2-qt. baking dish, layer the rice, ham and broccoli mixture. Combine the soup, cheese and milk; spoon over broccoli. Bake, uncovered, at 350° for 20 minutes.

Meanwhile, coarsely crumble bread. In a small skillet, cook crumbs in butter over medium-high heat until lightly browned. Sprinkle over casserole. Bake 15 minutes longer or until heated through. **YIELD:** 4 servings.

ham and broccoli supper

home-style meat loaf

home-style meat loaf

Down-home meat loaf is hard to resist, and with this recipe I can make sure that loads of friends and family get a chance to enjoy such a specialty. Guests seem to like the fact that this version uses both ground beef and ground pork. Freezing the extra loaves saves me so much time.

—Allison Craig, Ormstown, Quebec

6	eggs, lightly beaten
4	cups milk
4	cups dry bread crumbs
2-1/2	cups shredded carrots
1-1/4	cups chopped onions
5	teaspoons salt
4	teaspoons pepper
10	pounds ground beef
5	pounds ground pork

In two very large bowls, combine the first seven ingredients. Crumble meat over the top and mix well.

Shape into five loaves; place each in an ungreased 13-in. x 9-in. baking pan. Bake, uncovered, at 350° for 75-85 minutes or until a meat thermometer reads 160° and meat juices run clear. Drain; let stand for 10 minutes before slicing. **YIELD:** 5 meat loaves (12 servings each).

meatball sub sandwiches

Making these saucy meatballs in advance and reheating them saves me precious moments when expecting company. These sandwiches are a great casual treat for just about any get-together.

—Deena Hubler, Jasper, Indiana

2	eggs, lightly beaten
1	cup dry bread crumbs
2	tablespoons grated Parmesan cheese
2	tablespoons finely chopped onion
1	teaspoon salt
1/2	teaspoon pepper
1/2	teaspoon garlic powder
1/4	teaspoon Italian seasoning
2	pounds ground beef
1	jar (28 ounces) spaghetti sauce

Additional Parmesan cheese, sliced onion and green peppers, optional

12   sandwich rolls, split

In a large bowl, combine the first eight ingredients. Crumble beef over mixture and mix well. Shape into 1-in. balls. Place in a single layer in a 3-qt. microwave-safe dish.

Cover and microwave on high for 3-4 minutes. Turn meatballs; cook 3-4 minutes longer or until no longer pink. Drain. Add spaghetti sauce.

Cover and microwave on high for 2-4 minutes or until heated through. Top with Parmesan cheese, onion and green peppers if desired. Serve on rolls. **YIELD: 12 servings.**

editor's note: This recipe was tested in a 1,100-watt microwave.

quick calzones

These individual stuffed pizzas taste delectable with or without the sauce on the side. Prepare half of the calzones with ham and the other half with pepperoni to satisfy all of the diners at your table.

—Clarice Brender, North Liberty, Iowa

2	cups (8 ounces) shredded part-skim mozzarella cheese
1	carton (15 ounces) ricotta cheese
6	ounces diced fully cooked ham *or* sliced pepperoni
1	teaspoon garlic powder
2	loaves (1 pound *each*) frozen bread dough, thawed

Warmed spaghetti *or* pizza sauce, optional

In a large bowl, combine the cheeses, ham and garlic powder. Divide each loaf into eight pieces.

On a floured surface, roll each portion into a 5-in. circle. Place filling in the center of each circle. Bring dough over filling; pinch seams to seal.

Place seam side down on greased baking sheets. Bake at 375° for 30-35 minutes or until golden brown. Serve warm with sauce if desired. Refrigerate leftovers. **YIELD: 16 servings.**

meatball sub sandwiches

kielbasa bow tie skillet

Combine cornstarch and milk until smooth; gradually add to the skillet. Bring to a boil; cook and stir for 2 minutes or until thickened. Drain pasta; add to sausage mixture. Stir in the peas and cheese; cook until cheese is melted. **YIELD: 4 servings.**

kielbasa bow tie skillet

This meal couldn't make dinnertime simpler! Not only is Kielbasa Bow Tie Skillet a real crowd pleaser, it comes together in just one pan. It freezes and reheats beautifully, too, so you'll want to fix extras for a fast entree later. My daughters are picky eaters, but this reminds them of macaroni and cheese. I toss in their favorite veggies, and they gobble it up!

—Lori Daniels, Beverly, West Virginia

8	ounces uncooked bow tie pasta
1	pound smoked kielbasa *or* smoked Polish sausage, cut into 1/4-inch slices
1	jar (4-1/2 ounces) sliced mushrooms, drained
2	teaspoons minced garlic
2	tablespoons butter
1	tablespoon cornstarch
1-1/2	cups milk
1-1/2	cups fresh *or* frozen snow peas
1	cup (4 ounces) shredded cheddar cheese

Cook pasta according to package directions. Meanwhile, in a large skillet, saute the sausage, mushrooms and garlic in butter.

marmalade baked ham

My family loves the flavor that orange marmalade, beer and brown sugar give this ham. Scoring the ham and inserting whole cloves gives it an appealing look with little effort. It couldn't be easier!

—Clo Runco, Punxsutawney, Pennsylvania

1	boneless fully cooked ham (3 to 4 pounds)
12	to 15 whole cloves
1	can (12 ounces) beer *or* beef broth
1/4	cup packed brown sugar
1/2	cup orange marmalade

Place ham on a rack in a shallow roasting pan. Score the surface of the ham, making diamond shapes 1/2 in. deep; insert a clove in each of the diamonds.

Pour beer or broth over ham. Rub brown sugar over surface of ham. Cover and bake at 325° for 1-1/4 hours.

Spread with marmalade. Bake, uncovered, for 15-25 minutes longer or until a meat thermometer reads 140°. **YIELD: 12-14 servings.**

marmalade baked ham

simple salisbury steak

simple salisbury steak

Fresh mushrooms and cream of mushroom soup create the speedy simmered sauce that covers these ground beef patties. The family-pleasing entree is always perfect for a busy weeknight.

—Elouise Bonar, Hanover, Illinois

1	egg
1/3	cup dry bread crumbs
1	can (10-3/4 ounces) reduced-fat reduced-sodium condensed cream of mushroom soup, undiluted, *divided*
1/4	cup finely chopped onion
1	pound lean ground beef
1/2	cup fat-free milk
1/4	teaspoon browning sauce, optional
1/4	teaspoon salt
1-1/2	cups sliced fresh mushrooms

In a large bowl, combine the egg, bread crumbs, 1/4 cup soup and onion. Crumble the beef over mixture and mix well. Shape into six patties. In a large nonstick skillet, brown the patties on both sides; drain.

In a small bowl, combine the milk, browning sauce if desired, salt and remaining soup; stir in mushrooms. Pour over patties. Reduce heat; cover and simmer for 15-20 minutes or until a meat thermometer reads 160° and meat is no longer pink. YIELD: 6 servings.

stovetop hamburger casserole

Here is comfort food at its best! It's not only loaded with ground beef, pasta, veggies and cheddar cheese, but it also goes together in a jiffy.

—Edith Landinger, Longview, Texas

1	package (7 ounces) small pasta shells
1-1/2	pounds ground beef
1	large onion, chopped
3	medium carrots, chopped
1	celery rib, chopped
3	garlic cloves, minced
3	cups cubed cooked red potatoes
1	can (15-1/4 ounces) whole kernel corn, drained
2	cans (8 ounces *each*) tomato sauce
1-1/2	teaspoons salt
1/2	teaspoon pepper
1	cup (4 ounces) shredded cheddar cheese

Cook pasta according to package directions. Meanwhile, in a large skillet, cook beef and onion over medium heat until meat is no longer pink; drain. Add the carrots, celery and garlic; cook and stir for 5 minutes or until vegetables are crisp-tender.

Stir in the potatoes, corn, tomato sauce, salt and pepper; heat through. Drain pasta and add to skillet; toss to coat. Sprinkle with cheese. Cover and cook until cheese is melted. YIELD: 6 servings.

stovetop hamburger casserole

grilled fish sandwiches

4   cod fillets (4 ounces *each*)
1   tablespoon lime juice
1/2   teaspoon lemon-pepper seasoning
1/4   cup mayonnaise
2   teaspoons Dijon mustard
1   teaspoon honey
4   hamburger buns, split
4   lettuce leaves
4   tomato slices

Brush both sides of fillets with lime juice; sprinkle with lemon-pepper. Coat grill rack with cooking spray before starting the grill. Grill fillets, covered, over medium heat for 5-6 minutes on each side or until fish flakes easily with a fork.

In a small bowl, combine the mayonnaise, mustard and honey. Spread over the bottom of each bun. Top with a fillet, lettuce and tomato; replace bun tops. **YIELD: 4 servings.**

grilled fish sandwiches

These fish fillets are seasoned with lime juice and lemon-pepper before charbroiling them on the grill. A simple mayonnaise and honey-mustard sauce puts the sandwiches ahead of the rest.

—Violet Beard, Marshall, Illinois

beef enchiladas

This spicy entree is a good dish to feed a large group of people. I appreciate the make-ahead convenience.

—Rosemary Gonser, Clay Center, Kansas

2-1/2   pounds ground beef
2/3   cup chopped onion
2   cans (15 ounces *each*) enchilada sauce
1   can (10-3/4 ounces) condensed cream of mushroom soup, undiluted
1   can (10-3/4 ounces) condensed tomato soup, undiluted
20   flour tortillas (8 inches), warmed
2-1/2   cups (10 ounces) shredded cheddar cheese

Additional shredded cheddar cheese

In a large skillet, cook beef and onion over medium heat until meat is no longer pink; drain. Combine enchilada sauce and soups; pour 1 cup into each of two ungreased 13-in. x 9-in. baking dishes. Stir 1-1/2 cups of sauce into beef mixture; set remaining sauce aside.

Spoon 1/4 cup beef mixture down the center of each tortilla; top with 2 tablespoons cheese. Roll up tightly; place 10 enchiladas seam side down in each prepared dish. Top with remaining sauce. Cover and freeze one pan for up to 3 months.

Cover and bake the remaining pan at 350° for 25-30 minutes. Uncover; sprinkle with additional cheese. Bake 5-10 minutes longer or until cheese is melted.

To use frozen enchiladas: Thaw in the refrigerator overnight. Bake as directed. **YIELD: 2 pans (10 enchiladas each).**

ravioli skillet

It's easy to dress up store-bought ravioli and make it really special. Our home economists used prosciutto and mozzarella to do the trick.

ravioli skillet

1	pound ground beef	3/4	cup water
3/4	cup chopped green pepper	1	package (25 ounces) frozen cheese ravioli
1	ounce prosciutto *or* deli ham, chopped	1	cup (4 ounces) shredded part-skim mozzarella cheese
3	cups spaghetti sauce		

In a large skillet, cook the beef, green pepper and prosciutto over medium heat until meat is no longer pink; drain.

Stir in spaghetti sauce and water; bring to a boil. Add ravioli. Reduce heat; cover and simmer for 7-9 minutes or until ravioli is tender, stirring once. Sprinkle with cheese. Simmer, uncovered, 1-2 minutes longer or until cheese is melted. **YIELD: 4 servings.**

saucy skillet lasagna

Thanks to no-cook lasagna noodles, this is an effortless take on an all-time classic. It makes a fresh, filling, flavorful and fast entree for any Italian meal.

—Meghan Crihfield, Ripley, West Virginia

1	**pound ground beef**
1	**can (14-1/2 ounces) diced tomatoes, undrained**
2	**eggs, lightly beaten**
1-1/2	**cups ricotta cheese**
4	**cups Italian baking sauce**
1	**package (9 ounces) no-cook lasagna noodles**
1	**cup (4 ounces) shredded part-skim mozzarella cheese, optional**

In a large skillet, cook beef over medium heat until no longer pink; drain. Transfer to a large bowl; stir in tomatoes. In a small bowl, combine eggs and ricotta cheese.

Return 1 cup meat mixture to the skillet; spread evenly. Layer with 1 cup ricotta mixture, 1-1/2 cups sauce and half of the noodles. Repeat layers. Top with remaining sauce.

saucy skillet lasagna

Bring to a boil. Reduce heat; cover and simmer for 15-17 minutes or until noodles are tender. Remove from the heat. Sprinkle with mozzarella cheese if desired; let stand for 2 minutes or until cheese is melted. **YIELD: 6-8 servings.**

editor's note: This recipe was tested with Barilla Al Forno Italian Baking Sauce.

hamburger goulash

When I was growing up, my birthday meal of choice was always goulash over mashed potatoes. Now I make my mother's tangy recipe for my own family to enjoy.

—Jennifer Willingham, Kansas City, Missouri

2-1/2	**pounds ground beef**
1	**medium onion, chopped**
2	**cups water**
3/4	**cup ketchup**
2	**tablespoons Worcestershire sauce**
2	**teaspoons paprika**
1	**to 2 teaspoons sugar**
1	**teaspoon salt**
1/2	**teaspoon ground mustard**
1/4	**teaspoon garlic powder**
2	**tablespoons all-purpose flour**
1/4	**cup cold water**

Hot cooked noodles *or* mashed potatoes

In a Dutch oven, cook beef and onion over medium heat until meat is no longer pink; drain. Add the water, ketchup, Worcestershire sauce, paprika, sugar, salt, mustard and garlic powder. Bring to a boil. Reduce heat; simmer the mixture, uncovered, for 20 minutes.

In a small bowl, combine flour and cold water until smooth; stir into the meat mixture. Bring to a boil; cook and stir for 2 minutes or until thickened. Serve over noodles or potatoes; or cool and freeze for up to 3 months.

To use frozen casserole: Thaw in the refrigerator; place in a saucepan and heat through. **YIELD: 6 cups.**

moist ham loaf

moist ham loaf

Not only is this main dish special enough for entertaining, but I can assemble it early in the day and pop it in the oven before dinnertime. It seems much fancier than meat loaf, but it's just as easy to make. Plus the cherry sauce really dresses it up, so guests think I fussed.

—Nancy Brown, Dahinda, Illinois

1	egg, lightly beaten
1/2	cup milk
1/3	cup dry bread crumbs
1/2	teaspoon onion powder
1/4	teaspoon pepper
1	pound ground fully cooked ham
1/2	pound ground turkey

CHERRY SAUCE:

1/2	cup cherry preserves
1	tablespoon cider vinegar
1/8	teaspoon ground cloves

In a large bowl, combine the first five ingredients. Crumble ham and turkey over mixture and mix well. Press into a greased 9-in. x 5-in. loaf pan. Bake, uncovered, at 375° for 50-55 minutes or until a meat thermometer reads 160°.

In a small saucepan, combine sauce ingredients. Cook and stir over medium heat for 5 minutes or until heated through. Serve with ham loaf. **YIELD: 6 servings.**

stovetop pork dinner

Sometimes it's nice to combine a recipe's ingredients into one pan and simmer it on the stove, instead of turning on the oven and that's why I appreciate this recipe.

—Connie Moore, Medway, Ohio

4	bone-in pork loin chops (1/2 inch thick and 4 ounces *each*)
8	small new potatoes, optional
1	small onion, chopped
1	can (10-3/4 ounces) condensed cream of chicken soup, undiluted
1	can (4 ounces) sliced mushrooms, drained
1/4	cup water
1/2	teaspoon garlic salt
1/2	teaspoon Worcestershire sauce
1/4	teaspoon dried thyme
2	cups frozen peas and carrots

In a large skillet, cook pork for 3-4 minutes on each side or until a meat thermometer reads 160°; drain. Add potatoes if desired and onion.

In a large bowl, combine the soup, mushrooms, water, garlic salt, Worcestershire sauce and thyme; pour into skillet. Bring to a boil. Reduce heat; cover and simmer for 1 hour.

Stir in the peas and carrots; cover and simmer for 10 minutes or until heated through. **YIELD: 4 servings.**

stovetop pork dinner

cranberry pork roast

cranberry pork roast

Everyone raves about this tender roast, and I love preparing it because it's so simple. The gravy is delicious over creamy mashed potatoes.

—Audrey Thibodeau, Gilbert, Arizona

1	boneless rolled pork loin roast (2-1/2 to 3 pounds)
1	can (16 ounces) jellied cranberry sauce
1/2	cup sugar
1/2	cup cranberry juice
1	teaspoon ground mustard
1/4	teaspoon ground cloves
2	tablespoons cornstarch
2	tablespoons cold water

Salt to taste

Place pork roast in a 5-qt. slow cooker. In a small bowl, mash cranberry sauce; stir in the sugar, cranberry juice, mustard and cloves. Pour over roast. Cover and cook on low for 6-8 hours or until meat is tender.

Remove roast and keep warm. Skim fat from juices. Pour into a 2-cup measuring cup; add water if necessary to measure 2 cups. Pour into a small saucepan. Bring to a boil over medium-high heat. Combine cornstarch and cold water until smooth; stir into pan juices. Bring to a boil. Cook and stir for 2 minutes or until thickened. Season with salt. Serve with sliced pork. **YIELD: 4-6 servings.**

chicken parmesan

This easy combination of chicken breasts in spaghetti sauce makes a pretty dish, and it's so flavorful.

—Mary Dennis, Bryan, Ohio

2	boneless skinless chicken breast halves (8 ounces *each*)
2	teaspoons canola oil
1-1/2	cups spaghetti sauce
1	can (4 ounces) mushroom stems and pieces, drained
1/2	cup shredded part-skim mozzarella cheese
2	tablespoons grated Parmesan cheese

Hot cooked linguine

In a large ovenproof skillet, brown chicken in oil over medium heat. Add spaghetti sauce and mushrooms. Bring to a boil. Reduce heat; cover and simmer for 10-15 minutes or until a meat thermometer reads 170°.

Sprinkle with cheeses. Broil 4-6 in. from the heat for 3-4 minutes or until cheese is melted. Serve with linguine. **YIELD: 2 servings.**

chicken parmesan

simple manicotti

I found this recipe in a cookbook from my mother's hometown. Since everyone there is a good cook, I knew this would be terrific. One taste proved me right!

—Pam Clemens, Wimbledon, North Dakota

1-1/2	pounds ground beef
2	cups spaghetti sauce, *divided*
1	tablespoon onion powder
1	teaspoon salt
1/2	teaspoon pepper
1	cup (4 ounces) shredded part-skim mozzarella cheese
14	large manicotti shells, cooked and drained

In a large skillet, cook beef over medium heat until no longer pink; drain. Remove from heat. Stir in 1 cup spaghetti sauce, onion powder, salt and pepper. Cool for 5 minutes. Set 1/2 cup aside. Add cheese to the remaining meat mixture.

Stuff into manicotti shells; arrange in a greased 13-in. x 9-in. baking dish. Combine remaining spaghetti sauce and reserved meat mixture; pour over shells.

Bake, uncovered, at 350° for 10 minutes or until heated through. **YIELD: 7 servings.**

chicken and dressing dish

I've always enjoyed trying new recipes, and now that our children are grown, I have more time to do just that!

—Anne Smith, Taylors, South Carolina

1	cup chopped onion
1	cup chopped celery
1/4	cup butter, cubed
2	cups chicken broth
1-1/2	teaspoons dried thyme
1	teaspoon poultry seasoning
1/2	teaspoon salt

chicken and dressing dish

1/2	teaspoon pepper
1/4	teaspoon ground nutmeg
2	eggs, lightly beaten *or* 1/2 cup egg substitute
1	package (12 ounces) unseasoned stuffing cubes
1/4	cup minced fresh parsley
3	cups cubed cooked chicken
1	can (10-3/4 ounces) condensed cream of chicken *or* mushroom soup, undiluted
1/3	cup water

In a large saucepan, saute onion and celery in butter until tender; remove from the heat. Stir in the broth, seasonings and eggs. Add stuffing cubes and parsley; toss to coat.

Transfer to a greased 13-in. x 9-in. baking dish. Top with chicken. Combine soup and water; spoon over chicken. Let stand for 10 minutes.

Cover and bake at 350° for 50 minutes. Uncover; bake 5-10 minutes longer or until a thermometer reads 160°. **YIELD: 8 servings.**

baked ham sandwiches

Minced onion and prepared mustard put a flavorful spin on these ham and cheese sandwiches. I simply take a few foil-wrapped favorites from the freezer and warm them in the oven for effort-less lunches. —Charlotte Rowe, Alto, New Mexico

baked ham sandwiches

1/3	cup butter, softened	8	hamburger buns, split
1/2	cup dried minced onion	16	slices deli ham
1/3	to 1/2 cup prepared mustard	8	slices Swiss cheese
2	tablespoons poppy seeds		

In a small bowl, combine the butter, onion, mustard and poppy seeds; spread about 2 tablespoons on each bun. Layer with ham and cheese; replace tops. Wrap each sandwich in foil.

Bake at 350° for 6-10 minutes or until cheese is melted, or freeze for up to 2 months.

To use frozen sandwiches: Bake at 350° for 30-35 minutes or until cheese is melted. **YIELD:** 8 servings.

Poultry must be completely thawed before roasting. It's best to thaw frozen poultry in the refrigerator. Plan on 24 hours per 5 pounds. Cold-water thawing is a quicker option. The poultry must be in a leakproof bag such as its original tightly sealed wrapper. Immerse the wrapped chicken in cold tap water. Make sure the water stays cold. Change the water every 30 minutes until the bird is thawed. Allow 30 minutes for every pound.

garlic-herb roasted chicken

- 1   roasting chicken (4 to 5 pounds)
- 2   teaspoons *each* minced fresh parsley, rosemary, sage and thyme
- 3/4   teaspoon salt
- 1/4   teaspoon pepper
- 20   garlic cloves, peeled and sliced
- 1   medium lemon, halved
- 1   large whole garlic bulb
- 1   fresh sprig *each* parsley, rosemary, sage and thyme

garlic-herb roasted chicken

With fingers, carefully loosen the skin around the chicken breast, leg and thigh. Combine minced parsley, rosemary, sage, thyme, salt and pepper; rub half under skin. Place whole garlic cloves under skin. Squeeze half of the lemon into the cavity and place the squeezed half in the cavity.

Remove paper outer skin from garlic bulb (do not peel or separate cloves). Cut top off garlic bulb. Place garlic bulb and fresh herb sprigs in the cavity. Skewer chicken openings; tie drumsticks together with kitchen string.

Place chicken breast side up on a rack in a roasting pan. Squeeze the remaining lemon over chicken; rub remaining herb mixture over chicken.

Bake, uncovered, at 350° for 1-1/2 to 1-3/4 hours or until chicken juices run clear and a meat thermometer reads 180° (cover loosely with foil if browning too quickly). Baste with pan drippings if desired.

Cover and let stand for 15 minutes. Remove and discard skin, garlic, lemon and herbs from cavity before carving. **YIELD: 8 servings.**

Seasonings baking in and on the bird make this succulent chicken so flavorful you can even eliminate the salt from the recipe if you like. The aroma in the kitchen while it's baking is tantalizing.

—Cindy Steffen, Cedarburg, Wisconsin

beef barley soup, page 96

side dishes

mom's best
side dishes

Rounding out a meal is a snap with the 50 dinner accompaniments found here. Turn the page and you'll find soups, sauces, salads and breads in addition to all of the savory veggie dishes you and your gang enjoy most...each made easy!

crusty french bread, page 105

vegetable medley, page 92

creamy macaroni 'n' cheese, page 90

creamy macaroni 'n' cheese

I prepare this cheesy recipe when I'm craving comfort food but trying to eat a little lighter. The hint of mustard adds zip to this creamy side dish—and it makes a pleasing meatless entree, too.

—Dawn Royer, Albany, Oregon

creamy macaroni 'n' cheese

1/3 cup finely chopped onion

3-1/2 cups cooked elbow macaroni

1-3/4 cups shredded reduced-fat cheddar cheese

2 tablespoons minced fresh parsley

1/2 cup fat-free evaporated milk

1-3/4 cups 2% cottage cheese

1 teaspoon Dijon mustard

1/2 teaspoon salt

1/4 teaspoon pepper

In a large microwave-safe bowl, cover and microwave onion on high for 1-1/4 minutes or until tender; drain. Add the macaroni, cheddar cheese and parsley; set aside.

In a blender, combine the milk, cottage cheese, mustard, salt and pepper; cover and process until smooth. Stir into macaroni mixture.

Pour into a 1-1/2-qt. baking dish coated with cooking spray. Bake, uncovered, at 350° for 20-25 minutes or until lightly browned. **YIELD: 8 servings.**

editor's note: This recipe was tested in a 1,100-watt microwave.

potato pancakes

3 cups finely shredded peeled potatoes
1-1/2 tablespoons all-purpose flour
1/8 teaspoon baking powder
1/2 to 1 teaspoon salt
2 eggs, beaten
1/2 teaspoon grated onion
Applesauce *or* maple syrup, optional

In a sieve or colander, drain the potatoes, squeezing to remove excess liquid. Pat dry; set aside.

In a large bowl, combine the flour, baking powder and salt. Stir in eggs until blended. Add onion and reserved potatoes; toss to coat.

Drop by tablespoonfuls onto a preheated greased skillet. Fry in batches until lightly browned on both sides. Drain on paper towels. Serve with applesauce or syrup if desired. **YIELD: 12 (2-inch) pancakes.**

potato pancakes

We grew our own potatoes on the small farm in New Hampshire where I was raised. These pancakes were always good served with pork dishes.

—Roseanna Budell, Dunnellon, Florida

mom's corn bread

mom's corn bread

1-1/2 cups yellow cornmeal
3/4 cup all-purpose flour
2 tablespoons sugar
2-1/4 teaspoons baking powder
1 teaspoon salt
2 eggs, lightly beaten
1-1/4 cups milk
1/4 cup shortening, melted

In a large bowl, combine the cornmeal, flour, sugar, baking powder and salt.

Whisk together the eggs, milk and shortening. Stir into dry ingredients just until blended.

Pour into a greased 8-in. square baking pan. Bake at 400° for 20-25 minutes, or until a toothpick inserted near the center of the corn bread comes out clean. **YIELD: about 9 servings.**

Mom always made a fresh batch of corn bread when she'd cook up a pot of chili. It just didn't seem right to have one without the other, so I rely on this recipe when I've got chili simmering on the stovetop.

—Norma Erne, Albuquerque, New Mexico

vegetable medley

vegetable medley

With its red pepper slices and green broccoli florets, this merry medley will brighten any table. I rely on mild seasonings to let the large variety of the vegetables' flavors shine through.

—Sara Lindler, Irmo, South Carolina

1	teaspoon chicken bouillon granules
1/4	cup water
1	teaspoon salt
1/4	teaspoon garlic powder
1/4	teaspoon pepper
1	teaspoon plus 1 tablespoon olive oil, *divided*
2	cups fresh broccoli florets
2	medium carrots thinly sliced
1	large onion, sliced and quartered
1	cup sliced celery
2	medium zucchini, halved lengthwise and thinly sliced
1	medium sweet red pepper, thinly sliced
1	cup sliced fresh mushrooms
2	cups thinly sliced cabbage

In a small saucepan, heat bouillon and water for 1 minute; stir well. Stir in the salt, garlic powder, pepper and 1 teaspoon oil.

In a large nonstick skillet or wok, stir-fry the broccoli, carrots, onion and celery in remaining oil for 2-3 minutes. Add the bouillon mixture; cook and stir for 3 minutes. Add zucchini and red pepper; stir-fry for 3 minutes. Add the mushrooms and cabbage; stir-fry 1-2 minutes longer or until crisp-tender. **YIELD: 8 servings.**

monkey bread

Both of my boys really enjoyed helping me make my Monkey Bread when they were young. It seemed to taste twice as good when they helped fix it.

—Carol Allen, McLeansboro, Illinois

1	package (3-1/2 ounces) cook-and-serve butterscotch pudding mix
3/4	cup sugar
3	teaspoons ground cinnamon
1/2	cup finely chopped pecans, optional
1/2	cup butter, melted
3	tubes (10 ounces *each*) refrigerated biscuits

In a large resealable plastic bag, combine the pudding mix, sugar, cinnamon and pecans if desired. Pour the butter into a shallow bowl. Cut the biscuits into quarters. Dip several pieces into the butter, then place in bag and shake to coat.

Arrange in a greased 10-in. fluted tube pan. Repeat until all the biscuit pieces are coated. Bake at 350° for 30-35 minutes or until browned. Cool for 30 minutes before inverting onto a serving plate. **YIELD: 10-12 servings.**

monkey bread

corn chowder

corn chowder

On cool days, this thick, popular chowder hits the spot as an addition to dinner or even a light lunch.

—Nancy Johnson, Connersville, Indiana

1	medium onion, chopped
6	cups fresh *or* frozen corn, *divided*
3	cups reduced-sodium chicken broth, *divided*
1/2	cup chopped sweet red pepper
1/2	teaspoon dried rosemary, crushed
1/2	teaspoon dried thyme
1/8	teaspoon pepper

Dash cayenne pepper

Coat a large saucepan with cooking spray. Add onion; cook and stir over medium heat for 4 minutes or until tender. Add 4 cups corn; cook and stir until corn is softened, about 5 minutes. Add 2 cups broth; bring to a boil. Reduce heat; cover and simmer for 10 minutes or until the corn is tender. Cool mixture slightly.

In a blender, process soup in batches until smooth; return all to pan. Add the red pepper, rosemary, thyme, pepper, cayenne and remaining corn and broth; cook and stir for 10 minutes or until the corn is tender. **YIELD: 4-6 servings (about 1-1/2 quarts).**

cheesy hash brown bake

This dish was so popular at the morning meetings of our Mothers of Preschoolers group that we published it in our newsletter. It's a great dish for busy moms because it can be prepared ahead of time. It's perfect for brunches. It's creamy, comforting and tasty.

—Karen Burns, Chandler, Texas

1	package (30 ounces) frozen shredded hash brown potatoes, thawed
2	cans (10-3/4 ounces *each*) condensed cream of potato soup, undiluted
2	cups (16 ounces) sour cream
2	cups (8 ounces) shredded cheddar cheese, *divided*
1	cup grated Parmesan cheese

In a large bowl, combine the potatoes, soup, sour cream, 1-3/4 cups of cheddar cheese and Parmesan cheese. Transfer to a greased 3-qt. baking dish. Sprinkle with remaining cheddar cheese.

Bake, uncovered, at 350° for 40-45 minutes or until bubbly and cheese is melted. Let stand for 5 minutes before serving. **YIELD: 10 servings.**

cheesy hash brown bake

broccoli cheese soup

The microwave makes this traditional soup very convenient. Carrots add a nice splash of color.
—Jean Paré, Vermilion, Alberta

broccoli cheese soup

1	cup thinly sliced carrots
2	tablespoons plus 1 cup water, *divided*
1	package (16 ounces) frozen broccoli florets, thawed
2-1/2	cups milk
1/4	cup all-purpose flour

2	teaspoons chicken bouillon granules
1/2	teaspoon salt
1/4	teaspoon pepper
1	cup (4 ounces) shredded cheddar cheese

In a 2-qt. microwave-safe dish, combine carrots and 2 tablespoons water. Cover and microwave on high for 2 minutes; stir. Cover and cook 2 minutes longer or until tender. Add broccoli. Cover and microwave for 2 minutes; stir. Cover and cook 1 to 1-1/2 minutes longer or until vegetables are tender. Stir in milk.

In a small bowl, combine the flour, bouillon, salt and pepper; stir in remaining water until smooth. Stir into broccoli mixture. Cover and microwave on high for 6-7 minutes or until mixture is boiling and thickened, stirring every minute. Stir in cheese until melted. **YIELD: 4-5 servings.**

editor's note: This recipe was tested in a 1,100-watt microwave.

corn pudding supreme

- 1 package (8 ounces) cream cheese, softened
- 2 eggs
- 1/3 cup sugar
- 2-1/3 cups fresh, frozen *or* canned sweet corn
- 1 can (14-3/4 ounces) cream-style corn
- 1 package (8-1/2 ounces) corn bread/muffin mix
- 1 cup milk
- 2 tablespoons butter, melted
- 1 teaspoon salt
- 1/2 teaspoon ground nutmeg

corn pudding supreme

In a small bowl, beat the cream cheese, eggs and sugar until blended. Stir in the remaining ingredients.

Transfer to a greased 13-in. x 9-in. baking pan. Bake at 350° for 45-50 minutes or until a thermometer reads 160°. **YIELD: 12-16 servings.**

When I'm hungry for a good corn recipe, I bake this golden pudding. Big on flavor, this classic, slightly sweet side dish always hits the spot.

—*Martha Fehl, Brookville, Indiana*

favorite broccoli salad

favorite broccoli salad

- 1 bunch broccoli, separated into florets
- 1 head cauliflower, separated into florets
- 8 bacon strips, cooked and crumbled
- 1 cup chopped seeded tomatoes
- 1/3 cup chopped onion
- 2 hard-cooked eggs, sliced
- 1 cup mayonnaise
- 1/3 cup sugar
- 2 tablespoons cider vinegar

In a large salad bowl, combine the broccoli, cauliflower, bacon, tomatoes, onion and eggs; set aside.

In another bowl, combine mayonnaise, sugar and vinegar. Just before serving, pour dressing over salad and toss. **YIELD: 6-8 servings.**

"Fresh tasting...so colorful...delicious dressing" are some of the compliments I get whenever I serve this broccoli salad with a meal or take it as my contribution to a church dinner.

—*Esther Shank, Harrisonburg, Virginia*

creamy red potatoes

creamy red potatoes

I know I can easily please guests with this four-ingredient side dish. It's a snap to double, and I always receive compliments when I take it to potlucks.

—Shelia Schmitt, Topeka, Kansas

2	pounds small red potatoes, quartered
1	package (8 ounces) cream cheese, softened
1	can (10-3/4 ounces) condensed cream of potato soup, undiluted
1	envelope ranch salad dressing mix

Place potatoes in a 3-qt. slow cooker. In a small bowl, beat cream cheese, soup and salad dressing mix until blended. Stir into potatoes. Cover and cook on low for 8 hours or until potatoes are tender. YIELD: 4-6 servings.

Kitchen Tip

Red potatoes hold their shape well, which is why they are so often used in slow-cooked dishes and recipes that call for boiled potatoes. They also save you time since their thin skin doesn't need peeling.

beef barley soup

This hearty soup is a favorite menu item in our house throughout the year. Everyone savors the classic flavor.

—Elizabeth Kendall, Carolina Beach, North Carolina

1	pound boneless beef top round steak, cut into 1/2-inch cubes
1	tablespoon canola oil
3	cans (14-1/2 ounces *each*) beef broth
2	cups water
1/3	cup medium pearl barley
1	teaspoon salt
1/8	teaspoon pepper
1	cup chopped carrots
1/2	cup chopped celery
1/4	cup chopped onion
3	tablespoons minced fresh parsley
1	cup frozen peas

In a Dutch oven or soup kettle, brown beef in oil; drain. Stir in the broth, water, barley, salt and pepper. Bring to a boil. Reduce heat; cover and simmer for 1 hour.

Add the carrots, celery, onion and parsley; cover and simmer for 45 minutes or until meat and vegetables are tender. Stir in peas; heat through. YIELD: 9 servings (2-1/4 quarts).

beef barley soup

heavenly crab cakes

When I switched to a low-fat diet, I thought I'd never be able to eat crab cakes again. But then I found this easy recipe. Now I can enjoy these little patties of paradise...without any guilt!

—Laura Letobar, Livonia, Michigan

1	cup Italian bread crumbs, *divided*
1/4	cup egg substitute
2	tablespoons fat-free mayonnaise
2	tablespoons Dijon mustard
1	tablespoon dill weed
1	tablespoon lime juice
1	teaspoon lemon juice
1	teaspoon Worcestershire sauce
1	pound imitation crabmeat, flaked

In a large bowl, combine the first eight ingredients. Fold in crab. Shape into patties. Place remaining bread crumbs in a shallow bowl; dip each patty into crumbs to cover. Refrigerate for 30 minutes.

In a large skillet coated with cooking spray over medium-high heat, cook crab cakes in batches or until golden brown on both sides. **YIELD: 8 servings.**

orange candied carrots

My son always asks for these carrot coins at Thanksgiving. The orange flavor in the sweet, mild sauce really comes through. This pleasant side dish is a great way to easily dress up a meal of leftovers.

—Lori Lockrey, West Hill, Ontario

1	pound carrots, cut into 1/2-inch slices
1/4	pound butter, softened
1/4	cup jellied cranberry sauce
1	orange peel strip (1 to 3 inches)
2	tablespoons brown sugar
1/2	teaspoon salt

orange candied carrots

Place 1 in. of water and carrots in a skillet; bring to a boil. Reduce heat; cover and simmer for 15-20 minutes or until crisp-tender.

Meanwhile, in a blender, combine the butter, cranberry sauce, orange peel, brown sugar and salt. Cover and process until blended. Drain carrots; drizzle with cranberry mixture. **YIELD: 3 servings.**

marinated brussels sprouts

This unique relish adds a lively twist to any party. And with only five ingredients, it comes together in a pinch.

—Marie Hattrup, The Dalles, Oregon

1	package (10 ounces) frozen brussels sprouts
1	cup Italian salad dressing
1	tablespoon finely chopped onion
1	garlic clove, minced
1/2	teaspoon dill weed

Cook brussels sprouts according to package directions; drain. Combine remaining ingredients; pour over sprouts and toss to coat. Cover and refrigerate. **YIELD: 2-1/2 cups.**

grandma's gelatin fruit salad

Whenever I'm hosting a family dinner, my sons and grandchildren ask me to make this fruit salad. The taste doesn't just run in my family...the salad is always popular at large get-togethers, too.

—Wilma McLean, Medford, Oregon

2	cups boiling water, *divided*
1	package (3 ounces) lemon gelatin
2	cups ice cubes, *divided*
1	can (20 ounces) crushed pineapple, liquid drained and reserved
1	package (3 ounces) orange gelatin
2	cups miniature marshmallows
1/2	cup sugar
2	tablespoons cornstarch
1	cup reserved pineapple juice
1	egg, lightly beaten
1	tablespoon butter
3	large bananas, sliced
1	cup whipped topping
1/2	cup finely shredded cheddar cheese

In a large bowl, combine 1 cup water and lemon gelatin. Add 1 cup ice cubes, stirring until melted. Stir in pineapple. Pour into a 13-in. x 9-in. dish coated with cooking spray; refrigerate until set but not firm.

Repeat with the orange gelatin, remaining water and ice. Stir in marshmallows. Pour over lemon layer; refrigerate until firm.

Meanwhile, in a small saucepan, combine sugar and cornstarch. Stir in reserved pineapple juice until smooth. Cook and stir over medium-high heat until thickened and bubbly. Reduce heat; cook and stir 2 minutes longer. Remove from the heat.

Stir a small amount of hot filling into egg; return all to the pan, stirring constantly. Bring to a gentle boil; cook and stir 2 minutes longer. Remove from the heat; stir in butter. Cool to room temperature without stirring. Refrigerate dressing for 1 hour or until chilled.

Arrange bananas over gelatin. Stir whipped topping into dressing. Spread over bananas. Sprinkle with cheese. **YIELD: 12-15 servings.**

grandma's gelatin fruit salad

traditional mashed potatoes

Mashed potatoes make a wonderful accompaniment to most any meal, so keep this classic recipe handy. The easy dish comes from our home economists.

6	medium russet potatoes (about 2 pounds), peeled and cubed
1/2	cup warm milk
1/4	cup butter, cubed
3/4	teaspoon salt

Dash pepper

Place potatoes in a saucepan and cover with water. Cover and bring to a boil; cook for 20-25 minutes or until very tender. Drain well.

Add the milk, butter, salt and pepper; mash until light and fluffy. **YIELD: 6 servings (about 5 cups).**

chicken tortellini soup

This simple soup is a fun twist on old-fashioned chicken noodle soup. It's extra special made with cheese tortellini. The seasonings give it an Italian flair without much effort.

—Jean Atherly, Red Lodge, Montana

chicken tortellini soup

2 cans (14-1/2 ounces *each*) chicken broth

2 cups water

3/4 pound boneless skinless chicken breasts, cut into 1-inch cubes

1-1/2 cups frozen mixed vegetables

1 package (9 ounces) refrigerated cheese tortellini

2 celery ribs, thinly sliced

1 teaspoon dried basil

1/2 teaspoon garlic salt

1/2 teaspoon dried oregano

1/4 teaspoon pepper

In a large saucepan, bring broth and water to a boil; add chicken. Reduce heat; cook for 10 minutes.

Add the remaining ingredients; cook 10-15 minutes longer or until chicken is no longer pink and vegetables are tender. **YIELD: 8 servings (about 2 quarts).**

cheesy tortilla soup

1	envelope chicken fajita seasoning mix
1	pound boneless skinless chicken breasts, diced
2	tablespoons canola oil
1/2	cup chopped onion
1/4	cup butter, cubed
1/3	cup all-purpose flour
2	cans (14-1/2 ounces *each*) chicken broth
1/3	cup canned diced tomatoes with chilies
1	cup cubed process cheese (Velveeta)
1-1/2	cups (6 ounces) shredded Monterey Jack cheese, *divided*
1-1/2	cups half-and-half cream

Guacamole

1/2	cup shredded cheddar cheese

Tortilla chips

Prepare fajita mix according to package directions; add chicken and marinate as directed. In a large skillet, cook chicken in oil until no longer pink; set aside.

In a large saucepan, saute onion in butter until tender. Stir in flour until blended. Gradually stir in broth. Bring to a boil. Cook and stir for 2 minutes or until thickened and bubbly. Add the tomatoes, process cheese and 1 cup Monterey Jack; cook and stir until cheese is melted.

Stir in cream and reserved chicken; heat through (do not boil). Garnish with the guacamole, cheddar cheese and remaining Monterey Jack cheese; add tortilla chips. YIELD: 8 servings (2 quarts).

cheesy tortilla soup

Here's an easy take on a restaurant staple. It gets raves whenever I serve it.

—Marilyn Paradis, Woodburn, Oregon

mock hollandaise

This quick version of hollandaise sauce dresses up any vegetable. It's especially good with asparagus, broccoli or even green beans.

—Millie Vickery, Lena, Illinois

3/4	cup mayonnaise
1/2	cup milk
1	teaspoon lemon juice
1	teaspoon grated lemon peel
1/4	teaspoon salt

Dash pepper

Cooked asparagus spears *or* vegetable of your choice

In a small heavy saucepan, whisk mayonnaise and milk until blended. Cook and stir over low heat for 3-4 minutes or until warmed. Add the lemon juice, peel, salt, and pepper; cook and stir until heated through. Serve immediately with asparagus or vegetable of your choice. Refrigerate leftovers. YIELD: 1 cup.

crunchy sweet potato casserole

Some tasty seasonings, like cinnamon and nutmeg, and a crunchy corn flake topping actually make it fun for kids to eat these nutritious sweet potatoes.

—Virginia Slater, West Sunbury, Pennsylvania

2	cups mashed sweet potatoes
1/2	cup butter, melted
1/4	cup sugar
1/4	cup packed brown sugar
2	eggs, lightly beaten
1/2	cup milk
1	teaspoon ground cinnamon
1/2	teaspoon ground nutmeg

TOPPING:

1	cup crushed cornflakes
1/2	cup chopped walnuts
1/4	cup packed brown sugar
1/4	cup butter

In a large bowl, combine the first eight ingredients. Spoon into a greased 1-1/2-qt. baking dish. Bake, uncovered, at 375° for 20 minutes or until a thermometer reads 160°.

Combine topping ingredients; sprinkle over potatoes. Bake 5-10 minutes longer or until the topping is lightly browned. **YIELD: 6 servings.**

crunchy sweet potato casserole

italian veggie skillet

italian veggie skillet

This colorful blend of sauteed vegetables is as pretty as it is tasty. The recipe was given to me by a dear friend, and it's become a family favorite. It's a fast summer side from our garden.

—Sue Spencer, Coarsegold, California

1	medium onion, halved and sliced
1	medium sweet red pepper, chopped
1	tablespoon olive oil
3	medium zucchini, thinly sliced
1	garlic clove, minced
1-1/2	cups frozen corn, thawed
1	large tomato, chopped
2	teaspoons minced fresh basil
1/2	teaspoon salt
1/2	teaspoon Italian seasoning
1/4	cup shredded Parmesan cheese

In a large nonstick skillet, saute onion and red pepper in oil for 2 minutes. Add the zucchini and garlic; saute 4-5 minutes longer or until vegetables are crisp-tender.

Add the corn, tomato, basil, salt and Italian seasoning; cook and stir until heated through. Sprinkle with Parmesan cheese. Serve immediately. **YIELD: 6 servings.**

luncheon pasta salad

1	cup uncooked spiral pasta
1	cup cubed fully cooked ham
1	small cucumber, diced
1	small tomato, seeded and diced
5	radishes, sliced
2	tablespoons finely chopped onion
1	bottle (8 ounces) cucumber ranch salad dressing, *divided*
1/4	teaspoon salt, optional
1/4	teaspoon pepper
4	cups torn lettuce
3/4	cup cubed Colby *or* cheddar cheese

Cook pasta according to package directions; drain and rinse in cold water. Transfer to a large bowl; add the ham, cucumber, tomato, radishes and onion. Add 1/2 cup dressing, salt if desired and pepper; toss to coat. Cover and refrigerate for at least 2 hours.

Just before serving, add the lettuce, cheese and remaining dressing; toss to coat. **YIELD: 8 servings.**

luncheon pasta salad

I first tasted this salad at a ladies luncheon at church. My husband and children ask for it regularly.

—*Julie Heitsch, St. Louis, Michigan*

grilled corn with chive butter

6	medium ears sweet corn in husks
1/2	cup butter, melted
2	tablespoons minced chives
1	tablespoon sugar
1-1/2	teaspoons lemon juice

Salt and pepper

Soak corn in cold water for 1 hour. In a small bowl, combine the butter, chives, sugar, lemon juice, salt and pepper. Carefully peel back corn husks to within 1 in. of bottom; remove silk. Brush with butter mixture. Rewrap corn in husks and secure with kitchen string.

Grill corn, uncovered, over medium heat for 25-30 minutes, turning occasionally. **YIELD: 6 servings.**

grilled corn with chive butter

When our son was young, corn was the only vegetable he'd eat. My husband and I soon got bored with the simple salt and butter topping, so I stirred in some lemon juice and chives.

—*Sue Kirsch, Eden Prairie, Minnesota*

mashed potatoes supreme

I received this recipe from my sister 60 years ago and so many people have requested it since then! The potatoes are rich, creamy and taste like twice-baked.

—Julia Daubresse, Sun City Center, Florida

mashed potatoes supreme

3	pounds medium red potatoes, quartered
2	packages (3 ounces *each*) cream cheese, cubed
1/2	cup butter, cubed
1/2	cup half-and-half cream *or* milk
1	medium green pepper, chopped
4	green onions, thinly sliced
1	jar (2 ounces) sliced pimientos, drained
1/2	teaspoon salt
1/4	teaspoon pepper
1/2	cup shredded cheddar cheese, *divided*
1/2	cup grated Parmesan cheese, *divided*

Place potatoes in a large saucepan; cover with water. Bring to a boil. Reduce heat; cover and cook for 15-20 minutes or until tender. Drain.

In a large bowl, mash the potatoes. Add the cream cheese, butter and cream; beat until blended. Stir in the green pepper, onions, pimientos, salt and pepper. Stir in 1/3 cup cheddar cheese and 1/3 cup Parmesan cheese.

Transfer to a greased 11-in. x 7-in. baking dish. Sprinkle with remaining cheeses. Bake, uncovered, at 350° for 20-25 minutes or until heated through. **YIELD: 8 servings.**

stuffed baked potatoes

My mom gave me the recipe for these twice-baked potatoes, and I altered them by adding garlic, bacon and green onions. My two boys absolutely love them!

—Kristyn Drews, Omaha, Nebraska

5	medium baking potatoes
1/4	cup butter, softened
2	cups (8 ounces) shredded cheddar cheese, *divided*
3/4	cup sour cream
1	envelope ranch salad dressing mix
1	tablespoon minced chives
1	garlic clove, minced

Crumbled cooked bacon and chopped green onion

Scrub and pierce potatoes. Bake at 375° for 1 hour or until tender. When cool enough to handle, cut a thin slice off the top of each potato and discard. Cut each potato in half lengthwise. Scoop out the pulp, leaving thin shells.

In a large bowl, beat the pulp with butter. Stir in 1 cup of cheese, sour cream, salad dressing mix, chives and garlic. Spoon into potato shells. Sprinkle with remaining cheese.

Place on a baking sheet. Bake at 375° for 15-20 minutes or until heated through. Top with bacon and green onions. **YIELD: 10 servings.**

microwave french onion soup

Enjoy the taste and comfort of this classic soup through the convenience of microwave cooking. It's a simple recipe that I turn to time and again. After one spoonful, you'll understand why. Serve it as a surprise before any main dish or try it for a light meal.

—Mina Dyck, Boissevain, Manitoba

3	cups boiling water
1	can (14-1/2 ounces) beef *or* vegetable broth
3	tablespoons butter
1	vegetable bouillon cube
1	teaspoon Worcestershire sauce
1/8	teaspoon salt
1/8	teaspoon pepper
3	cups thinly sliced onions
2	cups seasoned croutons
1-1/3	cups shredded part-skim mozzarella cheese

In a 3-qt. microwave-safe dish, combine the first eight ingredients. Cover and microwave at 50% power for 18-23 minutes or until onions are tender.

Ladle hot soup into four microwave-safe bowls. Top with croutons and cheese.

Cover and microwave on high for 45 seconds or until cheese is melted. Serve immediately. **YIELD: 4 servings.**

editor's note: This recipe was prepared with Knorr vegetable bouillon. A half-cube makes 1 cup prepared bouillon. The recipe was tested in a 1,100-watt microwave.

stuffed baked potatoes

in a warm place until doubled, about 1 hour. Punch dough down; return to bowl. Cover and let rise for 30 minutes.

Punch dough down. Turn onto a lightly floured surface. Shape into a 16-in. x 2-1/2-in. loaf with tapered ends. Sprinkle a greased baking sheet with cornmeal; place loaf on baking sheet. Cover and let rise until doubled, about 25 minutes.

Beat egg white and cold water; brush over dough. With a sharp knife, make diagonal slashes 2 in. apart across top of loaf. Bake at 375° for 25-30 minutes or until golden brown. Remove from pan to a wire rack to cool. **YIELD: 1 loaf (16 slices).**

bok choy salad

Depending on what I have at home, I sometimes use only the sunflower kernels or almonds in this salad. The recipe makes a big amount, perfect for cookouts or reunions.

—Stephanie Marchese, Whitefish Bay, Wisconsin

1	**head bok choy, finely chopped**
2	**bunches green onions, thinly sliced**
2	**packages (3 ounces *each*) ramen noodles, broken**
1/4	**cup slivered almonds**
2	**tablespoons sunflower kernels**
1/4	**cup butter**

DRESSING:

1/3	**to 1/2 cup sugar**
1/2	**cup canola oil**
2	**tablespoons cider vinegar**
1	**tablespoon soy sauce**

In a large bowl, combine the bok choy and green onions; set aside. Save seasoning packet from ramen noodles for another use. In a large skillet, saute the noodles, almonds and sunflower kernels in butter for 7 minutes or until browned. Remove from the heat; cool to room temperature. Add to bok choy mixture.

In a jar with a tight fitting lid, combine the dressing ingredients; shake well. Just before serving, drizzle over salad and toss to coat. **YIELD: 10 servings.**

crusty french bread

crusty french bread

A delicate texture makes this simple bread absolutely wonderful. I sometimes use the dough to make bread-sticks, which I brush with melted butter and sprinkle with garlic powder.

—Deanna Naivar, Temple, Texas

1	**package (1/4 ounce) active dry yeast**
1	**cup warm water (110° to 115°)**
2	**tablespoons sugar**
2	**tablespoons canola oil**
1-1/2	**teaspoons salt**
3	**to 3-1/4 cups all-purpose flour**

Cornmeal

1	**egg white**
1	**teaspoon cold water**

In a large bowl, dissolve yeast in warm water. Add the sugar, oil, salt and 2 cups flour. Beat until blended. Stir in enough remaining flour to form a stiff dough.

Turn onto a floured surface; knead until smooth and elastic, about 6-8 minutes. Place in a greased bowl, turning once to grease top. Cover and let rise

In a large bowl, combine the first six ingredients. In another bowl, combine the artichoke, salad dressing, basil, garlic powder, oregano and lemon-pepper. Add to corn mixture and toss gently. Cover and refrigerate for at least 6 hours before serving. YIELD: 10 servings.

cheesy spinach casserole

This quiche-like casserole is a wonderful way to include good-for-you spinach in your menu. Made with eggs and cheese, the easy-to-cut side dish would also be a welcome addition to a breakfast or brunch buffet.

—Marilyn Paradis, Woodburn, Oregon

- 3/4 **cup chopped onion**
- 1 **tablespoon butter**
- 2 **eggs**
- 1 **package (10 ounces) frozen chopped spinach, thawed and squeezed dry**
- 2 **cups (16 ounces) 2% cottage cheese**
- 1 **cup (4 ounces) shredded reduced-fat cheddar cheese**
- 3 **tablespoons all-purpose flour**
- 1/8 **teaspoon salt**

In a small nonstick skillet, saute onion in butter until tender. In large bowl, combine the eggs, egg white and spinach. Stir in the cottage cheese, cheddar cheese, flour, salt and onion mixture. Pour into a 1-1/2-qt. baking dish coated with cooking spray.

Bake, uncovered, at 350° for 50-60 minutes or until a thermometer reads 160°. YIELD: 6 servings.

Kitchen Tip

It's easy to squeeze spinach dry to avoid your dishes from watering out. Simply set the spinach in a colander. If the spinach was cooked, allow it to cool. With clean hands, squeeze out the water.

corn relish salad

corn relish salad

My family enjoys hiking in the mountains. This salad is great with chicken or trout grilled over a campfire. It's perfect for backyard picnics.

—Claudia Poynter, Augusta, Kansas

- 2 **cups fresh *or* frozen corn**
- 3 **medium tomatoes, seeded and chopped**
- 1 **medium green pepper, diced**
- 1/2 **cup chopped red onion**
- 1/2 **cup sliced celery**
- 1 **can (2-1/4 ounces) sliced ripe olives, drained**
- 1 **jar (6-1/2 ounces) marinated artichoke hearts, undrained**
- 1/4 **cup reduced-fat Italian salad dressing**
- 5 **fresh basil leaves, finely chopped *or* 1 teaspoon dried basil**
- 1/2 **teaspoon garlic powder**
- 1/2 **teaspoon dried oregano**
- 1/4 **teaspoon lemon-pepper seasoning**

chunky chicken noodle soup

Marjoram and thyme come through nicely in this old-fashioned soup that tastes just like Grandma used to make. You can modify the recipe to include vegetables your family enjoys. My kids love carrots, so I always toss in a few extra.

—Coleen Martin, Brookfield, Wisconsin

chunky chicken noodle soup

1/2 cup diced carrot	1/2 teaspoon dried marjoram
1/4 cup diced celery	1/2 teaspoon dried thyme
1/4 cup chopped onion	1/8 teaspoon pepper
1 teaspoon butter	1-1/4 cups uncooked medium egg noodles
6 cups chicken broth	
1-1/2 cups diced cooked chicken	1 tablespoon minced fresh parsley
1 teaspoon salt	

In a large saucepan, saute the carrot, celery and onion in butter until tender. Stir in the broth, chicken and seasonings; bring to a boil. Reduce heat. Add noodles; cook for 10 minutes or until the noodles are tender. Sprinkle with parsley. **YIELD: 6 servings.**

sweet potato salad

When I took this salad to a potluck dinner, several people asked me for the recipe. The sweet potatoes give it a refreshing flair on a buffet table. I think you'll agree it's a nice change of pace from traditional potato salads.

—Lettie Baker, Pennsboro, West Virginia

sweet potato salad

3 pounds sweet potatoes, cooked, peeled and cubed	1-1/2 teaspoons salt, optional
1 cup chopped green pepper	1/4 teaspoon pepper
1/2 cup finely chopped onion	1-1/2 cups mayonnaise
	Dash hot pepper sauce

Combine the first five ingredients in a large bowl. Stir in mayonnaise and pepper sauce. Cover and refrigerate for at least 1 hour before serving. **YIELD: 10 servings.**

chicken dumpling soup

This comforting soup with soft dumplings was one of Mom's mainstays. With only three items, it's a cinch.

—Brenda Risser, Willard, Ohio

2	cans (10-3/4 ounces *each*) condensed cream of chicken soup, undiluted
3-1/3	cups milk, *divided*
1-2/3	cups biscuit/baking mix

In a 3-qt. saucepan, combine soup and 2-2/3 cups of milk. Bring to a boil over medium heat; reduce heat.

Meanwhile, in a large bowl, combine biscuit mix with remaining milk just until blended. Drop by rounded tablespoons onto simmering soup. Cook, uncovered, for 10 minutes.

Cover and simmer for 10-12 minutes or until a toothpick inserted in a dumpling comes out clean (do not lift the cover while simmering). **YIELD: 4 servings.**

green bean casserole

Who doesn't love green beans when they're dressed up in a creamy sauce and topped with golden french-fried onions? With this version, the popular side dish is sized right for two.

—Christy Hinrichs, Parkville, Missouri

1/2	cup condensed cream of mushroom soup, undiluted
3	tablespoons milk
1/2	teaspoon soy sauce
Dash pepper	
1-1/3	cups frozen cut green beans *or* cut fresh green beans
1/2	cup french-fried onions, *divided*

In a large bowl, combine the soup, milk, soy sauce and pepper. Stir in beans and 1/4 cup onions.

Transfer to a 2 or 3 cup baking dish coated with cooking spray. Sprinkle with remaining onions.

Bake, uncovered, at 400° for 12-15 minutes or until bubbly. **YIELD: 2 servings.**

creamy sweet corn

The addition of cream is all it takes to jazz up fresh or frozen corn. The simple take on this classic side dish tastes rich, and it takes just minutes to simmer together.

—Florence Jacoby, Granite Falls, Minnesota

2	cups fresh *or* frozen corn
1/4	cup half-and-half cream
2	tablespoons butter
1	tablespoon sugar
1/2	teaspoon salt

In a large saucepan, combine all ingredients. Bring to a boil over medium heat; reduce heat. Simmer, uncovered, for 6-8 minutes or until heated through. **YIELD: 4 servings.**

creamy sweet corn

fiesta corn salad

This simple salad is great for covered-dish dinners since it travels well and goes with everything.

—Marian Platt, Sequim, Washington

2	cups fresh *or* frozen corn
3	tomatoes, chopped
1	can (2-1/4 ounces) sliced pitted ripe olives, drained
1/4	cup sliced green olives
2	tablespoons taco seasoning
1/4	cup canola oil
1/4	cup white vinegar
1/4	cup water

In a large bowl, combine the corn, tomatoes and olives. In a small bowl, combine the seasoning mix, oil, vinegar and water; pour over corn mixture and toss to coat. Chill several hours before serving. **YIELD: 8-10 servings.**

microwave german potato salad

This salad has big flavor for a quick recipe. It's a time-saver when I need an impressive item for a get-together.

—Barbara Erdmann, West Allis, Wisconsin

fiesta corn salad

2	pounds red potatoes, cooked and sliced
3	hard-cooked eggs, chopped
1/2	cup chopped onion
1/2	cup chopped celery
6	bacon strips, diced
2	tablespoons sugar
4	teaspoons all-purpose flour
2	tablespoons vinegar
1/2	teaspoon salt
1/8	teaspoon pepper
3/4	cup milk

In a large bowl, combine the potatoes, eggs, onion and celery; set aside. Place bacon in a microwave-safe bowl; cover and microwave on high for 1 minute. Stir. Microwave 2-3 minutes longer or until the bacon is crisp, stirring after each minute.

Remove bacon to paper towels to drain; reserve 2 tablespoons drippings. Stir the sugar, flour, vinegar, salt and pepper into drippings until smooth; gradually add milk.

Microwave on high for 3-4 minutes, stirring every 2 minutes until thickened. Pour over the potato mixture; toss. Top with bacon. **YIELD: 8 servings.**

editor's note: This recipe was tested in a 1,100-watt microwave.

lemon broccoli

Add a hint of citrus to your vegetables with my attractive recipe. Ideal with most any entree, this time-saving specialty dresses up broccoli, pimientos and onions with a dash of lemon.

—Tonya Farmer, Iowa City, Iowa

3	pounds fresh broccoli, cut into florets
1/4	cup butter
2	tablespoons diced onion
2	tablespoons diced pimientos
3	to 4 teaspoons lemon juice
2	teaspoons grated lemon peel
1/2	teaspoon seasoned salt

Dash pepper

lemon broccoli

Add 1 in. of water to a large saucepan; add the broccoli. Bring to a boil. Reduce the heat; cover and simmer for 5-8 minutes or until crisp-tender. Meanwhile, melt the butter; stir in the remaining ingredients. Drain broccoli; add butter mixture and toss to coat. YIELD: 8 servings.

sesame breadsticks

Try these breadsticks from our Test Kitchen. The not-too-spicy sticks have a mild herb flavor that goes great with pasta. Your family will love them, and you'll love the effortless preparation. Best of all, the popular bites come together with only five ingredients.

1	tube (11 ounces) refrigerated breadsticks
1	tablespoon butter, melted
1	tablespoon sesame seeds, toasted
1	to 2 teaspoons dried basil
1/4	to 1/2 teaspoon cayenne pepper

Unroll and separate breadsticks. Twist each breadstick two to three times and place on an ungreased baking sheet; brush with butter. Combine the sesame seeds, basil and cayenne; sprinkle over breadsticks. Bake at 375° for 10-12 minutes or until golden brown. Serve warm. YIELD: 1 dozen.

editor's note: This recipe was tested with Pillsbury refrigerated breadsticks.

picnic potato salad

What would a picnic be without potato salad? In this recipe, mint adds a tasty twist on the traditional version. Because it contains oil instead of mayonnaise, it keeps well at outdoor parties.

—*Sheri Neiswanger, Ravenna, Ohio*

10	medium red potatoes, cubed
2/3	cup canola oil
2	tablespoons cider vinegar
4	teaspoons honey
1	teaspoon dried basil
1	teaspoon ground mustard
1/2	teaspoon salt
1/2	teaspoon dried thyme
1/4	teaspoon dried marjoram
1/4	teaspoon dried mint

Dash cayenne pepper

Place potatoes in a large saucepan and cover with water. Cover and bring to a boil over medium-high heat; cook for 15-20 minutes or until tender.

Drain and place in a large bowl. Combine the remaining ingredients; pour over potatoes and toss to coat. Cool to room temperature. Cover and refrigerate until serving. YIELD: 12 servings.

picnic potato salad

creamy hash browns

No one will ever guess these saucy potatoes come together with only a handful of kitchen staples.

—Shirley Kidd, New London, Minnesota

1 package (28 ounces) frozen O'Brien potatoes
1 cup (4 ounces) shredded reduced-fat cheddar cheese
1 can (4 ounces) chopped green chilies
1 can (10-3/4 ounces) reduced-fat reduced-sodium condensed cream of chicken soup, undiluted
1 cup (8 ounces) reduced-fat sour cream

In a large bowl, combine the potatoes, cheese and chilies. Transfer to a 13-in. x 9-in. baking dish coated with cooking spray. Combine soup and sour cream; spread evenly over potato mixture. Bake, uncovered, at 350° for 50-55 minutes or until potatoes are tender. **YIELD: 10 servings.**

mother's rolls

mother's rolls

2 packages (1/4 ounce *each*) active dry yeast
1 cup warm water (110° to 115°)
1-1/2 cups warm milk (110° to 115°)
1/3 cup sugar
1/3 cup shortening
1 egg
2 teaspoons salt
7 to 7-1/2 cups all-purpose flour

In a large bowl, dissolve yeast in warm water. Add the milk, sugar, shortening, egg, salt and 3 cups flour. Beat on medium speed until mixture has a spongy texture. Let stand for 10 minutes.

Stir in enough remaining flour to form a soft dough. Turn onto a lightly floured surface; knead until smooth and elastic, about 6-8 minutes.

Place in a greased bowl, turning once to grease top. Cover and let rise in a warm place until doubled, about 1 hour.

Punch dough down. Turn onto a lightly floured surface; divide into three portions. Let rest for 5 minutes.

Divide each portion into 36 pieces. Shape each piece into a ball; place three balls in each greased muffin cup.

Cover and let rise until almost doubled, about 30 minutes. Bake at 375° for 12-15 minutes or until golden brown. Remove from pans to wire racks. Serve warm. **YIELD: 3 dozen.**

These golden cloverleaf dinner rolls were one of my mother's specialties. We always looked forward to them on holidays and special occasions.

—Patricia Baxter, Great Bend, Kansas

down home succotash

If you like fresh corn, you've got to try this no-fuss recipe. It's a traditional succotash that whips up in a hurry. Try it the next time you need something different for a menu.

—Marian Platt, Sequim, Washington

down home succotash

1/4	pound sliced bacon, chopped	1	medium onion, chopped
2	cups fresh *or* frozen corn	2	medium tomatoes, cut into wedges
1/2	pound lima beans		
1	medium green pepper, chopped		

In a large skillet, cook bacon until crisp. Remove bacon to paper towels and drain all but 1 tablespoon drippings.

In the same skillet, add the corn, beans, green pepper and onion. Simmer for 10-15 minutes or until vegetables are almost tender, adding water if necessary. Stir in tomatoes and bacon; cook just until tomatoes are heated through. **YIELD: 12-14 servings.**

minestone soup

Brimming with a harvest of garden bounty, this quick-to-fix soup is fresh-tasting and nutritious. The tomato-based broth is chock-full of everything from carrots and zucchini to garbanzo beans and elbow macaroni. It stirs up easily with prepared vegetable juice.

—Heather Ryan, Brown Deer, Wisconsin

minestrone soup

4	**medium carrots, chopped**
1	**medium zucchini, sliced**
1/4	**cup chopped onion**
1	**garlic clove, minced**
1	**tablespoon olive oil**
2	**cans (14-1/2 ounces *each*) vegetable broth**
3	**cups V8 juice**

1	**can (15 ounces) garbanzo beans *or* chickpeas, drained**
1	**can (14-1/2 ounces) diced tomatoes, undrained**
1	**cup frozen cut green beans**
1/2	**cup uncooked elbow macaroni**
1	**teaspoon dried basil**
1	**tablespoon minced fresh parsley**

In a Dutch oven, cook the carrots, zucchini, onion and garlic in oil for 7 minutes or until onion is tender. Add the broth, V8 juice, garbanzo beans, tomatoes, green beans, macaroni and basil. Bring to a boil.

Reduce heat; simmer, uncovered, for 15 minutes. Stir in parsley. Cook 5 minutes longer or until macaroni is tender. **YIELD: 8 servings.**

garlic bread

This popular dinner staple could not be tastier or simpler to make. Minced fresh garlic is key to these flavor-packed crusty slices, which our big family would snap up before they even had a chance to cool.

—Grace Yaskovic, Lake Hiawatha, New Jersey

1/2	cup butter, melted
3	to 4 garlic cloves, minced
1	loaf (1 pound) French bread, halved lengthwise
2	tablespoons minced fresh parsley

In a small bowl, combine butter and garlic. Brush over cut sides of bread; sprinkle with parsley. Place, cut side up, on a baking sheet.

Bake at 350° for 8 minutes. Broil 4-6 in. from the heat for 2 minutes or until golden brown. Cut into 2-in. slices. Serve warm. **YIELD: 8 servings.**

chili verde

chili verde

Leftover pork adds heartiness to this standby. It's great on a cool night with a stack of tortillas. I've taken it to many gatherings and it's always gone when the party's over.

—Jo Oliverius, Alpine, California

2	cups cubed cooked pork (about 1 pound)
1	can (16 ounces) kidney beans, rinsed and drained
1	can (15 ounces) pinto beans, rinsed and drained
1	can (15 ounces) chili with beans, undrained
1	can (14-1/2 ounces) stewed tomatoes
1-1/2	to 2 cups green salsa
1	large onion, chopped
2	cans (4 ounces each) chopped green chilies
2	garlic cloves, minced
1	tablespoon minced fresh cilantro
2	teaspoons ground cumin

In a large saucepan, combine all ingredients. Bring to a boil. Reduce heat; simmer, uncovered, for 10 minutes or until heated through. **YIELD: 8 servings.**

garlic bread

best-ever potato soup

Combine flour and milk until smooth; add to soup. Bring to a boil; boil and stir for 2 minutes. Add cheese; stir until cheese is melted and the soup is heated through. Garnish with green onions if desired. YIELD: 8 servings (2 quarts).

lemon-pepper green beans

The perfect partner for a rich main course, these delicious green beans from our home economists bring a light and refreshing flavor, as well as a dash of color, to the table. They're wonderful all year long.

1/2	pound fresh green beans, trimmed
1	tablespoon olive oil
1-1/2	teaspoons cider vinegar
1/4	to 1/2 teaspoon Italian seasoning
1/4	teaspoon onion salt
1/8	teaspoon lemon-pepper seasoning

Place beans in a steamer basket; place in a large saucepan over 1 in. of water. Bring to a boil; cover and steam for 8-10 minutes or until crisp-tender.

Meanwhile, in a small bowl, whisk the oil, vinegar and seasonings until blended. Transfer beans to a serving bowl; drizzle with seasoning mixture and toss to coat. YIELD: 2 servings.

best-ever potato soup

You'll be surprised at the taste of this rich, cheesy concoction. I came up with the no-fuss recipe after enjoying baked potato soup at one of our favorite restaurants. I added bacon, and we think that makes it even better.

—Coleen Morrissey, Sweet Valley, Pennsylvania

6	bacon strips, diced
3	cups cubed peeled potatoes
1	can (14-1/2 ounces) chicken broth
1	small carrot, grated
1/2	cup chopped onion
1	tablespoon dried parsley flakes
1/2	teaspoon *each* celery seed, salt and pepper
3	tablespoons all-purpose flour
3	cups milk
8	ounces process cheese (Velveeta), cubed
2	green onions, thinly sliced, optional

In a large saucepan, cook bacon until crisp; drain. Add the potatoes, broth, carrot, onion, parsley, celery seed, salt and pepper. Cover and simmer until potatoes are tender, about 15 minutes.

lemon-pepper green beans

clam chowder

Here's an effortless take on a hearty, all-time classic. People are always surprised how easy it is to create something so delicious.

—Rosemary Peterson, Archie, Missouri

clam chowder

2	cans (6-1/2 ounces *each*) minced clams	2	cans (12 ounces *each*) evaporated milk
6	medium potatoes, peeled and diced	2	cans (10-3/4 ounces *each*) condensed cream of mushroom soup, undiluted
6	medium carrots, diced	1	teaspoon salt
1/2	cup chopped onion	1/2	teaspoon pepper
1/2	cup butter, cubed		
1-1/2	cups water		

Drain clams, reserving liquid; set the clams aside. In a large kettle, combine the potatoes, carrots, onion, butter, water and reserved clam juice. Cook over medium heat for 15 minutes or until the vegetables are tender.

Stir in the milk, soup, salt and pepper. Simmer, uncovered, until heated through. Stir in clams. **YIELD: 12 servings (3 quarts).**

peanut butter 'n' jelly bars, page 141

desserts

mom's best
desserts

When it comes to tempting the sweet tooth, no one outshines Mom. Whether you crave a home-baked pie, chocolate brownie or buttery cookie, turn to this chapter to whip up goodies just as delightful as her's...with only a fraction of the work.

lemon meringue pie, page 132

fudgy brownies, page 120

jelly-topped sugar cookies, page 140

fudgy brownies

When I was growing up, I helped my mother make delicious, hearty meals and desserts like this for our farm family of eight. Today, I love to bake treats like these brownies to share with co-workers.

—Judy Cunningham, Max, North Dakota

fudgy brownies

1-1/3	cups butter, softened	2	cups all-purpose flour
2-2/3	cups sugar	1	cup baking cocoa
4	eggs	1/2	teaspoon salt
3	teaspoons vanilla extract		Confectioners' sugar, optional

In a large bowl, cream butter and sugar until light and fluffy. Beat in eggs and vanilla. Combine the flour, cocoa and salt; gradually add to the creamed mixture.

Spread into a greased 13-in. x 9-in. baking pan. Bake at 350° for 25-30 minutes or until the top is dry and the center is set. Cool completely. Dust with confectioners' sugar if desired. **YIELD: 2-1/2 dozen.**

frozen grasshopper torte

frozen grasshopper torte

4 cups crushed cream-filled chocolate cookies (about 40)
1/4 cup butter, melted
1 pint vanilla ice cream, softened
1/4 cup milk
1 jar (7 ounces) marshmallow creme
1/4 to 1/2 teaspoon peppermint extract
Few drops green food coloring
2 cups heavy whipping cream, whipped

Combine cookie crumbs and butter. Set aside 1/4 cup for garnish; press remaining crumbs onto the bottom of a 9-in. springform pan, two 9-in. pie plates or a 13-in. x 9-in. dish. Chill for 30 minutes. Spread ice cream over crust. Freeze.

Meanwhile, in a small bowl, combine milk and marshmallow creme; stir until well blended. Add extract and food coloring. Fold in whipped cream. Spoon over ice cream and sprinkle with reserved crumbs. Freeze until firm. **YIELD: 12-16 servings.**

I first made this tasty torte for a ladies' meeting at our church, and it went over very well. I've made it often since then and have received many compliments from young and old alike.
—Elma Penner, Oak Bluff, Manitoba

mamie eisenhower's fudge

My mother came across this effortless recipe in a newspaper some 40 years ago. One taste and you'll see why it doesn't take long for a big batch to disappear.
—Linda First, Hinsdale, Illinois

1 tablespoon plus 1/2 cup butter, *divided*
3 milk chocolate candy bars (two 7 ounces, one 1.55 ounces), broken into pieces
4 cups (24 ounces) semisweet chocolate chips
1 jar (7 ounces) marshmallow creme
1 can (12 ounces) evaporated milk
4-1/2 cups sugar
2 cups chopped walnuts

Line a 13-in. x 9-in. pan with foil and butter the foil with 1 tablespoon butter; set aside. In a large heat-proof bowl, combine the candy bars, chocolate chips and marshmallow creme; set aside.

In a large heavy saucepan over medium-low heat, combine the milk, sugar and remaining butter. Bring to a boil, stirring constantly. Boil and stir for 4-1/2 minutes. Pour over chocolate mixture; stir until chocolate is melted and mixture is smooth and creamy. Stir in walnuts. Pour into prepared pan. Cover and refrigerate until firm.

Using foil, lift fudge out of pan; cut into 1-in. squares. Store in an airtight container in the refrigerator. **YIELD: about 6 pounds.**

strawberry cheesecake pie

no-bake chocolate torte

Here's a delightful dessert that only looks like you fussed all day. With its attractive appearance and wonderful taste, no one will know that you saved time by spreading an easy-to-prepare frosting on a handy store-bought pound cake. The effortless idea comes from our home economists.

1	frozen pound cake (10-3/4 ounces), thawed
2	cups heavy whipping cream
6	tablespoons confectioners' sugar
6	tablespoons baking cocoa
1/2	teaspoon almond extract
1/2	cup sliced almonds, toasted, optional

Slice pound cake lengthwise into three layers and set aside. In a large bowl, beat cream until soft peaks form. Gradually add sugar and cocoa; beat until stiff peaks form. Stir in extract.

Place one layer of cake on a serving platter; top with 1 cup of the frosting. Repeat layers. Frost top and sides with remaining frosting. Garnish with almonds if desired. Chill at least 15 minutes. Refrigerate any leftovers. **YIELD: 4-6 servings.**

strawberry cheesecake pie

This creamy concoction is so refreshing on a hot day and also really easy to assemble. With its appealing look, company will never know how simple it is.

—Janis Plourde, Smooth Rock Falls, Ontario

2	cups sliced fresh strawberries
1/4	cup chopped almonds, toasted
1	tablespoon sugar
1	graham cracker crust (9 inches)
1	package (8 ounces) cream cheese, softened
2	cups cold milk, *divided*
1	package (3.4 ounces) instant vanilla pudding mix

In a small bowl, combine the strawberries, almonds and sugar. Pour into crust; set aside. In a large bowl, beat cream cheese until smooth; gradually add 1/2 cup of milk. Add pudding mix and remaining milk. Beat for 1 minute or until blended; pour over strawberries. Cover and refrigerate for 2 hours or until set. **YIELD: 8 servings.**

no-bake chocolate torte

mint chip freeze

mint chip freeze

I'm a retired home economics teacher and have quite a collection of recipes from my classes. My students really like this invigorating frozen treat made with ice cream and sandwich cookies.

—Mrs. Robert Lamb, Daleville, Indiana

---

2   packages (14 ounces *each*) cream-filled chocolate sandwich cookies, crushed
1/2 cup butter, melted
1   can (12 ounces) evaporated milk
1   cup sugar
1/2 cup butter, cubed
2   squares (1 ounce *each*) unsweetened baking chocolate
1   gallon mint chocolate chip ice cream, softened
1   carton (16 ounces) frozen whipped topping, thawed

Shaved chocolate

In a large bowl, combine the cookie crumbs and butter. Press into two 13-in. x 9-in. dishes. Refrigerate for 30 minutes.

In a small saucepan, combine the milk, sugar, butter and chocolate. Cook and stir over medium heat until thickened and bubbly, about 12 minutes. Remove from the heat; cool completely.

Spread ice cream over each crust. Spoon cooled chocolate sauce over top; evenly spread to cover. Freeze until firm. Spread with whipped topping. Desserts may be frozen for up to 2 months. Remove from freezer 10 minutes before cutting. Garnish with shaved chocolate. **YIELD: 2 desserts (15-18 servings each).**

country apple coffee cake

I love to cook for my husband and three children, but my rule is "the simpler the better." Convenient refrigerated biscuits make this apple-pecan delight a breeze to prepare for dessert or brunch.

—Katie Strzyzewski, Midlothian, Illinois

---

2   medium tart apples, peeled and chopped, *divided*
1   tube (12 ounces) refrigerated buttermilk biscuits
1   egg
1/3 cup corn syrup
1/3 cup packed brown sugar
1   tablespoon butter, softened
1/2 teaspoon ground cinnamon
1/2 cup chopped pecans
GLAZE:
1/3 cup confectioners' sugar
1/4 teaspoon vanilla extract
1   to 2 teaspoons milk

Place 1-1/2 cups of apples in a greased 9-in. round baking pan. Separate biscuits into 10 pieces; cut each biscuit into quarters. Place over apples with point side up. Top with remaining apples.

In a small bowl, combine the egg, corn syrup, brown sugar, butter and cinnamon. Stir in pecans. Spoon over apples. Bake at 350° for 30-35 minutes or until biscuits are browned.

For glaze, combine the confectioners' sugar, vanilla and enough milk to achieve desired consistency. Drizzle mixture over the warm coffee cake. **YIELD: 8-10 servings.**

cherry cream puff ring

This creative and decadent dessert will leave your family wanting more. Its creamy filling is the perfect end to a delicious meal.

—James Korzenowski, Dearborn, Michigan

- 1/2 cup water
- 1/2 cup milk
- 1/2 cup butter, cubed
- 1/4 teaspoon salt
- 1 cup all-purpose flour
- 4 eggs

FILLING:

- 2 cups cold milk
- 3/4 cup sour cream
- 1 package (3.4 ounces) instant vanilla pudding mix
- 1/2 teaspoon almond extract, *divided*
- 1 cup heavy whipping cream
- 2 tablespoons confectioners' sugar
- 1 can (21 ounces) cherry pie filling

Additional confectioners' sugar

In a large saucepan, bring the water, milk, butter and salt to a boil. Add flour all at once and stir until a smooth ball forms. Remove from the heat; let stand for 5 minutes. Add eggs, one at a time, beating well after each addition. Continue beating until mixture is smooth and shiny.

cherry cream puff ring

Drop by 1/4 cupfuls into a 10-in. ring on a greased 12-in. pizza pan (mounds should be slightly touching). Bake at 400° for 40-45 minutes or until golden brown.

Remove to a wire rack. Immediately cut a slit in the side of each puff to allow steam to escape. Carefully cut ring in half horizontally and set top aside; remove soft dough from inside with a fork. Cool.

In a small bowl, whisk the milk, sour cream, pudding mix and 1/4 teaspoon extract for 2 minutes. Let stand for 2 minutes or until soft-set.

Just before serving, place bottom of cream puff ring on a serving plate. Fill with pudding mixture. In a small mixing bowl, beat the cream, confectioners' sugar and remaining extract until stiff peaks form. Spread over pudding. Top with pie filling. Replace cream puff ring top. Sprinkle with confectioners' sugar. **YIELD: 12-16 servings.**

couldn't-be-simpler bars

Every time I take these sweet, chewy bars to a gathering or serve them to guests, I get lots of compliments. They're easy to make, too—just sprinkle a few ingredients in a pan and bake!

—Kerry Bouchard, Augusta, Montana

- 1/2 cup butter, melted
- 1 cup graham cracker crumbs (about 16 squares)
- 1 cup flaked coconut
- 1 cup (6 ounces) semisweet chocolate chips
- 1 cup butterscotch chips
- 1 can (14 ounces) sweetened condensed milk
- 1 cup chopped walnuts

Pour butter into a greased 13-in. x 9-in. baking pan. Sprinkle with crumbs and coconut. Top with chips. Pour milk over all. Sprinkle with walnuts.

Bake at 350° for 23-28 minutes or until browned and bubbly. Cool completely on a wire rack before cutting. **YIELD: about 3-1/2 dozen.**

marble brownies

In a large microwave-safe bowl, beat cream cheese until fluffy. Beat in the sugar, egg and vanilla until smooth. Spoon over the brownie batter; cut through the batter with a knife to swirl. Sprinkle with chocolate chips.

Cook, uncovered, at 70% power for 8-10 minutes or until a toothpick inserted near the center comes out clean. Cook on high for 1 minute longer. Remove to a wire rack to cool completely. Store in the refrigerator. **YIELD: 1 dozen.**

editor's note: This recipe was tested in a 1,100-watt microwave.

marble brownies

I like to bake and enjoy trying all sorts of new recipes, and the cream cheese topping in these delights made them a fast favorite in my house.

—Diana Coppernoll, Linden, North Carolina

5	tablespoons butter
2	squares (1 ounce *each*) unsweetened chocolate
2/3	cup sugar
2	eggs
1	teaspoon vanilla extract
2/3	cup all-purpose flour
1/2	teaspoon baking powder

CHEESECAKE LAYER:

1	package (8 ounces) cream cheese, softened
1/2	cup sugar
1	egg
1	teaspoon vanilla extract
1	cup (6 ounces) semisweet chocolate chips

In a large microwave-safe bowl, combine butter and chocolate. Cover and microwave on high for 30-60 seconds; stir until smooth. Beat in sugar, eggs and vanilla. Combine flour and baking powder; gradually add to chocolate mixture until blended. Spread into a greased microwave-safe 8-in. square dish; set aside.

frozen fudge pops

Kids of all ages will enjoy these cool, chocolaty treats, especially on hot summer days. The frosty fudge pops start with a simple homemade mix that can be stored in the fridge or freezer.

—Angie Hall, Newport, North Carolina

4	cups nonfat dry milk powder
1-1/2	cups sugar
1	cup all-purpose flour
1/2	cup baking cocoa
1/2	cup cold butter, cubed

ADDITIONAL INGREDIENTS (for each batch of fudge pops):

2-1/2	cups water
1	teaspoon vanilla extract

In a large bowl, combine the milk powder, sugar, flour and cocoa. Cut in butter until the mixture resembles coarse crumbs. Freeze in an airtight container for up to 6 months or refrigerate for up to 3 months. **YIELD: 3 batches (6-1/2 cups total).**

To prepare fudge pops: In a saucepan, whisk 2 cups mix and water. Bring to a boil. Reduce heat; simmer for 1-2 minutes or until thickened, stirring frequently. Remove from the heat; stir in vanilla. Cool slightly. Fill 3-oz. molds or cups three-fourths full; top with holders or insert Popsicle sticks. Freeze for up to 3 months. **YIELD: 10 fudge pops.**

berry pineapple parfaits

berry pineapple parfaits

3 cups whole fresh strawberries
3 to 4 tablespoons sugar
12 scoops vanilla ice cream
1 can (8 ounces) crushed pineapple, drained
Whipped topping

Set aside six strawberries for garnish. Slice the remaining strawberries and toss with sugar; let stand for 10 minutes.

Spoon half of the sliced berries into six parfait glasses. Top with half of the ice cream and half of the pineapple. Repeat layers. Top with whipped topping and reserved strawberries. **YIELD: 6 servings.**

Here's a surefire winner that's bound to satisfy all of the taste buds that sit at your table.

—Ruth Andrewson, Leavenworth, Washington

peanut butter cookie cups

1 package (17-1/2 ounces) peanut butter cookie mix
36 miniature peanut butter cups, unwrapped

Prepare cookie mix according to package directions. Roll the dough into 1-in. balls. Place in greased miniature muffin cups. Press dough evenly onto bottom and up sides of each cup.

Bake at 350° for 11-13 minutes or until set. Immediately place a peanut butter cup in each cup; press down gently. Cool for 10 minutes; carefully remove from pans. **YIELD: 3 dozen.**

editor's note: 2-1/4 cups peanut butter cookie dough of your choice can be substituted for the mix.

peanut butter cookie cups

I'm a busy schoolteacher and pastor's wife who always looks for shortcuts. I wouldn't dare show my face at a church dinner or bake sale without these tempting peanut butter treats. They're quick and easy to make and always a hit.

—Kristi Tackett, Banner, Kentucky

granola apple crisp

Tender apple slices are tucked beneath a sweet crunchy topping in this classic, comforting crisp. For variety, replace the apples with your favorite fruit.

—*Barbara Schindler, Napoleon, Ohio*

granola apple crisp

8	medium tart apples, peeled and sliced	2-1/2	cups granola with fruit and nuts
1/4	cup lemon juice	1	cup sugar
1-1/2	teaspoons grated lemon peel	1	teaspoon ground cinnamon
		1/2	cup butter, melted

In a large bowl, toss the apples, lemon juice and lemon peel. Transfer to a greased 3-qt. slow cooker. Combine granola, sugar and cinnamon; sprinkle over apples. Drizzle with butter. Cover and cook on low for 5-6 hours or until the apples are tender. Serve warm. **YIELD: 6-8 servings.**

raspberry swirl cupcakes

I truly love cooking and baking. These cupcakes are an all-time favorite of mine.

—Christine Sohm, Newton, Ontario

1	package (18-1/4 ounces) white cake mix
1/4	cup raspberry pie filling
1/2	cup shortening
1/3	cup milk
1	teaspoon vanilla extract
1/4	teaspoon salt
3	cups confectioners' sugar

Fresh raspberries and mint, optional

Prepare and bake cake mix according to package directions. Fill paper-lined muffin cups two-thirds full. Drop 1/2 teaspoon of pie filling in the center of each; cut through batter with a knife to swirl.

Bake at 350° for 20-25 minutes or until a toothpick comes out clean. Cool for 10 minutes before removing from pans to wire racks to cool completely.

In a large bowl, beat shortening until fluffy. Add the milk, vanilla, salt and confectioners' sugar; beat until smooth. Frost cupcakes. Garnish with fresh raspberries and mint if desired. **YIELD: about 1-1/2 dozen.**

chocolate chip blondies

chocolate chip blondies

Folks who love chocolate chip cookies will enjoy that same great flavor in these bars. These golden treats can be mixed up in a jiffy and taste wonderful. They're perfect for occasions when company drops by unexpectedly or you need a treat in a hurry.

—Rhonda Knight, Hecker, Illinois

1-1/2	cups packed brown sugar
1/2	cup butter, melted
2	eggs, lightly beaten
1	teaspoon vanilla extract
1-1/2	cups all-purpose flour
1/2	teaspoon baking powder
1/2	teaspoon salt
1	cup (6 ounces) semisweet chocolate chips

In a large bowl, combine the brown sugar, butter, eggs and vanilla just until blended. Combine the flour, baking powder and salt; add to brown sugar mixture. Stir in chocolate chips.

Spread into a greased 13-in. x 9-in. baking pan. Bake at 350° for 18-20 minutes or until a toothpick inserted near the center comes out clean. Cool on a wire rack. Cut into bars. **YIELD: 3 dozen.**

raspberry swirl cupcakes

cherry danish

These delightful Danish are so quick to fix, you don't even have to uncoil the refrigerated breadsticks. We prefer them with cherry pie filling, but you can use peach or blueberry instead.

—Margaret McNeil, Germantown, Tennessee

2	tubes (11 ounces *each*) refrigerated breadsticks
1/3	cup butter, melted
1	tablespoon sugar
1	cup cherry pie filling
1	cup confectioners' sugar
1-1/2	teaspoons water

Separate each tube of breadsticks into six sections but leave coiled. Place in a greased 15-in. x 10-in. x 1-in. baking pan. Brush generously with butter and sprinkle with sugar.

Make an indentation in the top of each coil; fill with about 1 tablespoon of pie filling. Bake at 400° for 15-20 minutes or until golden brown. Combine confectioners' sugar and water; drizzle over warm rolls. **YIELD: 1 dozen.**

editor's note: This recipe was tested with Pillsbury refrigerated breadsticks.

cherry danish

jumbo chocolate chip cookies

jumbo chocolate chip cookies

These huge cookies are a family favorite. No one can resist their sweet chocolaty taste.

—Lori Sporer, Oakley, Kansas

2/3	cup shortening
2/3	cup butter, softened
1	cup sugar
1	cup packed brown sugar
2	eggs
2	teaspoons vanilla extract
3-1/2	cups all-purpose flour
1	teaspoon baking soda
1	teaspoon salt
2	cups (12 ounces) semisweet chocolate chips
1	cup chopped pecans

In a large bowl, cream shortening, butter and sugars until light and fluffy. Beat in eggs and vanilla. Combine the flour, baking soda and salt; add to creamed mixture and mix well. Fold in the chocolate chips and pecans. Chill for at least 1 hour.

Drop by 1/4 cupfuls at least 1-1/2 in. apart onto greased baking sheets. Bake at 375° for 13-15 minutes or until golden brown. Cool for 5 minutes before removing to a wire rack. **YIELD: 2 dozen.**

delicate chocolate cake

1/4	cup baking cocoa
1	cup water
1	cup canola oil
1/2	cup butter, cubed
2	cups self-rising flour
2	cups sugar
1/2	cup buttermilk
2	eggs

FROSTING:

1/2	cup butter, cubed
1/4	cup baking cocoa
1/4	cup milk
4	to 4-1/2 cups confectioners' sugar
1	teaspoon vanilla extract

In a small saucepan over medium heat, combine the cocoa and water until smooth; add the oil and butter. Bring to a boil; cook and stir for 1 minute. Remove from the heat.

In a large bowl, combine flour and sugar; gradually add cocoa mixture, beating well. Add buttermilk and eggs; mix well. Pour mixture into a greased 15-in. x 10-in. x 1-in. baking pan.

Bake at 350° for 28-30 minutes or until a toothpick inserted near the center comes out clean. Cool on a wire rack. Cut cake into four 7-1/2-in. x 5-in. rectangles. Wrap two of the rectangles separately in foil; refrigerate or freeze. Set the other two rectangles aside.

For frosting, combine the butter, cocoa and milk in a saucepan. Bring to a boil; cook and stir for 1 minute (the mixture will appear curdled). Pour into a large bowl. Gradually add confectioners' sugar and vanilla; beat until frosting achieves spreading consistency. Frost the top of one cake rectangle; top with the second rectangle. Frost top and sides of cake. **YIELD: 1 two-layer cake (6-8 servings) plus 2 plain cake portions.**

editor's note: As a substitute for each cup of self-rising flour, place 1-1/2 teaspoons baking powder and 1/2 teaspoon salt in a measuring cup. Add all-purpose flour to measure 1 cup.

delicate chocolate cake

A special friend gave me this recipe more than 20 years ago. The cake has a light cocoa flavor, and the frosting is rich and delicious. Best of all, it's a from-scratch cake that comes together quite easily. If you are short on time, however, you can feel free to pop open a can of prepared frosting and use that instead of the homemade variety suggested here.

—Annette Foster, Taylors, South Carolina

magic apple pie

This pie is unique—it forms its own crust on top as it bakes, and it has a chewy cake-like consistency. It's inexpensive, too.

—Helen Hassler, Reinholds, Pennsylvania

1	egg
3/4	cup sugar
1/2	cup all-purpose flour
1	teaspoon baking powder

Pinch salt

1	medium tart apple, peeled and diced
1/2	cup raisins

Whipped cream *or* ice cream, optional

In a large bowl, beat egg. Add the sugar, flour, baking powder and salt. Stir in apple and raisins. Spread into a greased 9-in. pie plate.

Bake at 350° for 25-30 minutes or until golden brown and a toothpick inserted near the center comes out clean. Serve with whipped cream or ice cream if desired. **YIELD: 8 servings.**

easy hot fudge sauce

This fudge sauce is the perfect topping for ice cream. It's so easy to make, you won't ever need to buy hot fudge sauce from the store again!

—Nancy Nielson, Cambridge, Ohio

2	squares (1 ounce *each*) unsweetened chocolate
1	can (14 ounces) sweetened condensed milk
1/4	to 1/3 cup milk

Place all ingredients in a heavy saucepan; cook and stir over medium heat until chocolate is melted. Serve warm. Store in the refrigerator. **YIELD: 1-1/2 cups.**

ice cream sandwich dessert

ice cream sandwich dessert

No one will believe this awesome dessert is simply dressed-up ice cream sandwiches. For my son's birthday party, I decorated it with racecars and checkered flags because he's a big racing fan. It was a huge success!

—Jody Koerber, Caledonia, Wisconsin

19	ice cream sandwiches
1	carton (12 ounces) frozen whipped topping, thawed
1	jar (11-3/4 ounces) hot fudge ice cream topping
1	cup salted peanuts

Cut one ice cream sandwich in half. Place one whole and one half sandwich along a short side of an ungreased 13-in. x 9-in. pan. Arrange eight sandwiches in opposite direction in the pan. Spread with half of the whipped topping. Spoon fudge topping by teaspoonfuls onto whipped topping. Sprinkle with 1/2 cup peanuts. Repeat layers with remaining ice cream sandwiches, whipped topping and peanuts (pan will be full).

Cover and freeze for up to 2 months. Remove from the freezer 20 minutes before serving. Cut into squares. **YIELD: 15 servings.**

lemon meringue pie

lemon meringue pie

My father loves lemon meringue pie and always wants one for his birthday. I rely on this recipe, which won first place at our county fair. It has a light flaky crust, refreshing lemon filling and soft meringue with pretty golden peaks. It's much easier than it seems.

—Susan Jones, Bradford, Ohio

1-1/2	cups all-purpose flour
1/2	teaspoon salt
1/2	cup shortening
1/4	cup cold water

FILLING:

1-1/2	cups sugar
1/4	cup cornstarch
3	tablespoons all-purpose flour
1/4	teaspoon salt
1-1/2	cups water
3	egg yolks, lightly beaten
2	tablespoons butter
1/3	cup lemon juice
1	teaspoon grated lemon peel
1	teaspoon lemon extract

MERINGUE:

3	egg whites
1/4	teaspoon cream of tartar
6	tablespoons sugar

In a small bowl, combine flour and salt; cut in the shortening until crumbly. Gradually add water, tossing with a fork until dough forms a ball. Roll out pastry to fit a 9-in. pie plate. Transfer pastry to pie plate. Trim pastry to 1/2 in. beyond edge of pie plate; flute edges.

Line with a double thickness of heavy-duty foil. Bake at 450° for 8 minutes or until lightly browned. Remove foil; cool on a wire rack.

For filling, in a small saucepan, combine the sugar, cornstarch, flour and salt. Gradually stir in water. Cook and stir over medium heat until thickened and bubbly, about 2 minutes. Reduce heat; cook and stir 2 minutes longer. Remove from the heat. Gradually stir 1 cup hot filling into egg yolks; return all to pan. Bring to a gentle boil; cook and stir for 2 minutes. Remove from the heat. Stir in the butter, lemon juice, peel and extract until butter is melted. Pour hot filling into crust.

In a small bowl, beat egg whites and cream of tartar on medium speed until soft peaks form. Gradually beat in sugar, 1 tablespoon at a time, on high until stiff glossy peaks form and sugar is dissolved. Spread meringue evenly over hot filling, sealing edges to crust.

Bake pie at 350° for 12-15 minutes or until the meringue is golden brown. Cool pie on a wire rack for 1 hour. Refrigerate for at least 3 hours before serving. Store leftovers in the refrigerator. **YIELD:** 6-8 servings.

Kitchen Tip

To keep your meringue from forming beads of moisture on the top, try not to make a meringue dessert on a humid day. Sugar absorbs moisture and excess moisture may cause beading on the meringue. Also, be certain the sugar is completely dissolved during beating. Test it by rubbing a small amount between your fingers—if it's grainy, continue to beat the mixture.

honeymoon mousse

This elegant dessert is sure to delight. The light and chocolaty mousse is so wonderful, I enclose the recipe with every bridal shower gift I give.

—Beverly Carter, Beechwood, New Jersey

honeymoon mousse

1 cup cold evaporated milk
3 teaspoons vanilla extract
1 cup sugar
4 squares (1 ounce *each*) unsweetened chocolate, finely chopped

1/4 teaspoon salt
2 cups heavy whipping cream
Chocolate curls, optional

In a blender, combine the milk, vanilla, sugar, chocolate and salt; cover and process until smooth, about 1 minute. Transfer to a large bowl.

In a small bowl, beat cream until soft peaks form. Fold into chocolate mixture. Spoon into dessert dishes. Refrigerate until serving. Garnish with chocolate curls if desired. **YIELD: 6-8 servings.**

fun marshmallow bars

These colorful kid-tested treats sell fast at bake sales. A cake mix really cuts your prep time, making these bars an instant hit with busy moms.

—Debbie Brunssen, Randolph, Nebraska

1	package (18-1/4 ounces) devil's food cake mix
1/4	cup water
1/4	cup butter, melted
1	egg
3	cups miniature marshmallows
1	cup milk chocolate M&M's
1/2	cup chopped peanuts

In a large bowl, combine the cake mix, water, butter and egg. Press into a greased 13-in. x 9-in. baking pan. Bake at 375° for 20-22 minutes or until a toothpick inserted near the center comes out clean.

Sprinkle with marshmallows, M&M's and peanuts. Bake 2-3 minutes longer or until the marshmallows begin to melt. Cool on a wire rack. Cut into bars. YIELD: 3-1/2 dozen.

fun marshmallow bars

Kitchen Tip

To easily cut bars and brownies, line the baking pan with foil, leaving 3 inches hanging over each end. Grease the foil if the recipe instructs. After the baked bars have cooled, use the foil to lift them out of the pan. Use a serrated knife and cut downward, avoiding a sawing motion.

pineapple upside-down cake

I dole out slices of this sunny-colored dessert while it's still warm from the oven. The moist cake gets fruity flavor from crushed pineapple and lemon gelatin.

—Anna Polhemus, North Merrick, New York

1	can (20 ounces) unsweetened crushed pineapple
1	package (.3 ounce) sugar-free lemon gelatin
1/2	cup egg substitute
1	egg white
3/4	cup sugar
1	teaspoon vanilla extract
3/4	cup all-purpose flour
1	teaspoon baking powder

Drain pineapple, reserving 1/3 cup juice (discard or save remaining juice for another use). Line a 9-in. round baking pan with waxed paper; coat with cooking spray. Spread pineapple over waxed paper; sprinkle with gelatin.

In a large bowl, beat egg substitute and egg white. Beat in the sugar, reserved pineapple juice and vanilla. Combine flour and baking powder; add to egg mixture and mix well. Pour over gelatin.

Bake at 350° for 25-30 minutes or until a toothpick inserted near the center comes out clean. Cool for 5 minutes; invert onto a serving plate. Serve warm. YIELD: 10 servings.

mixed nut bars

mixed nut bars

One pan of these bars goes a long way. They get a nice flavor from butterscotch chips.

—Bobbi Brown, Waupaca, Wisconsin

1-1/2 cups all-purpose flour
  3/4 cup packed brown sugar
  1/4 teaspoon salt
  1/2 cup plus 2 tablespoons cold butter, *divided*
    1 can (11-1/2 ounces) mixed nuts
    1 cup butterscotch chips
  1/2 cup light corn syrup

In a small bowl, combine flour, sugar and salt. Cut in 1/2 cup butter until mixture resembles coarse crumbs. Press into a greased 13-in. x 9-in. baking pan. Bake at 350° for 10 minutes. Sprinkle with the nuts.

In a microwave, melt butterscotch chips and remaining butter at 70% power for 1 minute; stir. Microwave at additional 10- to 20-second intervals, stirring until smooth. Stir in corn syrup. Pour over nuts. Bake for 10 minutes or until set. Cool in pan on a wire rack. **YIELD: about 3-1/2 dozen.**

editor's note: This recipe was tested in a 1,100-watt microwave.

angel food cake roll

There's always room for dessert—especially when it's this eye-catching, make-ahead treat. We love the strawberry yogurt filling, but different flavors work as well.

—Joan Colbert, Sigourney, Iowa

  1 package (16 ounces) angel food cake mix
  5 teaspoons confectioners' sugar
  1 carton (8 ounces) reduced-fat strawberry yogurt
  1 package (1 ounce) instant sugar-free vanilla pudding mix
  3 drops red food coloring, optional
  2 cups reduced-fat whipped topping

Line a 15-in. x 10-in. x 1-in. baking pan with waxed paper. Prepare the cake according to the package directions.

Pour batter into prepared pan. Bake at 350° for 15-20 minutes or until cake springs back when lightly touched. Cool for 5 minutes.

Turn cake onto a kitchen towel dusted with confectioners' sugar. Gently peel off waxed paper. Roll up jelly-roll style in the towel, starting with a short side. Cool on a wire rack.

In a large bowl, whisk the yogurt, pudding mix and food coloring if desired. Fold in whipped topping.

Unroll cake; spread filling evenly over cake to within 1/2 in. of edges. Roll up. Cover and freeze. Remove from freezer 30 minutes before slicing. **YIELD: 10 servings.**

angel food cake roll

black forest freezer pie

black forest freezer pie

A delightful dessert is never far off when you have this layered ice cream pie in the freezer. For variety, use strawberry pie filling and a chocolate crust.

—Angie Helms, Pontotoc, Mississippi

1	pint chocolate *or* vanilla ice cream, softened
1	extra-servings-size graham cracker crust (9 ounces)
4	ounces cream cheese, softened
1	cup confectioners' sugar
1	carton (8 ounces) frozen whipped topping, thawed
1	can (21 ounces) cherry pie filling, chilled
3	tablespoons chocolate syrup

Spoon ice cream into pie crust; cover and freeze for 15 minutes.

Meanwhile, in a large bowl, beat cream cheese and confectioners' sugar until smooth; fold in whipped topping. Set aside 1-1/2 cups for garnish.

Spread remaining cream cheese mixture over ice cream. Using the back of a spoon, make an 8-in. diameter well in the center of the pie for the pie filling. Pipe reserved cream cheese mixture around the pie.

Cover and freeze for 3-4 hours or until firm. May be frozen for up to 2 months. Just before serving, spoon pie filling into the well; drizzle with chocolate syrup. Serve immediately. **YIELD: 6-8 servings.**

butterscotch snickerdoodles

This recipe is a combination of the traditional Snickerdoodle recipe and my mother's best spritz recipe. Everyone comments on the unique combination of ingredients.

—Nancy Radenbaugh, White Lake, Michigan

1	cup butter, softened
1/3	cup canola oil
1-1/4	cups sugar
1/3	cup confectioners' sugar
2	eggs
3	tablespoons plain yogurt
1-1/2	teaspoons almond extract
1/8	teaspoon lemon extract
3-1/2	cups all-purpose flour
1	cup whole wheat flour
1	teaspoon cream of tartar
1	teaspoon baking soda
1/2	teaspoon salt
1	cup butterscotch chips
1/2	cup chopped almonds
Additional sugar	

In a large bowl, cream the butter, oil and sugars until light and fluffy. Add eggs, one at a time, beating well after each addition. Beat in yogurt and extracts. Combine flours, cream of tartar, baking soda and salt; gradually add to the creamed mixture and mix well. Stir in butterscotch chips and almonds.

Roll into 1-in. balls, then in sugar. Place 2 in. apart on ungreased baking sheets. Flatten with a fork dipped in sugar. Bake at 350° for 12-15 minutes or until lightly browned. Remove to wire racks to cool. **YIELD: 8 dozen.**

pumpkin cake roll

This lovely cake is delicious—especially if you like cream cheese and pumpkin. It tastes so good in fall and makes a fancy finale at Thanksgiving, too.

—Elizabeth Montgomery, Cambridge, Massachusetts

3	eggs
1	cup sugar
2/3	cup canned pumpkin
1	teaspoon lemon juice
3/4	cup all-purpose flour
2	teaspoons ground cinnamon
1	teaspoon baking powder
1/2	teaspoon salt
1/4	teaspoon ground nutmeg
1	cup finely chopped walnuts

CREAM CHEESE FILLING:

2	packages (3 ounces *each*) cream cheese, softened
1	cup confectioners' sugar
1/4	cup butter, softened
1/2	teaspoon vanilla extract

Additional confectioners' sugar

In a large bowl, beat eggs on high for 5 minutes. Gradually beat in sugar until thick and lemon-colored. Add pumpkin and lemon juice. Combine the flour, cinnamon, baking powder, salt and nutmeg; fold into the pumpkin mixture.

Grease a 15-in. x 10-in. x 1-in. baking pan and line with waxed paper. Grease and flour the paper. Spread batter into pan; sprinkle with walnuts. Bake at 375° for 15 minutes or until cake springs back when lightly touched. Immediately turn out onto a linen towel dusted with confectioners' sugar. Peel off paper and roll cake up in towel, starting with a short end. Cool.

Meanwhile, in a bowl, beat cream cheese, sugar, butter and vanilla until fluffy. Carefully unroll the cake. Spread filling over cake to within 1 in. of edges. Roll up again. Cover and chill until serving. Dust with the confectioners' sugar. **YIELD: 8-10 servings.**

pecan pie

This pie was always a favorite for birthdays while my children were growing up. They never liked the typical party cakes. My mother gave me an old-fashioned recipe for a crust but this pie uses a premade pastry shell.

—Virginia Jung, Milwaukee, Wisconsin

4	eggs
1	cup sugar
1/8	teaspoon salt
1-1/2	cups dark corn syrup
2	tablespoons plus 1 teaspoon butter, melted and cooled
1	teaspoon vanilla extract
1	cup pecan halves
1	unbaked pastry shell (9 inches)

In a large bowl, beat eggs just until blended but not frothy. Add the sugar, salt and corn syrup. Stir butter and vanilla just until blended. Spread pecans in the bottom of pie shell. Pour in filling.

Place in a 350° oven and immediately reduce heat to 325°. Bake for 50-60 minutes or until a knife inserted near the center comes out clean. Refrigerate leftovers. **YIELD: 8-10 servings.**

pumpkin cake roll

cherry-lemon icebox pie

This recipe makes a nice and refreshing finish to a heavy meal. The cherry and lemon combination leave your taste buds wanting more.

—*Mary Weller, Twin Lake, Michigan*

cherry-lemon icebox pie

Pastry for single-crust pie (9 inches)
- **1   can (14 ounces) sweetened condensed milk**
- **1/2 cup lemon juice**
- **1/2 teaspoon vanilla extract**
- **1/2 teaspoon almond extract**
- **1-1/2 cups heavy whipping cream**
- **1   can (21 ounces) cherry pie filling**

 Line a 9-in. deep-dish pie plate with pastry; trim and flute edges. Line pastry shell with a double thickness of heavy-duty foil. Bake at 450° for 8 minutes. Remove foil; bake 5-7 minutes longer or until lightly browned. Cool on a wire rack.

In a large bowl, whisk the milk, lemon juice and extracts until thickened, about 2 minutes. Beat cream until stiff peaks form; fold into milk mixture. Pour into crust.

Refrigerate for 30 minutes; spoon pie filling over the top. Refrigerate for at least 2 hours before serving. **YIELD: 8 servings.**

no-bake cereal bars

2 cups sugar
2 cups corn syrup
1 jar (40 ounces) chunky peanut butter
6 cups Cheerios
6 cups crisp rice cereal

In a large saucepan, cook and stir sugar and corn syrup until the sugar is dissolved. Remove from the heat. Add peanut butter; mix well. Stir in cereals. Spread quickly into two lightly greased 15-in. x 10-in. x 1-in. pans. Cut into bars while warm. **YIELD: about 10 dozen.**

no-bake cereal bars

With crisp rice cereal and peanut butter, these oven-free bars taste almost like candy.

—Pauline Christiansen, Columbus, Kansas

blueberry lemon trifle

blueberry lemon trifle

3 cups fresh blueberries, *divided*
2 cans (15-3/4 ounces *each*) lemon pie filling
2 cartons (8 ounces *each*) lemon yogurt
1 prepared angel food cake (8 inches), cut into 1-inch cubes
1 carton (8 ounces) frozen whipped topping, thawed

Lemon slices and fresh mint, optional

Set aside 1/4 cup blueberries for garnish. In a large bowl, combine pie filling and yogurt.

In a 3-1/2-qt. serving or trifle bowl, layer a third of the cake cubes, lemon mixture and blueberries. Repeat layers twice. Top with whipped topping. Cover and refrigerate for at least 2 hours. Garnish with reserved blueberries, and lemon and mint if desired. **YIELD: 12-14 servings.**

A refreshing lemon filling and fresh blueberries give this sunny dessert plenty of color. Don't worry about heating up the oven—this doesn't require baking.

—Ellen Peden, Houston, Texas

jelly-topped sugar cookies

On busy days, I appreciate this fast-to-fix drop sugar cookie. Top each cookie with your favorite flavor of jam or jelly for a delicious treat!

—June Quinn, Kalamazoo, Michigan

3/4	cup sugar
3/4	cup canola oil
2	eggs
2	teaspoons vanilla extract
1	teaspoon lemon extract
1	teaspoon grated lemon peel
2	cups all-purpose flour
2	teaspoons baking powder
1/2	teaspoon salt
1/2	cup jam *or* jelly

In a large bowl, beat sugar and oil until blended. Beat in eggs, extracts and lemon peel. Combine the flour, baking powder, and salt; gradually add to sugar mixture and mix well.

Drop by rounded tablespoonfuls 2 in. apart onto ungreased baking sheets. Coat bottom of a glass with cooking spray, then dip in sugar. Flatten the cookies with the prepared glass, redipping in sugar as needed.

Place 1/4 teaspoon jelly in the center of each cookie. Bake at 400° for 8-10 minutes or until set. Remove cookies to wire racks to cool. **YIELD: about 3-1/2 dozen.**

jelly-topped sugar cookies

carrot cake

We made this for our daughter's wedding. We stirred it all by hand and baked it in frying pans of varied sizes. After decorating it with pink frosting roses, we transported it 50 miles to the church in the back of a car!

—Anna Aughenbaugh, Fort Collins, Colorado

1-1/3	cups canola oil
4	eggs
1-1/2	cups sugar
2	cups all-purpose flour
2	teaspoons baking powder
2	teaspoons baking soda
2	teaspoons ground cinnamon
2-1/2	cups finely shredded carrots
1/2	cup chopped walnuts

CREAM CHEESE ICING:

1	package (3 ounces) cream cheese, softened
3	cups confectioners' sugar

Dash salt

1	teaspoon vanilla extract
2	tablespoons milk

In a large bowl, combine the oil, eggs and sugar. Combine the flour, baking powder, baking soda and cinnamon; add to wet ingredients and beat well. Stir in carrots and nuts.

Pour into a greased 13-in. x 9-in. baking pan. Bake at 350° for about 50 minutes or until the cake tests done.

For frosting, beat cream cheese and sugar in a medium bowl. Gradually add the salt, vanilla and milk, beating until smooth. Add additional milk if needed to reach desired consistency. Spread over cooled cake. **YIELD: 12 servings.**

quick coffee torte

peanut butter 'n' jelly bars

My two young sons are crazy about these simple, fast-fixing cookie bars. And as an on-the-go mom, easy preparation makes this one scrumptious dessert I can rely on—even at the last minute. You might want to vary the jam or jelly to suit your own family's tastes.

—Carolyn Mulloy, Davison, Michigan

1	tube (16-1/2 ounces) refrigerated peanut butter cookie dough
1/2	cup peanut butter chips
1	can (16 ounces) buttercream frosting
1/4	cup creamy peanut butter
1/4	cup seedless raspberry jam *or* grape jelly

Let dough stand at room temperature for 5-10 minutes to soften. Press into an ungreased 13-in. x 9-in. baking dish; sprinkle with peanut butter chips.

Bake at 375° for 15-18 minutes or until lightly browned and edges are firm to the touch. Cool on a wire rack.

In a small bowl, beat frosting and peanut butter until smooth. Spread over bars. Drop jam by teaspoonfuls over frosting; cut through frosting with a knife to swirl the jam. **YIELD: 2 dozen.**

quick coffee torte

When I've had a hectic day, but still would like to serve dessert, I turn to this delicious standby. This easy-to-prepare torte really hits the spot.

—Karen Gardiner, Eutaw, Alabama

1/4	cup sugar
1/4	cup water
1	tablespoon instant coffee granules
1-1/2	teaspoons butter
1/8	teaspoon rum extract
1	frozen pound cake (10-3/4 ounces), thawed
1	carton (8 ounces) frozen whipped topping, thawed

Grated chocolate, optional

In a small saucepan, combine the sugar, water and coffee. Bring to a boil; cook for 3 minutes, stirring occasionally. Remove from the heat; stir in butter and rum extract. Cool slightly.

Split cake into three horizontal layers. Place bottom layer on a serving plate. Brush with about 1 tablespoon coffee mixture; spread with 1 cup whipped topping. Repeat layers. Brush remaining coffee mixture over cut side of remaining cake layer; place coffee side down over topping. Spread remaining whipped topping over top of torte. Garnish with grated chocolate if desired. Chill until serving. **YIELD: 6-8 servings.**

peanut butter 'n' jelly bars

cereal cookie bars

cereal cookie bars

These chewy crowd-pleasers feature all sorts of goodies, including chocolate chips, raisins, coconut and candy-coated baking bits. For a more colorful look, press the baking bits on top of the bars instead of stirring them into the cereal mixture.

—Connie Craig, Lakewood, Washington

9	cups crisp rice cereal
6-1/2	cups quick-cooking oats
1	cup cornflakes
1	cup flaked coconut
2	packages (one 16 ounces, one 10-1/2 ounces) miniature marshmallows
1	cup butter, cubed
1/2	cup honey
1/2	cup chocolate chips
1/2	cup raisins
1/2	cup M&M's miniature baking bits

In a large bowl, combine the cereal, oats, cornflakes and coconut; set aside.

In a large saucepan, cook and stir the marshmallows and butter over low heat until melted and smooth. Stir in honey. Pour over cereal mixture; stir until coated. Cool for 5 minutes.

Stir in chocolate chips, raisins and baking bits. Press into two greased 15-in. x 10-in. x 1-in. pans. Cool bars for 30 minutes before cutting. **YIELD:** 6 dozen.

make-ahead shortcake

This family favorite has all the satisfaction of traditional strawberry shortcake with just a dash of distinction.

—Karen Ann Bland, Gove, Kansas

1	loaf (14 ounces) angel food cake, cut into 1-inch slices
1/2	cup cold milk
1	package (5.1 ounces) instant vanilla pudding mix
1	pint vanilla ice cream, softened
1	package (6 ounces) strawberry gelatin
1	cup boiling water
2	packages (10 ounces *each*) frozen sweetened sliced strawberries

Sliced fresh strawberries, optional

Arrange cake slices in a single layer in an ungreased 13-in. x 9-in. dish. In a large bowl, beat milk and pudding mix for 2 minutes or until thickened; beat in ice cream. Pour over cake. Chill.

Meanwhile, in a bowl, dissolve gelatin in boiling water; stir in frozen strawberries. Chill until partially set. Spoon over pudding mixture. Chill until firm. Garnish with fresh strawberries if desired. YIELD: 12 servings.

make-ahead shortcake

great pumpkin dessert

I rely on canned pumpkin and a yellow cake mix to fix this effortless alternative to pumpkin pie. It's a tried-and-true dessert that always elicits compliments and requests for the recipe.

—Linda Guyot, Fountain Valley, California

1	can (15 ounces) solid-pack pumpkin
1	can (12 ounces) evaporated milk
3	eggs
1	cup sugar
4	teaspoons pumpkin pie spice
1	package (18-1/4 ounces) yellow cake mix
3/4	cup butter, melted
1-1/2	cups chopped walnuts

Vanilla ice cream or whipped cream

In a large bowl, beat first five ingredients until smooth.

Transfer to a greased 13-in. x 9-in. baking dish. Sprinkle with dry cake mix and drizzle with butter. Top with walnuts. Bake at 350° for 1 hour or until a knife inserted near the center comes out clean. Serve with ice cream or whipped cream. **YIELD: 12-16 servings.**

brownies in a cone

brownies in a cone

These brownie-filled ice cream cones are a fun addition to any summer get-together. They always seem to appeal to the child in everyone.

—Mitzi Sentiff, Annapolis, Maryland

1	package fudge brownie mix (13-inch x 9-inch pan size)
17	ice cream cake cones (about 2-3/4 inches tall)
1	cup (6 ounces) semisweet chocolate chips
1	tablespoon shortening

Colored sprinkles

Prepare brownie batter according to package directions, using 3 eggs. Place the ice cream cones in muffin cups; spoon about 3 tablespoons batter into each cone.

Bake at 350° for 25-30 minutes or until a toothpick comes out clean and top is dry (do not overbake). Cool completely.

In a microwave, melt chocolate chips and shortening; stir until smooth. Dip tops of brownies in melted chocolate; allow excess to drip off. Decorate with sprinkles. **YIELD: 17 servings.**

editor's note: This recipe was tested with Keebler ice cream cups. These brownie cones are best served the day they're prepared.

great pumpkin dessert

crunchy apple salad, page 146

10-minute dishes

mom's best
10-minute dishes

When you're tight on time, turn to this chapter! You'll find more than two dozen recipes that come together in just 10 minutes or less. With quick takes on everything from breakfasts to dessert, beating the kitchen clock has never been so delicious.

elegant mushroom soup, page 152

turkey tortilla roll-ups, page 153

chocolate fondue, page 155

crunchy apple salad

crunchy
apple salad

4   **large red apples, diced**
1   **cup chopped celery**
1   **cup raisins**
1   **cup chopped walnuts**
1/2 **cup mayonnaise**

In a large bowl, combine the apples, celery, raisins and walnuts. Add mayonnaise; toss to coat. Cover and refrigerate until serving. **Yield: 16 servings.**

This old-fashioned salad is part of my favorite meal that Mom used to make. Crunchy apples, celery and walnuts blend well with the creamy mayonnaise.

—Julie Pearsall, Union Springs, New York

cinnamon carrots

1   **package (16 ounces) frozen sliced carrots**
1/4 **cup honey**
1   **to 2 tablespoons butter**
1/2 **to 1 teaspoon ground cinnamon**

Cook carrots according to package directions. Meanwhile, in a saucepan, heat the honey, butter and cinnamon until butter is melted; stir to blend.

Drain carrots; place in a serving bowl. Drizzle with honey mixture. **YIELD: 6 servings.**

cinnamon carrots

When my daughter was a little girl, the only vegetable she ate were carrots covered in a packaged glaze. I ran out of glaze one day and created this taste-tempting recipe. I never bought a prepared glaze again.

—Charlene Kalb, Catonsville, Maryland

dijon-walnut spinach salad

These greens have so much flavor for so few ingredients! This family favorite has a great fresh taste, a lot of different textures and can be tossed together in a heartbeat. For variety, change the dressing to honey mustard or any other flavor you like best.

—*Chris DeMontravel, Mohegan Lake, New York*

dijon-walnut spinach salad

1 **package (9 ounces) fresh baby spinach**

1 **package (4 ounces) crumbled feta cheese**

1 **cup dried cranberries**

1 **cup walnut halves, toasted**

1/2 **cup honey Dijon vinaigrette**

In a large salad bowl, combine the spinach, feta cheese, cranberries and walnuts. Drizzle with vinaigrette; toss to coat. Serve immediately. **YIELD: 13 servings.**

easy cheesy nachos

There's no need to brown ground beef when fixing this satisfying snack. I just top crunchy chips with warm canned chili and melted cheese, then sprinkle it all with chopped tomato and onions for fresh flavor and color.

—Laura Jirasek, Howell, Michigan

- 1 package (14-1/2 ounces) tortilla chips
- 2 cans (15 ounces *each*) chili without beans
- 1 pound process cheese (Velveeta), cubed
- 4 green onions, sliced
- 1 medium tomato, chopped

Divide chips among six plates; set aside. In a saucepan, warm chili until heated through.

Meanwhile, in another saucepan, heat cheese over medium-low heat until melted, stirring frequently. Spoon chili over chips; drizzle with cheese. Sprinkle with onions and tomato. **YIELD: 6 servings.**

herb-buttered corn

herb-buttered corn

My husband and I love fresh corn on the cob, and this is an easy, change-of-pace way to serve it.

—Donna Smith, Victor, New York

- 1/2 cup butter, softened
- 1 tablespoon minced chives
- 1 tablespoon minced fresh dill
- 1 tablespoon minced fresh parsley
- 1/2 teaspoon dried thyme
- 1/4 teaspoon salt
- Dash garlic powder
- Dash cayenne pepper
- Hot cooked corn on the cob

In a small bowl, combine the first eight ingredients. Serve with corn. Refrigerate leftovers. **YIELD: 10 servings.**

Kitchen Tip

It's a cinch to give corn on the cob a fun twist. Follow the recipe above, replacing the thyme and dill with the herbs and seasonings your family likes best.

easy cheesy nachos

california clubs

Ranch dressing and Dijon mustard create a tasty sauce to top this sandwich. Pairing tomato and avocado with the chicken and bacon is just the right combination on toasted sourdough bread.

—Diane Cigel, Stevens Point, Wisconsin

1/2	cup ranch salad dressing
1/4	cup Dijon mustard
8	slices sourdough bread, toasted
4	boneless skinless chicken breast halves, cooked and sliced
1	large tomato, sliced
1	medium ripe avocado, peeled and sliced
12	bacon strips, cooked and drained

In a small bowl, combine salad dressing and mustard; spread on each slice of bread. On four slices of bread, layer the chicken, tomato, avocado and bacon. Top with the remaining slices of bread. YIELD: 4 servings.

fluffy strawberry dessert

I've been a cake decorator for years but really enjoy taking it easy with a no-fuss dessert such as this one. It's very light and refreshing.

—Linette Arnold, Simsbury, Connecticut

2	packages (10 ounces *each*) frozen sweetened strawberries, thawed
2-1/2	cups miniature marshmallows
1	cup chopped pecans
1	cup heavy whipping cream
1	teaspoon vanilla extract

In a large bowl, combine the strawberries, marshmallows and pecans. In another large bowl, beat cream and vanilla until stiff peaks form; fold into strawberry mixture. Spoon into dessert dishes. YIELD: 8-10 servings.

mock caesar salad

This quick version of the classic salad is a tasty complement to a soup or main dish. Best of all, the thick, creamy dressing has all the flavor you'd expect with just a fraction of the work involved.

—Sue Yaeger, Boone, Iowa

1/3	cup plain yogurt
1/4	cup mayonnaise
1	tablespoon red wine vinegar
2	teaspoons Dijon mustard
1	teaspoon Worcestershire sauce
1/4	teaspoon garlic powder
1/8	teaspoon pepper
6	cups torn romaine
1/2	cup fat-free salad croutons
2	tablespoons shredded Parmesan cheese

In a small bowl, whisk together the first seven ingredients. In a salad bowl, combine the romaine, croutons and cheese. Drizzle with dressing; toss to coat. YIELD: 5 servings.

mock caesar salad

taco dip platter

To make this zesty appetizer, you simply layer beans, salsa, cheese and other taco-like ingredients onto a platter. What could be easier?

—Marieann Johansen, Desert Hot Springs, California

1	can (15 ounces) refried beans
1	cup chunky salsa
1	cup guacamole
2	cups (16 ounces) sour cream
1	can (4 ounces) chopped green chilies
1	can (2-1/4 ounces) sliced ripe olives, drained
1/2	cup finely shredded cheddar cheese
1/2	cup finely shredded Monterey Jack cheese

Tortilla chips

Spread beans on a 12-in. serving plate. Layer the salsa, guacamole and sour cream over beans, within 1 in. of edges for each layer. Sprinkle with chilies, olives and cheeses.

Refrigerate until ready to serve. Serve with tortilla chips. **YIELD: 16-20 servings.**

speedy salsa

With a small list of ingredients, this salsa is a snap to prepare on a moment's notice. I've also served it over baked potatoes for a light lunch.

—Carolyn Hayes, Johnston City, Illinois

2	cans (10 ounces *each*) diced tomatoes and green chilies, undrained
1	can (15 ounces) black beans, rinsed and drained
1	can (11 ounces) Mexicorn, drained

Sour cream and sliced green onions
Tortilla *or* corn chips

In a serving bowl, combine the tomatoes, beans and corn. Garnish with sour cream and green onions. Serve with chips. **YIELD: 3 cups.**

taco dip platter

fast fiesta soup

This spicy soup was served at a very elegant lunch, and the hostess was overwhelmed with requests for the recipe. The colorful combination is a snap to throw together. Just open the cans and heat.

—Patricia White, Monrovia, California

- 2 cans (10 ounces *each*) diced tomatoes and green chilies
- 1 can (15-1/4 ounces) whole kernel corn, drained
- 1 can (15 ounces) black beans, rinsed and drained

Shredded cheddar cheese and sour cream, optional

In a large saucepan, combine the tomatoes, corn and beans; heat through. Garnish individual servings with cheese and sour cream if desired. **YIELD: 4 servings.**

fast fiesta soup

10-minute tomato soup

Here's a from-scratch soup that's table-ready in mere moments! You just can't go wrong with that!

—Ada Ryger, Beresford, South Dakota

- 2 cups crushed canned tomatoes
- 1/2 teaspoon baking soda
- 2 cups milk
- 2 tablespoons butter

In a large heavy saucepan, cook tomatoes over medium heat; bring to a boil. Remove from heat; add remaining ingredients. Return to heat and cook and stir over medium heat until butter is melted and soup is heated through. **YIELD: 3-4 servings (1 quart).**

cinnamon-spice french toast

The cinnamon and nutmeg give this single-serve recipe an extra tasty twist, which just goes to prove that breakfast for one can be fun!

—Angela Sansom, New York, New York

- 1 egg
- 1/4 cup milk
- 1/2 teaspoon sugar
- 1/4 to 1/2 teaspoon ground cinnamon
- 1/8 teaspoon ground nutmeg
- 2 slices day-old whole wheat *or* white bread
- 2 teaspoons butter

Maple syrup

In a shallow bowl, beat the egg, milk, sugar, cinnamon and nutmeg. Add bread one slice at time, and soak both sides.

Melt butter on a griddle over medium heat; toast bread until golden brown on both sides and cooked through. Serve with syrup. **YIELD: 1 serving.**

elegant mushroom soup

This quick version of a classic standby turns commonplace ingredients into a wonderfully delicious soup. My family is delighted whenever they see it simmering on the stove.

—Marjorie Jaeger, Enderlin, North Dakota

elegant mushroom soup

1	large onion, chopped
1/2	pound fresh mushrooms, sliced
2	tablespoons butter
2	tablespoons all-purpose flour
1/4	teaspoon pepper
1/8	teaspoon salt

1	cup milk
1	cup chicken broth
1	tablespoon minced fresh parsley

Ground nutmeg, optional

Sour cream

In a large saucepan, saute onion and mushrooms in butter for 3 minutes or until onion is tender. Stir in the flour, pepper and salt; gradually add milk and broth. Bring to a boil; cook and stir for 2 minutes or until thickened. Add parsley and nutmeg if desired.

Top individual servings with a dollop of sour cream. **YIELD: 2-3 servings.**

turkey tortilla roll-ups

- **3/4** cup sour cream
- **6** flour tortillas (8 inches)
- **1-1/2** cups diced cooked turkey
- **1** cup (4 ounces) finely shredded cheddar cheese
- **1** cup shredded lettuce
- **1/2** cup chopped ripe olives
- **1/2** cup chunky salsa

Spread 2 tablespoons sour cream over each tortilla. Top with the turkey, cheese, lettuce, olives and salsa. Roll up each tortilla tightly; wrap in plastic wrap. Refrigerate until serving. **YIELD: 6 servings.**

turkey tortilla roll-ups

If you are on the run, you won't have to take along a grill (or even a fork and knife) to enjoy these tasty, hearty roll-ups.

—Darlene Brenden, Salem, Oregon

crisp side salad

crisp side salad

- **1/4** cup olive oil
- **2** tablespoons cider vinegar
- **4** teaspoons sugar
- **1/2** teaspoon salt
- **1/4** teaspoon pepper
- **4** cups torn salad greens
- **3/4** cup sliced zucchini
- **2** medium carrots, sliced
- **2** celery ribs, sliced
- **2** green onions, sliced
- **1/4** cup seasoned croutons
- **1** tablespoon whole almonds, toasted
- **1** tablespoon sesame seeds, toasted

In a jar with a tight-fitting lid, combine the oil, vinegar, sugar, salt and pepper; shake well.

In a large salad bowl, combine the greens, zucchini, carrots, celery and onions. Drizzle with dressing and toss to coat. Top with the croutons, almonds and sesame seeds. **YIELD: 4 servings.**

The light dressing I serve over a crunchy combination of salad fixings contains just a hint of sweetness. Make it ahead to let the flavors blend.

—Craig Miller, Torrance, California

tropical pineapple smoothies

Around our house, we often make these yummy shakes. They are fast and nutritious! For a creamier indulgence, substitute ice cream for the fat-free milk and ice cubes.

—Polly Coumos, Mogadore, Ohio

1	cup fat-free milk
1	can (8 ounces) unsweetened crushed pineapple
1/2	cup unsweetened pineapple juice
3	tablespoons sugar
1/2	teaspoon vanilla extract
1/4	teaspoon coconut extract
6	ice cubes

In a blender, place the first six ingredients; cover and process until smooth. Add ice cubes; cover and process until smooth. Pour into chilled glasses; serve immediately. **YIELD: 3 servings.**

cozy hot chocolate

Steaming mugs of these smooth beverages are a nice anytime treat with my husband.

—Marie Hattrup, The Dalles, Oregon

2	tablespoons baking cocoa
2	tablespoons sugar
1/4	cup water
2	cups milk
1/2	teaspoon vanilla extract
1/4	cup whipped cream

Ground cinnamon, optional

In a small saucepan, mix the cocoa and sugar; add water, and stir until smooth. Bring to a boil, stirring constantly. Boil for 1 minute. Reduce heat; stir in milk and heat through.

Remove from the heat and stir in vanilla. Pour into 2 cups; top with whipped cream and sprinkle with cinnamon if desired. **YIELD: 2 servings.**

tropical pineapple smoothies

crunchy raisin treats

Peanuts give an extra crunch to these crispy treats dotted with raisins. As an evening snack, they are irresistible with a tall, cold glass of milk.

—Bernice Morris, Marshfield, Missouri

    4   cups miniature marshmallows
    1/4 cup butter
    5-1/2 cups crisp rice cereal
    1-1/2 cups raisins
    1   cup salted dry roasted peanuts

In a microwave-safe bowl, melt marshmallows and butter; stir until smooth. Add the cereal, raisins and peanuts. Pat into a greased 13-in. x 9-in. pan. Cool completely; cut into squares. **YIELD: 3 dozen.**

hot spinach dip

For a different take on traditional spinach dip, warm this rich mixture in the microwave.

—Janie Obermier, St. Joseph, Missouri

    1   package (8 ounces) cream cheese, softened
    1/2 cup mayonnaise
    1/4 cup grated Parmesan cheese
    1   package (10 ounces) frozen chopped spinach, thawed and squeezed dry
    1   cup (4 ounces) shredded part-skim mozzarella cheese
Crackers *or* vegetables

In a small bowl, beat the cream cheese, mayonnaise and Parmesan cheese until blended. Stir in spinach and mozzarella cheese. Spoon into an ungreased microwave-safe 9-in. pie plate.

Microwave, uncovered, on high for 4-5 minutes or until bubbly, stirring twice. Serve with crackers or vegetables. **YIELD: 8-10 servings.**

editor's note: This recipe was tested in a 1,100-watt microwave.

chocolate fondue

chocolate fondue

I combine prepared chocolate frosting with sour cream to create a sweet dip that's perfect with fresh fruit. It's easy to keep the ingredients for this quick dessert on hand for company. It's also decadent served with sugar cookies and pound cake.

—Jane Franks, Spokane, Washington

    1   can (16 ounces) chocolate frosting
    1   cup (8 ounces) sour cream
Assorted fresh fruit

In a small bowl, combine frosting and sour cream; spoon into a serving bowl. Serve with fruit. Refrigerate leftovers. **YIELD: about 2-1/2 cups.**

cheese quesadillas

Three ingredients are all you need for this Mexican twist on grilled cheese. The tasty wedges are ideal as an after-school snack or with soup at lunchtime.

—Luke Walker, Unionville, Ontario

4	flour tortillas (6 inches)
1/2	cup salsa
2/3	cup shredded cheddar cheese

Place two tortillas on a greased baking sheet. Top each with salsa, cheese and remaining tortillas. Broil 4 in. from the heat for 3 minutes on each side or until golden brown. Cut into four wedges. **YIELD: 2-4 servings.**

fruit crumble

Fruit is a good dessert after almost any meal, but it seems to be even more unique when it's dressed up like this. Convenient canned pie filling and a microwave make this take on a classic crumble a snap to prepare.

—Jackie Heyer, Cushing, Iowa

1/3	cup butter, cubed
1-1/3	cups graham cracker crumbs
3	tablespoons sugar
1	can (21 ounces) raspberry *or* cherry pie filling
1/4	teaspoon almond extract

Whipped cream

In a skillet, melt the butter. Add cracker crumbs and sugar; cook and stir until crumbs are lightly browned.

Meanwhile, combine the pie filling and extract in a microwave-safe bowl. Cover and microwave on high for 1-2 minutes or until heated through. Spoon into individual dishes; sprinkle with crumbs. Top with whipped cream. **YIELD: 4-6 servings.**

editor's note: This recipe was tested in a 1,100-watt microwave.

cilantro chicken salad

Here's a perfect summer recipe that comes together in a pinch. A distinctive dressing of cilantro, cumin and lime is refreshing over crisp lettuce and tender chicken. Toss in cherry tomatoes, if you'd like, for a splash of color.

—Linda Schwab-Edmunsdson, Shokan, New York

2/3	cup olive oil
1/4	cup lime juice
1/4	cup minced fresh cilantro
1/2	teaspoon ground cumin
1/2	teaspoon salt
1/4	teaspoon crushed red pepper flakes
4	cups torn leaf lettuce
2	cups cubed cooked chicken
1	pint cherry tomatoes, optional

In a jar with a tight-fitting lid, combine the oil, lime juice, cilantro, cumin, salt and red pepper flakes; shake well.

In a large bowl, combine the lettuce, chicken and tomatoes if desired. Drizzle with dressing; toss to coat. **YIELD: 4 servings.**

cilantro chicken salad

vegetable scrambled eggs

I like to have friends and family over for a special Sunday brunch, especially when there's a "big game" on television. These colorful eggs go perfectly with sausage, toasted English muffins and fresh fruit. —Marilyn Ipson, Rogers, Arkansas

vegetable scrambled eggs

4	eggs, lightly beaten	1/2	teaspoon salt
1/2	cup chopped green pepper	1/8	teaspoon pepper
1/4	cup milk	1	small tomato, chopped and seeded
1/4	cup sliced green onions		

In a small bowl, combine the eggs, green pepper, milk, onions, salt and pepper. Pour into a lightly greased skillet. Cook and stir over medium heat until eggs are nearly set. Add the tomato; cook and stir until eggs are completely set. **YIELD: 2 servings.**

chicken pecan wraps

Pecans add a touch of crunch to the warm chicken mixture in my speedy wraps. Kick up the heat a notch or two by using medium or hot salsa.

—Judy Frakes, Blair, Nebraska

chicken pecan wraps

1	pound boneless skinless chicken breasts, cut into 1-inch cubes	3	tablespoons sour cream
1/4	cup chopped onion	4	flour tortillas (10 inches), warmed
1/4	teaspoon ground cumin	1	cup (4 ounces) shredded cheddar cheese
1	tablespoon butter	1	cup salsa
1/4	cup chopped pecans		Shredded lettuce, optional

In a large skillet, cook chicken, onion and cumin over medium heat in butter until chicken juices run clear. Reduce heat to low. Add pecans and sour cream; cook and stir until heated through. Spoon about 1/2 cupful down the center of each tortilla; layer with cheese, salsa and lettuce if desired. Roll up. **YIELD: 4 servings.**

deli vegetable roll-ups

deli vegetable roll-ups

1/2	cup garden vegetable cream cheese spread
4	flour tortillas (10 inches)
1	medium tomato, seeded and diced
2	sweet banana peppers, seeded and julienned
1	cup sliced ripe olives
4	slices Colby cheese
4	slices part-skim mozzarella cheese
8	thick dill pickle slices
1/4	cup ranch salad dressing
4	lettuce leaves
4	thin slices deli turkey
4	thin slices salami

Additional ranch salad dressing, optional

Spread about 2 tablespoons of cream cheese spread over each tortilla. Layer with tomato, peppers, olives, cheeses and pickle slices. Drizzle with salad dressing. Top with lettuce, turkey and salami.

Roll up tightly; wrap in plastic wrap. Refrigerate until ready to serve. Serve with additional dressing if desired. **YIELD: 4 servings.**

I would make these loaded tortilla sandwiches for my husband and son to take for lunch. My son thought I could peddle them on a street corner—and be sold out in an hour!

—Nancy Divelbiss, Leo, Indiana

fruity oatmeal

1/3	cup old-fashioned oats
1	teaspoon oat bran
1/3	cup diced unpeeled tart apple
1	medium firm banana, diced
1/4	cup halved seedless grapes
2	tablespoons raisins
1	tablespoon sliced almonds

Milk *or* yogurt, optional

Toss the first seven ingredients; divide between two bowls. Top with milk or yogurt if desired. Serve immediately. **YIELD: 2 servings.**

fruity oatmeal

I never liked oatmeal until my mom found this effortless combination of uncooked oats and fresh fruit. Now I often make it myself for breakfast or even a no-fuss snack on chilly days.

—Sarah Hunt, Everett, Washington

ham with creamed vegetables
swirled dill rolls
pecan baked apples,
page 170

30-minute meals

mom's best
30-minute meals

Mom never had a problem setting a hot and hearty meal on the table. Today, however, schedules are busier than ever and kitchen time is tight. Let this chapter show you how to surprise your gang with a complete menu in just half an hour.

smoked sausage kabobs, page 174

mint berry blast, page 189

brunch pizza squares, page 169

sometimes coming up with ideas for dinner is more difficult than actually preparing it. That's why the home economists in our Test Kitchen created this meal that takes the work out of menu planning.

It starts with Pasta Sausage Supper, a swift stove-top entree. While the pasta is cooking, it's a breeze to saute the meat and veggies. At the same time, you can warm the jarred spaghetti sauce in the microwave or in a saucepan.

Slices of Creamy Onion Garlic Bread are a delightful accompaniment to the main dish. A cheesy mixture seasoned with green onions and garlic powder adds rich flavor to Italian bread.

Complete the meal with Colorful Spinach Salad. Bagged spinach from the produce section hurries along the preparation of the salad that's topped with crunchy radishes, pretty slices of yellow summer squash and sweet chewy raisins.

Dress it with a simple homemade balsamic vinaigrette or choose your favorite bottled dressing for even quicker results.

pasta sausage supper

- 1 package (16 ounces) uncooked penne pasta
- 1 pound smoked kielbasa *or* Polish sausage, cut into 1/4-inch slices
- 1 medium green pepper, julienned
- 1 medium sweet red pepper, julienned
- 1 medium onion, halved and sliced
- 1 tablespoon canola oil
- 1 jar (26 ounces) meatless spaghetti sauce, warmed

Cook pasta according to package directions. Meanwhile, in large skillet, saute the sausage, peppers and onion in oil until vegetables are crisp-tender.

Drain pasta; divide among six serving plates. Top with spaghetti sauce. Using a slotted spoon, top with sausage mixture. **YIELD: 6 servings.**

creamy onion garlic bread

- 2 packages (3 ounces *each*) cream cheese, softened
- 1/4 cup butter, softened
- 1/4 cup grated Parmesan cheese
- 1/2 teaspoon garlic powder
- 8 green onions, chopped
- 1 loaf (1 pound) unsliced Italian bread, halved lengthwise

In a small bowl, beat the cream cheese, butter, Parmesan cheese and garlic powder until smooth. Beat in onions. Spread over cut sides of bread. Place on an ungreased baking sheet.

Broil 4 in. from the heat for 3-4 minutes or until lightly browned. Let stand for 5 minutes before cutting. **YIELD: 6-8 servings.**

colorful spinach salad

- 4 cups fresh baby spinach
- 3/4 cup sliced radishes
- 1/2 cup sliced yellow summer squash
- 1/2 cup raisins
- 1 tablespoon balsamic vinegar
- 1 teaspoon Dijon mustard
- 1/8 teaspoon salt
- 1/8 teaspoon pepper
- 3 tablespoons olive oil

In a large bowl, toss the spinach, radishes, yellow squash and raisins. In a small bowl, whisk the vinegar, mustard, salt and pepper. Gradually whisk in oil. Serve with salad. **YIELD: 6 servings.**

warm, sunny days can convince even the most dedicated cook to spend less time in the kitchen and more time outdoors. And since fresh air builds appetites, this fast-to-fix meal is especially appropriate.

Patti Beatty's Cocoa Mousse Pie is a snap to fix. Try it and you'll be amazed that something so easy could taste so wonderful. Patti sets the creamy dessert in her Hamilton, Ohio freezer for a bit, so start with the pie when preparing this supper.

Walnut Ham Linguine is a pleasing combination of textures and flavors. Shared by Mike Pickerel of Columbia, Missouri, it simmers to perfection on the stovetop, so there is no need to warm up the house or wait for the oven to preheat.

Next, toss the ingredients for Gay Nell Nicholas' salad. The Henderson, Texas cook creates an oil and vinegar dressing for torn salad greens. Use the salad to take advantage of any extra vegetables you may have on hand. Not only do fresh veggies add color and a nutritional boost, but they're a great way to turn an ordinary salad into something extra special on a busy weeknight.

walnut ham linguine

- 1 package (16 ounces) linguine *or* thin spaghetti
- 2 to 4 garlic cloves, minced
- 1/4 cup olive oil
- 1/2 cup coarsely chopped walnuts
- 1/2 pound fully cooked ham slices, cut into 1/2-inch strips
- 1/3 cup grated Parmesan cheese
- 1/4 cup minced fresh parsley

Cook pasta according to package directions. Meanwhile, in a large skillet, saute garlic in oil for 1 minute. Add walnuts; saute for 2 minutes. Stir in ham; cook until heated through, about 2 minutes. Drain pasta; toss with ham mixture. Sprinkle with Parmesan and parsley. **YIELD: 4-6 servings.**

french vinaigrette salad

- 1-1/2 cups vegetable oil
- 3/4 cup cider vinegar
- 4 teaspoons sugar
- 1 teaspoon salt
- 1 teaspoon paprika
- 1/2 teaspoon ground mustard
- 1/4 teaspoon pepper

Torn salad greens and vegetables of your choice

In a jar with a tight-fitting lid, combine the first seven ingredients; shake well. In a large salad bowl, combine the greens and vegetables. Drizzle with dressing. Serve immediately. **YIELD: 2-1/3 cups dressing.**

cocoa mousse pie

- 1 package (3 ounces) cream cheese, softened
- 2/3 cup sugar
- 1/3 cup baking cocoa
- 1/4 cup milk
- 1 teaspoon vanilla extract
- 1 carton (8 ounces) frozen whipped topping, thawed
- 1 graham cracker crust (9 inches)

Additional whipped topping and baking cocoa, optional

In a mixing bowl, beat cream cheese, sugar and cocoa. Beat in the milk and vanilla until smooth. Fold in the whipped topping. Spoon into the crust. Cover and freeze for 20 minutes. Garnish with additional whipped topping and cocoa if desired. **YIELD: 8 servings.**

meaty meals

come together as quickly as simple salads, particularly with help from deli meat and a few convenience items. Just ask Patricia Fredericks of Oak Creek, Wisconsin.

She starts dinner prep with her Seasoned Oven Fries. You'll never believe these tasty spuds call for only four ingredients. Once they're in the oven, Patricia turns her attention to the main dish.

In this menu, thinly sliced roast beef gets star treatment on a hoagie bun with sliced green peppers. "I simply jazz up a can of beef broth with some garlic and a bit of oregano and pepper for a fantastic au jus to serve on the side," Patricia explains.

As the beef simmers in its juices, she prepares her change-of-pace tomato slices. Once they are breaded, they fry up on the stovetop in just a few minutes. Top the slices with mozzarella cheese and they'll be ready to serve at the same time the fries come out of the oven.

Need an effortless dessert? Pick up a treat at the bakery before stopping by the deli for the beef.

italian beef sandwiches

- 1   can (14-1/2 ounces) beef broth
- 2   garlic cloves, minced
- 1   teaspoon dried oregano
- 1/8   teaspoon pepper
- 1   medium green pepper, thinly sliced into rings
- 1   pound thinly sliced deli roast beef
- 6   hoagie buns, split

In a large skillet, add the broth, garlic, oregano and pepper; bring to a boil. Add green pepper. Reduce heat; simmer, uncovered, about 5 minutes or until green pepper is tender. Remove green pepper with a slotted spoon; keep warm. Return broth to a boil.

Add roast beef; cover and remove from the heat. Let stand for 2 minutes or until heated through. Place beef and green pepper on buns; serve with broth for dipping. **YIELD: 6 servings.**

breaded tomato slices

- 1/2   cup seasoned bread crumbs
- 1   tablespoon finely chopped green onion
- 1   tablespoon grated Parmesan cheese
- 1   teaspoon salt
- 1   teaspoon Italian seasoning
- 1/4   cup milk
- 4   medium tomatoes, cut into 1/2-inch slices
- 2   tablespoons olive oil
- 1/3   to 1/2 cup shredded part-skim mozzarella cheese

In a shallow bowl, combine the bread crumbs, onion, Parmesan cheese, salt and Italian seasoning. Place milk in another bowl. Dip tomato slices in milk, then coat with crumb mixture.

In a large skillet, heat oil. Fry tomato slices for 2 minutes on each side or until golden brown. Sprinkle with mozzarella cheese. **YIELD: 6 servings.**

seasoned oven fries

- 6   medium baking potatoes
- 2   tablespoons butter, melted
- 2   tablespoons canola oil
- 1   teaspoon seasoned salt

Cut each potato lengthwise into thirds; cut each portion into thirds. In a large resealable plastic bag, combine the butter, oil and seasoned salt. Add potatoes; shake to coat.

Place in a single layer on a greased baking sheet. Bake, uncovered, at 450° for 10-12 minutes on each side or until tender. **YIELD: 6 servings.**

eye-opening

breakfasts don't always require hours in the kitchen. Perfect for a casual Saturday breakfast or formal Sunday brunch, this meal comes together in a snap. LaChelle Olivet of Pace, Florida relies on convenience items to give her menu all the flavor with only a fraction of work.

Crescent rolls make LaChelle's sunny Brunch Pizza Squares a snap to fix. "Use hot sausage if your family likes things on the spicy side," she suggests.

While the breakfast pizza is baking in the oven, assemble the fruit skewers. The creamy dipping sauce, sweetened with honey, is also a breeze to make. Its pleasant banana flavor complements any fresh fruit you choose.

To complete the meal, you'll need just three ingredients for chilly Pineapple Orange Drink. "The beverage is not too sweet and so easy," LaChelle says. "Just throw it in a blender and it's done."

Looking to save even more time? Call the family into the kitchen. Older kids can help you assemble the brunch pizza with just a bit of supervision, and little ones can help beat the eggs.

Get the entire family involved with the fruit kabobs. Set up an assembly line and you'll be amazed at how quickly the skewers stack up. (If hosting early morning guests, consider cutting the fruit the night before and storing in the refrigerator to save time the morning of your event.)

Because it's a no-cook recipe, the beverage comes together in a snap. Ask your teenager for some help, and you'll have breakfast on the table in a flash.

brunch pizza squares

- 1 pound bulk pork sausage
- 1 tube (8 ounces) refrigerated crescent rolls
- 4 eggs
- 2 tablespoons milk
- 1/8 teaspoon pepper
- 3/4 cup shredded cheddar cheese

In a skillet, cook sausage over medium heat until no longer pink; drain. Unroll crescent dough into a lightly greased 13-in. x 9-in. baking pan. Press dough 1/2 in. up the sides; seal seams. Sprinkle with sausage. In a bowl, beat the eggs, milk and pepper; pour over sausage. Sprinkle with cheese. Bake, uncovered, at 400° for 15 minutes or until the crust is golden brown and the cheese is melted. YIELD: 8 servings.

fruit kabobs with dip

Assorted fruit—green grapes, watermelon balls, cantaloupe balls and strawberry halves
- 1 cup (8 ounces) plain yogurt
- 1/2 medium ripe banana
- 4 teaspoons honey
- 1/8 teaspoon ground cinnamon

Thread the fruit alternately onto skewers. In a blender, combine the remaining ingredients; cover and process until smooth. Serve with the kabobs. YIELD: 1-1/2 cups dip.

pineapple orange drink

- 6 cups orange juice
- 2 cans (8 ounces *each*) crushed unsweetened pineapple, undrained
- 16 ice cubes

Place half of the orange juice, pineapple and ice cubes in a blender; cover and process until smooth. Repeat with remaining ingredients. Pour into chilled glasses. Serve immediately. YIELD: 8 servings.

nothing soothes the spirit after a long day like a hot home-cooked meal. Our Test Kitchen put together this mouthwatering menu that you can have on the table in only a few minutes.

Start by setting the four-ingredient rolls in the oven. With their fresh-from-the-oven aroma and mild dill flavor, they complement the main course nicely. Or serve the rolls with most any entree.

It's easy to fix a hearty skillet entree of Ham with Creamed Vegetables. Loaded with garden flavor, it's sure to warm your family right down to their toes on chilly nights.

Cooked in the microwave, Pecan Baked Apples offer a time-saving twist on a dinner tradition. The down-home apples are stuffed with dried cherries, nuts and brown sugar, drizzled with their own juices and served warm for a homey dessert. Feel free to experiment with your fillings such as chocolate chips or caramel. Top them with a scoop of frozen whipped topping if you'd like or serve with a small bowl of vanilla ice cream on the side.

ham with creamed vegetables

1/4	cup julienned sweet red pepper
1/4	cup julienned sweet yellow pepper
1/4	cup chopped onion
2	tablespoons sliced celery
2	tablespoons chopped carrot
2	tablespoons butter
1	tablespoon all-purpose flour
1/8	teaspoon pepper
1	cup milk
1-1/2	teaspoons chicken bouillon granules
1	boneless fully cooked ham steak (1 pound)

In a large skillet, saute the peppers, onion, celery and carrot in butter for 3-4 minutes or until crisp-

tender. Sprinkle with flour and pepper. Gradually whisk in milk and bouillon until smooth. Bring to a boil; cook and stir for 2 minutes or until thickened.

Meanwhile, cut the ham steak into four pieces. Cook in a large skillet coated with cooking spray over medium heat for 2-4 minutes or until browned on both sides. Serve with vegetable mixture. **YIELD: 4 servings.**

swirled dill rolls

1	tube (8 ounces) refrigerated crescent rolls
2	tablespoons butter, softened
1/4	teaspoon onion powder
1/4	teaspoon snipped fresh dill

Do not unroll crescent dough; cut into eight equal slices. Place cut side down on an ungreased baking sheet. Bake at 375° for 11-13 minutes or until golden brown. Meanwhile, in a small bowl, combine the butter, onion powder and dill. Spread over warm rolls. **YIELD: 8 rolls.**

pecan baked apples

1/4	cup butter, softened
1/4	cup chopped pecans
1/4	cup packed brown sugar
1/4	cup dried cherries
1/2	teaspoon ground cinnamon
1/8	teaspoon ground nutmeg
4	medium tart apples

In a small bowl, combine first six ingredients. Core apples and peel top third; fill with pecan mixture.

Place in a greased 8-in. square microwave-safe dish. Microwave, uncovered, on high for 8-12 minutes or until apples are tender. Drizzle with pan juices. **YIELD: 4 servings.**

editor's note: This recipe was tested in a 1,100-watt microwave.

working late, attending after-school events, running errands...they all add up to less time in the kitchen. But it takes only 30 minutes to put this special meal on the table.

For this delightful menu, start by boiling the water for Scott Jones' comforting tortellini side dish and prepare the creamy cheese sauce. He sends the recipe from Tulsa, Oklahoma.

Next, grab your blender and whip up Frosty Almond Dessert shared by Phyllis Schmalz of Kansas City, Kansas. Pour the creamy mixture into dessert glasses and set them in the fridge. Save the toppings until you're ready to serve the cool treat.

Last but not least, mix up the rub for the fish. You'll find that the fillets fry up quickly in a skillet. The recipe is from Windy Byrd of Freeport, Texas.

By now the tortellini should be ready to combine with the cheese sauce. Finish the side dish and serve it with the change-of-pace snapper for a dinner that's sure to become a fast favorite.

pepper-rubbed red snapper

1/2	teaspoon onion powder
1/2	teaspoon garlic powder
1/2	teaspoon dried thyme
1/2	teaspoon white pepper
1/2	teaspoon cayenne pepper
1/2	teaspoon pepper
1/8	teaspoon salt
4	red snapper fillets (8 ounces *each*)
3	tablespoons butter, melted

In a small bowl, combine the first seven ingredients. Dip fillets in butter, then rub with spice mixture.

In a large nonstick skillet, cook fillets over medium-high heat for 2-4 minutes on each side or until fish flakes easily with a fork. **YIELD: 4 servings.**

prosciutto tortellini

1	package (19 ounces) frozen cheese tortellini
1	tablespoon all-purpose flour
1	cup half-and-half cream
1/2	cup shredded part-skim mozzarella cheese
1/2	cup shredded Parmesan cheese
10	thin slices prosciutto, chopped
1	package (10 ounces) frozen peas
1/4	teaspoon white pepper

Cook tortellini according to package directions. Meanwhile, in a large skillet, combine flour and cream until smooth; stir in the cheeses. Bring to a boil; cook and stir for 2 minutes or until thickened. Reduce heat.

Drain tortellini; add to the cheese sauce. Stir in the prosciutto, peas and pepper. Cook for 5 minutes or until heated through. **YIELD: 4 servings.**

frosty almond dessert

4	cups vanilla frozen yogurt
1	cup ice cubes
1/2	cup hot fudge ice cream topping
1/4	teaspoon almond extract

Whipped topping and baking cocoa, optional

In a blender, place half of the yogurt, ice cubes, fudge topping and extract; cover and process for 1-2 minutes or until smooth. Stir if necessary. Pour into chilled dessert glasses.

Repeat with remaining yogurt, ice, fudge topping and extract. Garnish with whipped topping and baking cocoa if desired. **YIELD: 4 servings.**

a balancing act likely takes place in your kitchen daily. That's why you'll just love this hearty meal from Ruth Lee of Troy, Ontario.

Ruth's Smoked Sausage Kabobs are a convenient entree since the ingredients can be cut, marinated and threaded ahead of time. Then they go immediately from the fridge to the broiler.

"It takes no time to toss together the greens, corn and red peppers for my Corny Lettuce Salad," adds Ruth. "Keep the recipe in mind the next time you need a covered-dish contribution."

For dessert, few things dress up a family meal or special occasion faster than Banana Pineapple Sundaes. Vanilla is a nice alternative to rum extract in the sauce, or you could include other flavors such as ginger, allspice or mint. "Try the topping over pound cake or a plain yellow cake," Ruth adds.

smoked sausage kabobs

1/3	cup honey
1/4	cup spicy brown mustard
2	tablespoons canola oil
1	tablespoon soy sauce
2	garlic cloves, minced
1/2	teaspoon minced fresh gingerroot
1-1/4	pounds smoked sausage, cut into 1-inch pieces
16	cherry tomatoes
8	medium fresh mushrooms
1	large green pepper, cut into 1-inch pieces
1	medium onion, cut into eight wedges
1	small zucchini, cut into 1-inch pieces

In a large bowl, combine the first six ingredients. Add the sausage and vegetables; toss to coat. Drain and reserve marinade.

On eight metal or soaked wooden skewers, alternately thread sausage and vegetables. Broil 3-4 in. from the heat for 3-4 minutes on each side or until vegetables are tender and the sausage is heated through, basting occasionally with reserved marinade. **YIELD: 4 servings.**

corny lettuce salad

3	cups shredded lettuce
3/4	cup fresh *or* frozen corn, thawed
2	tablespoons sugar
2	tablespoons cider vinegar
1-1/2	teaspoons poppy seeds
1/2	teaspoon grated onion
1/4	teaspoon salt
1/4	teaspoon ground mustard
1/4	cup vegetable oil
1/4	cup finely chopped sweet red pepper

In a salad bowl, toss the lettuce and corn. In a small bowl, combine the sugar, vinegar, poppy seeds, onion, salt and mustard; gradually whisk in oil. Pour over salad and toss to coat. Sprinkle with red pepper. **YIELD: 4 servings.**

banana pineapple sundaes

6	tablespoons brown sugar
1/4	cup orange juice
1-1/2	teaspoons butter
1/8	teaspoon ground cinnamon
2	small firm bananas, sliced
1	cup cubed fresh pineapple
1/2	teaspoon rum extract
2	cups vanilla ice cream

In a large saucepan, combine the brown sugar, orange juice, butter and cinnamon. Bring to a boil. Reduce heat to medium; cook and stir for 2 minutes. Add the bananas and pineapple; cook and stir 1-2 minutes longer. Remove from the heat; stir in extract. Serve with ice cream. **YIELD: 4 servings.**

herbed pork medallions

1-1/2	pounds pork tenderloin
2	tablespoons butter, melted
1/4	teaspoon garlic powder
1/2	teaspoon salt
1/2	teaspoon dried tarragon
1/2	teaspoon dried thyme
1/2	teaspoon paprika
1/8	teaspoon pepper
1/8	teaspoon cayenne pepper
1	tablespoon honey

Cut pork into 1/2-in. slices and pound to flatten. Combine butter and garlic powder; brush over pork. Combine the seasonings; sprinkle over pork.

Broil 4-6 in. from the heat for 4 minutes on each side. Brush with honey; broil for 1 minute longer or until meat juices run clear. **YIELD: 6 servings.**

vinaigrette vegetables

4	cups fresh broccoli florets
1	medium zucchini, cut into 1/4-inch slices
1/3	cup julienned sweet yellow *or* red pepper
3	tablespoons olive oil
4	to 5 teaspoons red wine vinegar
1	garlic clove, minced
1/2	teaspoon salt
1/4	to 1/2 teaspoon dried thyme

Place broccoli in a steamer basket. Place in a saucepan over 1 in. of water. Bring to a boil; cover and steam for 5 minutes. Add zucchini and yellow pepper; cover and steam for 2 minutes or until vegetables are crisp-tender.

In a jar with a tight-fitting lid, combine the oil, vinegar, garlic, salt and thyme; shake well. Transfer vegetables to a serving bowl; add dressing and toss to coat. **YIELD: 6 servings.**

toasted coconut pudding

1/2	cup sugar
3	tablespoons cornstarch
3	cups milk
3	egg yolks, lightly beaten
3	tablespoons butter
1-1/2	teaspoons vanilla extract
3/4	cup flaked coconut, toasted
3/4	cup miniature semisweet chocolate chips

In a large saucepan, combine the sugar and cornstarch. Stir in milk until smooth. Cook and stir over medium-high heat until thickened and bubbly. Reduce heat; cook and stir 2 minutes longer. Remove from heat. Stir a small amount of hot filling into egg yolks; return all to pan, stirring constantly. Bring to a gentle boil; cook and stir 2 minutes longer. Remove from the heat. Gently stir in butter and vanilla. Cool to room temperature without stirring.

Sprinkle 2 teaspoons each of coconut and chips into dessert dishes. Top with pudding mixture and remaining coconut and chips. Refrigerate until serving. **YIELD: 6 servings.**

dinnertime rolls around in a hurry, but action-packed evenings won't stop you when Renee Endress' meal is on the planner.

The Galva, Illinois mom serves her menu in 30 minutes, by working backward, fixing the dessert first so it has time to chill.

Cookies 'n' Cream Fluff goes together in a flash with ingredients that many family cooks already have on hand. Consider it whenever you need a fast dessert or an effortless after-school surprise. You can even replace the cookies with whatever kind your little ones like best.

Next, Renee mixes up a batch of Creamy Coleslaw. "A package of shredded cabbage really cuts down on prep time," she adds. "Feel free to toss in some shredded carrots, chopped onion or finely diced green pepper for extra crunch and a bit of color."

To complete the meal, Renee assembles tangy Pineapple Chicken Stir-Fry. Frozen veggies and canned pineapple chunks make the chicken dish a convenient solution to the dinner rush Renee and so many other moms face today.

In a small bowl, combine the first six ingredients; set aside. In a large skillet or wok, stir-fry chicken in oil for 5-6 minutes or until juices run clear. Add the vegetables; stir-fry for 3-4 minutes or until crisp-tender. Stir in the pineapple and the reserved soy sauce mixture; heat through. Serve the stir-fry over rice. **YIELD: 6 servings.**

creamy coleslaw

1	package (16 ounces) coleslaw mix
3/4	cup mayonnaise *or* salad dressing
1/3	cup sour cream
1/4	cup sugar
3/4	teaspoon seasoned salt
1/2	teaspoon ground mustard
1/4	teaspoon celery salt

Place coleslaw mix in a large bowl. In a small bowl, combine the remaining ingredients; stir until blended. Pour over coleslaw mix and toss to coat. Refrigerate until serving. **YIELD: 6 servings.**

pineapple chicken stir-fry

1/4	cup soy sauce
2	tablespoons sugar
1	tablespoon vinegar
1	tablespoon ketchup
1/2	teaspoon ground ginger
2	garlic cloves, minced
1	pound boneless skinless chicken breasts, cut into strips
2	tablespoons vegetable oil
1	package (16 ounces) frozen stir-fry vegetables
1	can (8 ounces) unsweetened pineapple chunks, drained

Hot cooked rice

cookies 'n' cream fluff

2	cups cold milk
1	package (3.4 ounces) instant vanilla pudding mix
1	carton (8 ounces) frozen whipped topping, thawed
15	chocolate cream-filled sandwich cookies, broken into chunks

Additional broken cookies, optional

In a bowl, whisk the milk and pudding mix for 2 minutes or until slightly thickened. Fold in the whipped topping and cookies. Spoon into dessert dishes. Top with additional cookies if desired. Refrigerate until serving. **YIELD: 6 servings.**

searching for quick-to-fix fare with old-fashioned appeal? This comforting menu takes advantage of the microwave and the stove.

Start by preparing Karen Kurtz's meaty main dish. While she zaps the sirloin strips in the microwave, the Muskegon, Michigan mom boils water for the noodles on the stovetop.

To complement the entree, toss together Wilted Lettuce Salad from Cheryl Newendorp, Pella, Iowa.

Cap off the meal with ice cream and Eleanor Martens' warm fruit sauce. Six ingredients create the speedy treat in her Rosenort, Manitoba home.

microwave stroganoff

2	tablespoons butter
1-1/2	pounds boneless beef sirloin steak, cut into thin strips
1/4	cup all-purpose flour
1	envelope onion soup mix
2-1/4	cups hot water
1	can (4 ounces) mushroom stems and pieces, drained
1/2	cup sour cream

Hot cooked noodles

Melt butter in a 2-qt. microwave-safe dish; arrange meat evenly in dish. Microwave, uncovered, on high for 4-1/2 minutes, stirring once. Remove meat with a slotted spoon and keep warm.

Stir the flour and soup mix into the drippings until blended. Gradually add water, stirring until smooth. Add mushrooms and beef.

Cover and microwave on high for 13-14 minutes or until the meat is tender and the sauce is thickened, stirring several times. Stir in the sour cream. Serve with noodles. **YIELD: 6-8 servings.**

editor's note: This recipe was tested in a 1,100-watt microwave.

wilted lettuce salad

6	cups torn leaf lettuce
3	tablespoons finely chopped onion
3	bacon strips, diced
2	tablespoons red wine vinegar
2-1/4	teaspoons sugar
1-1/2	teaspoons water

Salt and pepper to taste

1	hard-cooked egg, sliced

In a large salad bowl, combine the lettuce and onion; set aside.

Place bacon on a microwave-safe plate lined with paper towels. Cover with another paper towel; microwave on high for 5-7 minutes or until crisp. Using a slotted spoon, remove bacon to paper towels.

In a small microwave-safe dish, combine 1-1/2 teaspoons bacon drippings, vinegar, sugar and water. Microwave, uncovered, on high for 45 seconds or until sugar is dissolved; stir until smooth.

Pour over lettuce; sprinkle with salt and pepper. Add bacon and egg; toss to coat. **YIELD: 6 servings.**

editor's note: This recipe was tested in a 1,100-watt microwave.

apricot pecan sauce

1/2	cup apricot spreadable fruit
1/2	cup heavy whipping cream
2	tablespoons butter
1/2	cup chopped pecans
1/2	teaspoon vanilla extract
1/4	to 1 teaspoon rum extract, optional

Vanilla ice cream

In a large saucepan, combine the spreadable fruit, cream and butter. Bring to a boil. Reduce heat; simmer, uncovered, for 3-5 minutes or until blended. Stir in pecans, vanilla and rum extract if desired. Remove from the heat. Serve over ice cream. **YIELD: 1 cup.**

it's wonderful when family meals turn into elaborate spreads. But when reality comes knocking at your front door and you need to get dinner on the table in minutes instead of hours, here's a menu to reach for.

Start with Honey Peach Freeze from Dorothy Smith of El Dorado, Arkansas. The tang of orange and lemon juices blends nicely with the desssert's honey, making it a cool, refreshing end to any meal.

It's great for anyone who is on a restricted diet, and those who aren't won't know the difference. Let it freeze while you get the rest of the supper going.

It's nearly impossible to resist the entree in this lineup. "Crispy Chicken Cutlets are moist and tender with a golden nutty coating," says Debra Smith of Brookfield, Missouri. The sensational main course seems like you fussed, but it couldn't be easier to whip up.

Keep the cutlets warm by covering them in the skillet briefly before the side dish is ready.

Jeanette Lawrence sent her recipe for Stir-Fried Asparagus from Vacaville, California. It should be served as soon as it's done, so complete your meal preparation with her asparagus dish.

It's a cinch to fix and it puts good use to spring asparagus, plus it goes well with just about any main course. If you don't have time to whip up this side dish, however, simply serve the chicken with hot egg noodles instead.

crispy chicken cutlets

4	boneless skinless chicken breast halves
1	egg white
3/4	cup finely chopped pecans
3	tablespoons all-purpose flour
1/4	teaspoon salt
1/4	teaspoon pepper
1	tablespoon butter
1	tablespoon canola oil

Flatten chicken to 1/4-in. thickness. In a shallow bowl, lightly beat the egg white. In another shallow bowl, combine the pecans, flour, salt and pepper. Dip chicken in egg white, then coat with the pecan mixture. In a large skillet, brown chicken in butter and oil over medium heat for 4-6 minutes on each side or until juices run clear. **YIELD: 4 servings.**

stir-fried asparagus

3	tablespoons butter
1	teaspoon chicken bouillon granules
1/8	teaspoon celery salt
1/8	teaspoon pepper
1-1/2	pounds fresh asparagus, trimmed and cut into 2-inch slices (about 4 cups)
1	teaspoon soy sauce

In a large skillet, melt butter. Add bouillon, celery salt and pepper; mix well. Add asparagus and toss to coat. Cover and cook for 2 minutes over medium-high heat, stirring occasionally. Stir in soy sauce and serve immediately. **YIELD: 4 servings.**

honey peach freeze

1	package (20 ounces) frozen sliced peaches, partially thawed
1/4	cup honey
2	tablespoons orange juice
1	tablespoon lemon juice

Set aside a few peach slices for garnish if desired. Place remaining peaches in a blender or food processor; add honey and juices. Cover and process until smooth. Pour into four freezer-proof dishes. Freeze. Remove from the freezer 5 minutes before serving. Garnish with reserved peaches. YIELD: 4 servings.

herb-coated cod

1/4	cup butter, melted
2/3	cup butter-flavored cracker crumbs
2	tablespoons grated Parmesan cheese
1/2	teaspoon dried oregano
1/2	teaspoon dried basil
1/4	teaspoon garlic powder
1	pound cod fillets

Place butter in a shallow bowl. In another bowl, combine the next five ingredients. Dip fillets in butter, then coat with crumbs. Place in a greased 13-in. x 9-in. baking dish. Bake, uncovered, at 400° for 15-20 minutes or until fish flakes easily with a fork. YIELD: 4 servings.

monterey green beans

1/2	cup chopped green onions
3	tablespoons butter
1	package (9 ounces) frozen cut green beans
1	can (4 ounces) mushroom stems and pieces, drained
1/2	teaspoon lemon-pepper seasoning
1/4	teaspoon salt
1/2	cup shredded Monterey Jack cheese

In a saucepan, saute onions in butter until tender. Add beans, mushrooms, lemon-pepper and salt. Cover and cook over medium heat for 5 minutes or until beans are tender. Sprinkle with cheese; cover and let stand for 1 minute or until cheese is melted. YIELD: 6 servings.

microwave oatmeal cake

1	cup quick-cooking oats
1-1/2	cups water
1/2	cup butter, softened
1	cup packed brown sugar
1/2	cup sugar
2	eggs
1-1/2	teaspoons vanilla extract
1-1/3	cups all-purpose flour
1	teaspoon baking soda
1	teaspoon ground cinnamon
1/2	teaspoon salt
1/4	teaspoon ground nutmeg

TOPPING:

1	cup flaked coconut
1/2	cup chopped nuts
1/2	cup packed brown sugar
1/2	cup milk
1/4	cup butter

Dash salt

In a microwave-safe bowl, combine oats and water. Microwave, uncovered, on high for 2-3 minutes or until thickened, stirring once; set aside. Cream butter and sugars. Add eggs; beat well. Beat in vanilla and oat mixture. Combine dry ingredients; gradually add to oat mixture and mix well. Pour into a greased 11-in. x 7-in. microwave-safe dish. Shield corners with small triangles of foil. Microwave, uncovered, at 50% power for 8 minutes. Cook on high for 6 minutes or until cake clings to finger while area underneath is almost dry. Place on a wire rack. Combine topping ingredients in a microwave-safe dish; heat, uncovered, on high for 6-7 minutes or until thick and bubbly, stirring every 2 minutes. Spread over warm cake. YIELD: 8 servings.

editor's note: Shielding with small pieces of foil prevents overcooking of food in the corners of a square or rectangular dish. Secure foil firmly to dish and do not allow it to touch insides of microwave. This recipe was tested in an 850-watt microwave.

there's no chance

Gaylene Anderson's family gets bored when she sets this meal on the table in her Sandy, Utah home.

Pantry staples create her crowd-pleasing Beef-Topped Bean Enchiladas. Once the zesty entree is in the oven, she whips up the rest of her meal.

Next, she turns to yummy Peanut Cookie Bars, prepared on the stovetop. While her no-fuss bars cool, she tosses Ready-to-Serve Salad.

"The unique combination of salad ingredients relies on canned mandarin oranges, mozzarella cheese, bacon and almonds for a delightful specialty everyone will crave," Gaylene promises.

beef-topped bean enchiladas

1-1/2	pounds ground beef
1	medium onion, chopped
1	jar (16 ounces) salsa
1	can (8 ounces) tomato sauce
1	to 2 teaspoons ground cumin
1/8	teaspoon garlic salt
1	can (16 ounces) refried beans
12	flour tortillas (7 inches)
1-1/2	cups (6 ounces) shredded cheddar cheese, *divided*
1-1/2	cups (6 ounces) shredded Monterey Jack cheese, *divided*
2	cans (2-1/4 ounces *each*) sliced ripe olives, drained, *divided*

In a skillet, cook beef and onion until meat is no longer pink; drain. Stir in the salsa, tomato sauce, cumin and garlic salt; cook for 3 minutes or until heated through. Meanwhile, spread 2-3 tablespoons refried beans over each tortilla. Sprinkle each with 1 tablespoon cheddar cheese, 1 tablespoon of Monterey Jack cheese and 1 tablespoon olives. Roll up. Place seam side down in a greased 13-in. x 9-in. baking dish. Top with beef mixture. Sprinkle with remaining cheeses and olives. Bake, uncovered, at 350° for 20 minutes or until heated through. **YIELD: 6 servings.**

ready-to-serve salad

1	package (16 ounces) ready-to-serve salad
8	bacon strips, cooked and crumbled
1	can (11 ounces) mandarin oranges, drained
1/2	cup chopped red onion
1/4	cup sliced almonds
1	cup (4 ounces) shredded mozzarella cheese, optional
1/2	cup canola oil
2	tablespoons sugar
2	tablespoons vinegar
1/4	to 1/2 teaspoon salt

In a large salad bowl, toss the first six ingredients. Combine the remaining ingredients in a jar with a tight-fitting lid; shake well. Pour over salad and toss to coat. **YIELD: 6 servings.**

peanut cookie bars

12	cups cornflakes, crushed
1	jar (16 ounces) dry roasted peanuts
1-1/2	cups corn syrup
1	cup sugar
1	cup packed brown sugar
1	cup peanut butter

In a large bowl, combine cornflakes and peanuts; mix well. In a saucepan, combine corn syrup and sugars; bring to a boil. Boil for 1 minute. Remove from the heat; stir in peanut butter. Pour over cornflake mixture and mix gently. Press into a greased 15-in. x 10-in. x 1-in. baking pan. Cool slightly; cut into bars. **YIELD: 2 dozen.**

pork chops in orange sauce

1/4	teaspoon paprika
1/4	teaspoon pepper
4	boneless pork loin chops (6 ounces *each*)
3/4	cup orange juice
2	tablespoons sugar
6	whole cloves
1/2	teaspoon grated orange peel
2	tablespoons all-purpose flour
1/4	cup cold water

Combine paprika and pepper; rub over both sides of pork chops. In a large nonstick skillet, brown chops over medium heat.

Combine the orange juice, sugar, cloves and orange peel; pour over pork. Cover and simmer for 18-22 minutes or until a meat thermometer reads 160°. Remove chops and keep warm.

In a small bowl, combine flour and water until smooth; stir into cooking juices. Bring to a boil; cook and stir for 2 minutes or until thickened. Discard cloves. Serve sauce with pork chops. **YIELD:** 4 servings.

snap peas 'n' mushrooms

1/2	pound fresh sugar snap peas
8	medium fresh mushrooms, sliced
1	tablespoon canola oil
1	tablespoon teriyaki sauce

In a skillet or wok, stir-fry the peas and mushrooms in oil and teriyaki sauce until crisp-tender. **YIELD:** 4 servings.

mint berry blast

1	cup *each* fresh raspberries, blackberries, blueberries and halved strawberries
1	tablespoon minced fresh mint
1	tablespoon lemon juice
Whipped topping, optional	

In a large bowl, combine the berries, mint and lemon juice; gently toss to coat. Cover and refrigerate until serving. Garnish with whipped topping if desired. **YIELD:** 4 servings.

mint berry blast

settle in for a comfortable evening when this seemingly extravagate dinner is on the menu. It may look like you fussed, but this entire meal is made up of recipes that can be prepared in a hurry. Virginia Conley of Milwaukee, Wisconsin shares her secrets here.

Chicken with Mushroom Sauce is baked in a flavorful mixture that's easily made with canned soup and mushrooms. The impressive entree is then served over hot noodles that simmer on their own on the stovetop.

Next, toss together Red and Green Salad. Virginia's change-of-pace medley features crisp greens and colorful fruit for a refreshing addition to any meal.

She ends her supper with Peppermint Ice Cream Dessert. The sundae-like treats are a snap to make with a quart of peppermint or mint chocolate chip ice cream that you can simply pick up from the grocery store on your way home from work. Crumbled sandwich cookies and a dollop of chocolate-flavored whipped cream make these frosty treats perfect after-dinner delights.

chicken with mushroom sauce

4   boneless skinless chicken breast halves
2   tablespoons butter
1   can (10-3/4 ounces) condensed cream of mushroom soup, undiluted
1   cup (8 ounces) sour cream
1   can (4 ounces) mushroom stems and pieces, drained
1/4   cup white wine *or* chicken broth
1/2   teaspoon garlic powder
1/2   teaspoon salt
1/2   teaspoon pepper
Hot cooked noodles *or* rice
Sliced almonds, toasted, optional

In a skillet, brown chicken on both sides in butter; drain. Place in a greased 11-in. x 7-in. baking dish. In a bowl, combine the soup, sour cream, mushrooms, wine, garlic powder, salt and pepper; pour over the chicken. Bake, uncovered, at 375° for 20 minutes or until meat juices run clear. Serve chicken and sauce over noodles or rice. Garnish with almonds if desired. **YIELD: 4 servings.**

red and green salad

4   cups torn mixed salad greens
2   tablespoons sliced green onion
2   medium red apples, diced
2   kiwifruit, peeled and sliced
1   cup unsweetened raspberries
1/2   cup poppy seed *or* French salad dressing

In a bowl, toss the salad greens, onion and fruit. Drizzle with dressing. Serve immediately. **YIELD: 4 servings.**

peppermint ice cream dessert

4   chocolate cream-filled sandwich cookies, broken
1   quart peppermint stick *or* mint chocolate chip ice cream
1/2   cup whipping cream
1   tablespoon confectioners' sugar
2   teaspoons baking cocoa
Miniature candy canes and additional cookies, optional

Sprinkle the broken cookies into four dessert dishes. Top with scoops of ice cream. In a mixing bowl, beat the cream, confectioners' sugar and cocoa until soft peaks form. Dollop over ice cream. Garnish with candy canes and additional cookies if desired. **YIELD: 4 servings.**

win raves from your whole family with a satisfying meal of steak, green beans and cheesy breadsticks. Believe it or not, this simple but hearty supper can be on the table in just half an hour. It's perfect for the hectic holiday season when cookie baking and shopping dominate the schedule, but it makes a fantastic dinner all year long.

Quick-to-fix Cheddar Bread Twists will become an instant hit at your home, just as they did for Tracy Travers of Fairhaven, Massachusetts. Convenient frozen puff pastry makes the cheesy bites a sure-fire success. Assemble the twists first, then let them bake while you prepare the rest of dinner.

Karen Haen's Saucy Skillet Steaks couldn't be easier to make. "Try the versatile sauce recipe with everything from chicken breasts and fish to veal and hamburgers," she writes from Sturgeon Bay, Wisconsin. It's hard to believe something so succulent calls for just a handful of kitchen staples.

Serve the steaks alongside Special Green Beans. "Dried cranberries may seem like a unique ingredient, but after one bite you'll add them to green beans time and again," explains Darlene Brenden from her home in Salem, Oregon. A touch of sweet honey complements the tart cranberries.

saucy skillet steaks

4	beef rib eye steaks (3/4 inch thick)
1	large onion, chopped
4	garlic cloves, minced
1/4	cup butter, cubed
2	tablespoons Dijon mustard

Salt and pepper to taste

1/3	cup beef broth
1	tablespoon minced fresh parsley

In a large nonstick skillet, brown the beef rib eye steaks over medium-high heat for 1-2 minutes on each side. Remove and keep warm. In the same skillet, saute the onion and garlic in butter until tender, stirring to loosen browned bits.

Brush the steaks with mustard; sprinkle with salt and pepper. Return to the pan. Stir in broth. Cook for 5-7 minutes on each side or until meat reaches desired doneness (for medium-rare, a meat thermometer should read 145°; medium, 160°; well-done, 170°). Spoon the onion mixture over steaks; sprinkle with parsley. **YIELD: 4 servings.**

special green beans

1	package (16 ounces) frozen cut green beans
1	teaspoon grated orange peel
1/2	cup dried cranberries
1/2	cup real bacon bits
2	tablespoons honey

Cook the green beans according to package directions, adding the orange peel during cooking; drain. Add the cranberries, bacon and honey; toss to combine. **YIELD: 4 servings.**

cheddar bread twists

1	sheet frozen puff pastry, thawed
1	egg white
1	tablespoon cold water
1/2	cup shredded cheddar cheese

Dash salt

Place the puff pastry on a greased baking sheet. In a small bowl, beat the egg white and water; brush over pastry. Sprinkle with cheese and salt.

Cut into ten 1-in. strips; twist each strip three times. Bake at 400° for 10-13 minutes or until golden brown. **YIELD: 10 breadsticks.**

speedy minestrone
tomato olive salad
mini rum cakes,
page 213

weeknight meals

mom's best
weeknight meals

Heartwarming meals are the centerpieces of family memories. With the menus found here, you won't have trouble creating those special moments at your table—even during the week. Turn the page for effortless suppers made special…just like Mom's.

family-pleasing pizza, page 205

broiled sirloin steaks, page 198

chicken a la king, page 210

while most people enjoy curling up with a novel, Barbara Keith of Faucett, Missouri likes to read a good cookbook. "I love to cook and have been collecting cookbooks for years," she says. Her husband, four adult children, 10 grandchildren and seven great-grandchildren couldn't be happier about Barbara's passion for cooking, and enjoy it on a very regular basis.

Here, Barbara shares a favorite weeknight meal that features her popular fried fish. "I make this meal on a monthly basis," she says of her Mustard Fried Catfish. "The fish is so delicious and flaky, and it's easy to prepare, too." If you can't find catfish, buy orange roughy or cod instead.

Tender fried fish just wouldn't be the same without a side of creamy coleslaw. Barbara's Sweet 'n' Sour Coleslaw comes together in just 5 minutes and brings bright flavor and crunch to the menu. "This was my mother's recipe, and I'm always asked to share it," she explains.

To round out the menu, Barbara turns to buttery Garlic New Potatoes. "I have yet to meet a person who doesn't like this side dish," she says. "The potatoes complement just about any entree and are quick to assemble."

To speed things up, start by preparing the coleslaw. Set it in the fridge and work on the potatoes. While the potatoes boil, you can turn your attention to the catfish. Dinner will be ready before you know it.

mustard fried catfish

2/3	cup yellow cornmeal
1/3	cup all-purpose flour
1/2	teaspoon salt
1/4	teaspoon paprika
1/4	teaspoon pepper
1/8	teaspoon cayenne pepper
1/2	cup prepared mustard

4	catfish fillets (6 ounces *each*)

Oil for frying

In a shallow bowl, combine the first six ingredients. Spread mustard over both sides of fillets; coat with cornmeal mixture.

In an electric skillet or deep-fat fryer, heat oil to 375°. Fry fillets, a few at a time, for 2-3 minutes on each side or until fish flakes easily with a fork. Drain on paper towels. **YIELD: 4 servings.**

garlic new potatoes

16	small red potatoes
3	tablespoons butter, melted
1-1/2	teaspoons minced garlic
1-1/2	teaspoons dried parsley flakes

Salt and pepper to taste

Place potatoes in a steamer basket; place in a large saucepan over 1 in. of water. Bring to a boil; cover and steam for 15-20 minutes or until tender. Transfer to a serving bowl.

Combine the butter, garlic, parsley, salt and pepper; pour over potatoes and toss to coat. **YIELD: 4 servings.**

sweet 'n' sour coleslaw

5-1/2	cups coleslaw mix
1/2	cup heavy whipping cream
1/3	cup sugar
3	tablespoons white vinegar
1/2	teaspoon salt

Place coleslaw mix in a serving bowl. In a jar with a tight-fitting lid, combine the remaining ingredients; shake well. Pour over coleslaw mix and toss to coat. Chill until serving. **YIELD: 4 servings.**

time is of the essence for Karol Chandler-Ezell of Nacogdoches, Texas. "I usually work late, so I need to cook dinner quickly for my busy family and me."

She begins this supper with tasty Tomato-Stuffed Avocados. Each attractive avocado is packed with chopped tomatoes, onion and basil.

Karol then pairs the avocados with Broiled Sirloin Steaks, a family favorite. "Broiling is a fast cooking method for lean cuts like this."

What goes better with steak than potatoes? Twice-Baked Deviled Potatoes double the pleasure. This delicious side dish is flavored with bacon, cheddar and a hint of Dijon mustard. "The microwave makes them very quick to fix," Karol says. "Best of all, you can leave them while they're cooling if the kids need your attention for a while."

broiled sirloin steaks

2	tablespoons lime juice
1	teaspoon onion powder
1	teaspoon garlic powder
1/4	teaspoon ground mustard
1/4	teaspoon dried oregano
1/4	teaspoon dried thyme
4	boneless beef sirloin steaks (5 ounces *each*)
1	cup sliced fresh mushrooms

In a small bowl, combine the first six ingredients; rub over both sides of steaks. Broil 4 in. from the heat for 7 minutes. Turn steaks; top with mushrooms. Broil 7-8 minutes longer or until meat reaches desired doneness (for medium-rare, a meat thermometer should read 145°; medium, 160°; well-done, 170°) and mushrooms are tender. **YIELD: 4 servings.**

twice-baked deviled potatoes

4	small baking potatoes
1/4	cup butter, softened
1/4	cup milk
1	cup (4 ounces) shredded cheddar cheese
1/3	cup real bacon bits
2	green onions, chopped
1	teaspoon Dijon mustard

Dash paprika

Scrub and pierce potatoes; place on a microwave-safe plate. Microwave, uncovered, on high for 7-10 minutes or until tender, turning once. Let stand for 5 minutes. Cut a thin slice off of the top of each potato and discard. Scoop out the pulp, leaving a thin shell.

In a large bowl, mash the pulp with butter and milk. Stir in the cheese, bacon, onions, mustard and paprika. Spoon into potato shells. Return to the microwave-safe plate. Microwave, uncovered, on high for 1-2 minutes or until cheese is melted. **YIELD: 4 servings.**

editor's note: This recipe was tested in a 1,100-watt microwave.

tomato-stuffed avocados

2	plum tomatoes, seeded and chopped
3/4	cup thinly sliced red onion, quartered
1	teaspoon fresh basil leaves, julienned
1/2	teaspoon salt
1/4	teaspoon pepper
2	medium ripe avocados, halved and pitted
2	teaspoons lime juice

In a large bowl, gently toss the tomatoes, onion, basil, salt and pepper. Spoon into avocado halves; drizzle with lime juice. **YIELD: 4 servings.**

sweet-and-sour scallops

2	cans (8 ounces *each*) pineapple chunks
1	pound sea scallops (about 16)
1	tablespoon canola oil
1/3	cup chopped onion
1/3	cup julienned green pepper
1/4	cup butter, cubed
1/4	cup sugar
2	tablespoons cornstarch
1/2	teaspoon ground mustard
1/4	teaspoon salt
1/2	cup white vinegar
2	tablespoons soy sauce
2/3	cup cherry tomatoes, halved

Drain pineapple, reserving juice; set pineapple and juice aside. In a large skillet, saute scallops in oil until firm and opaque; drain. Remove from pan and keep warm.

In the same pan, saute onion and green pepper in butter for 3-4 minutes or until crisp-tender.

Meanwhile, in a small bowl, combine the sugar, cornstarch, ground mustard and salt. Whisk in the vinegar, soy sauce and reserved pineapple juice until smooth.

Gradually stir into pan. Bring to a boil; cook and stir for 2 minutes or until thickened. Stir in the tomatoes, scallops and reserved pineapple; heat through. **YIELD: 4 servings.**

almond rice

1-1/2	cups water
1-1/2	cups uncooked instant rice
1	tablespoon butter
1/2	cup slivered almonds, toasted
1/4	teaspoon salt
1/4	teaspoon pepper
1	tablespoon minced fresh parsley

In a large saucepan, bring the water, rice and butter to a boil. Remove from the heat. Cover and let stand for 5 minutes or until water is absorbed. Stir in the almonds, salt and pepper. Sprinkle with parsley. **YIELD: 4 servings.**

dream clouds

dream clouds

1	pint vanilla ice cream, softened
1	pint orange sherbet, softened
2	cups whipped topping
1	can (11 ounces) mandarin oranges, drained

Place ice cream and sherbet in a large bowl. Using a knife, swirl sherbet into ice cream. Spoon 1/2 cup whipped topping into each of four serving dishes. Top with ice cream mixture and mandarin oranges. **YIELD: 4 servings.**

rosemary lamb chops

- 2 teaspoons dried rosemary, crushed
- 1 teaspoon dried thyme
- 1/2 teaspoon salt
- 1/4 teaspoon pepper
- 1/4 cup olive oil
- 8 lamb loin chops (1 inch thick and 6 ounces *each*)

Combine the rosemary, thyme, salt and pepper. Pour oil over both sides of chops; rub chops with spice mixture.

In a large skillet, cook chops over medium heat for 6-7 minutes on each side or until the meat reaches desired doneness (for medium-rare, a meat thermometer should read 145°; medium, 160°; well-done, 170°). **YIELD: 4 servings.**

mediterranean couscous

- 2 tablespoons chopped onion
- 3 teaspoons minced garlic
- 2 tablespoons olive oil, *divided*
- 1-1/4 cups water
- 1 package (5.6 ounces) couscous with toasted pine nuts
- 1-1/2 teaspoons chicken bouillon granules
- 1/2 cup cherry tomatoes, halved
- 2 tablespoons grated Parmesan cheese

In a small skillet, saute onion and garlic in 1 tablespoon oil for 3-4 minutes or until tender. Meanwhile, in a large saucepan, combine the water, contents of seasoning packet from couscous mix, bouillon and remaining oil. Bring to a boil.

Stir in the onion mixture and couscous. Cover and remove from the heat; let stand for 5 minutes. Fluff with a fork. Stir in tomatoes and Parmesan cheese. **YIELD: 4 servings.**

blueberry crumble

- 3 cups fresh *or* frozen blueberries
- 3 tablespoons sugar
- 1 tablespoon cornstarch
- 1/3 cup old-fashioned oats
- 1/3 cup packed brown sugar
- 3 tablespoons all-purpose flour
- 2 tablespoons chopped almonds
- 1/8 teaspoon ground cinnamon
- 3 tablespoons cold butter

Vanilla ice cream

In a greased 9-in. microwave-safe pie plate, combine the blueberries, sugar and cornstarch. Cover and microwave on high for 7-8 minutes or until thickened, stirring twice.

Meanwhile, in a small bowl, combine the oats, brown sugar, flour, almonds and cinnamon. Cut in butter until mixture resembles coarse crumbs. Sprinkle over blueberry mixture.

Microwave, uncovered, on high for 2-3 minutes or until butter is melted. Serve with ice cream. **YIELD: 4 servings.**

editor's note: This recipe was tested in a 1,100-watt microwave.

as a busy volunteer, Judy Sellgren of Wyoming, Michigan doesn't always have time to cook. That's why this pizza recipe is a favorite. "I've used it for years," she notes.

Judy dresses up spinach with bacon and chow mein noodles for a quick accompaniment, and she relies on a prepared angel food cake for a no-fuss dessert that rounds out just about any meal.

family-pleasing pizza

1/2 pound bulk pork sausage
1 tube (13.8 ounces) refrigerated pizza crust
2 teaspoons butter, melted
2 tablespoons grated Parmesan cheese
1 teaspoon garlic powder
2 cups (8 ounces) shredded part-skim mozzarella cheese
2 medium Roma tomatoes, thinly sliced
2 teaspoons Italian seasoning

In a large skillet, cook sausage over medium heat until no longer pink. Drain and set aside.

Meanwhile, press pizza dough into a greased 13-in. x 9-in. baking dish. Brush with butter; sprinkle with Parmesan cheese and garlic powder. Layer with 1 cup mozzarella, sausage and tomatoes. Sprinkle with remaining mozzarella and Italian seasoning.

Bake at 400° for 20-25 minutes or until the crust is golden brown and cheese is melted. **YIELD: 6 servings.**

tangy spinach salad

3 tablespoons sugar
3 tablespoons cider vinegar
3 tablespoons canola oil
3 tablespoons ketchup
1-1/2 teaspoons Worcestershire sauce
1 teaspoon dried minced onion
1 package (6 ounces) fresh baby spinach
3 hard-cooked eggs, chopped
1/3 cup chow mein noodles
1/3 cup real bacon bits

In a jar with a tight-fitting lid, combine the first six ingredients; shake well. In a large bowl, combine the spinach, eggs, chow mein noodles and bacon. Drizzle with dressing; toss to coat. Refrigerate leftovers. **YIELD: 6 servings.**

cake with pineapple pudding

cake with pineapple pudding

2 cups milk
1 package (3.4 ounces) instant French vanilla pudding mix
1 can (8 ounces) unsweetened crushed pineapple, drained
1 cup whipped topping
6 slices angel food cake

In a large bowl, whisk milk and pudding mix for 2 minutes. Let stand for 2 minutes or until soft-set. Fold in pineapple and whipped topping. Chill until serving. Serve with cake. **YIELD: 6 servings.**

"on-the-go" is just one way that people who know Nella Parker are apt to describe her. Ask any of her family or friends in Hersey, Michigan, and they'll likely say that Nella is one active cook. After all, she fills much of her free time with gardening, river rafting and volunteering for various organizations. No matter how full her days are, however, she always finds time to prepare a sit-down meal.

"I'm constantly looking for recipes that come together without much fuss," she says. "My recipe box is full of easy fixes for dinner. The meal that I share here can be on the table in a matter of minutes," Nella promises.

To speed preparations, she fixes dessert first. "The trifle calls for just five ingredients and is a breeze to put together. You can even assemble it a few hours ahead of time," she adds.

After preparing and refrigerating the trifle, Nella starts on her Flavorful Fish Fillets. "I like to make this entree whenever there's a special occasion in my family. The fish has an impressive taste without the time-consuming preparation of other dishes, and people always ask for the recipe."

While the fillets cook, Dilled Green Beans are a snap to saute. "I serve this side dish quite often," Nella says. "It tastes delicious with just about any meal, and it can easily be reheated in the microwave." For extra flavor, she suggests crumbling bacon on top.

flavorful fish fillets

- 1 package (18.7 ounces) frozen breaded fish fillets
- 3 tablespoons olive oil
- 1 jar (26 ounces) spaghetti sauce
- 3 tablespoons prepared horseradish
- 1 cup (4 ounces) shredded part-skim mozzarella cheese

In a large skillet, cook fish in oil for 4 minutes on each side or until crisp and golden brown. Meanwhile, in a large saucepan, combine the spaghetti sauce and horseradish; cook until heated through.

Spoon over fish; sprinkle with cheese. Cover and remove from the heat. Let stand for 5 minutes or until cheese is melted. **YIELD: 4-5 servings.**

dilled green beans

- 1 cup water
- 1/4 cup chopped green pepper
- 2 tablespoons chopped onion
- 2 teaspoons beef bouillon granules
- 1/2 teaspoon dill seed
- 2 packages (9 ounces *each*) frozen cut green beans

In a large saucepan, combine the water, green pepper, onion, bouillon and dill. Bring to a boil. Reduce heat; cover and simmer for 5 minutes.

Add the beans. Cover and simmer 8-10 minutes longer or until the beans are crisp-tender; drain. YIELD: 5 servings.

strawberry yogurt trifle

- 5 cups cubed angel food cake
- 1 carton (8 ounces) vanilla yogurt
- 1 cup whipped topping, *divided*
- 3 cups sliced fresh strawberries
- 1 tablespoon flaked coconut, toasted

Place cake cubes in a 2-qt. bowl. Combine the yogurt and 3/4 cup whipped topping; spoon over the cake.

Top with the strawberries and remaining whipped topping. Sprinkle with the flaked coconut. YIELD: 4-5 servings.

grabbing a bite

on the run could be tempting for Robin Stevens and her family, but the Cadiz, Kentucky mom is a master of preparing dinners in a dash.

A popular menu at Robin's supper table is Chicken Parmigiana. "This version bakes in about a half hour," she promises. "You just throw a few ingredients together and pop the dish in the oven."

As a pretty complement to the flavorful chicken, Robin serves Broccoli Fettuccine Alfredo. "Instead of broccoli, you can use green beans, carrots or your family's favorite vegetable," she says. "You can even add cubed cooked chicken for a main dish."

To top off the meal, Robin uses refrigerated biscuits for easy turnovers. A fast filling made with chopped apple and applesauce tastes delicious, especially when a craving for old-fashioned apple pie hits.

broccoli fettuccine alfredo

1	package (12 ounces) fettuccine
1	cup chopped fresh *or* frozen broccoli
3	tablespoons butter *or* margarine
1	tablespoon all-purpose flour
2/3	cup milk
1/4	cup grated Parmesan cheese

Cook fettuccine according to package directions. Meanwhile, in a saucepan over medium heat, cook broccoli in a small amount of water until crisp-tender, about 5 minutes; drain. In a saucepan over medium heat, melt butter. Stir in flour until smooth. Gradually whisk in milk. Bring to a boil; cook and stir for 2 minutes or until thickened. Remove from the heat; stir in Parmesan cheese and broccoli. Drain fettuccine; top with the broccoli mixture. **YIELD: 4 servings.**

chicken parmigiana

4	boneless skinless chicken breast halves
1	can (6 ounces) tomato paste
3/4	cup water
2	garlic cloves, minced
1	tablespoon dried parsley flakes
1	teaspoon salt
1/4	teaspoon pepper
1/2	teaspoon Italian seasoning
1/2	teaspoon dried oregano
1/4	teaspoon crushed red pepper flakes, optional
2	cups (8 ounces) shredded mozzarella cheese
1/4	cup grated Parmesan cheese

Place the chicken in a greased 8-in. square baking dish. In a saucepan, combine tomato paste, water, garlic and seasonings; bring to a boil. Pour over chicken. Bake, uncovered, at 400° for 15-20 minutes or until chicken juices run clear. Sprinkle with cheeses; bake 10 minutes longer or until the cheese is melted. **YIELD: 4 servings.**

apple cinnamon turnovers

1	medium tart apple, peeled and chopped
1/2	cup applesauce
3/4	teaspoon ground cinnamon, *divided*
Dash	ground nutmeg
1	tube (7-1/2 ounces) refrigerated biscuits
1	tablespoon butter *or* margarine, melted
2	tablespoons sugar

In a bowl, combine the apple, applesauce, 1/4 teaspoon cinnamon and nutmeg. Separate biscuits; roll out each into a 6-in. circle. Place on greased baking sheets. Place a heaping tablespoonful of apple mixture in the center of each. Fold in half and pinch edges to seal. Brush with butter.

Combine sugar and remaining cinnamon; sprinkle over tops. Bake at 400° for 8-10 minutes or until edges are golden brown. **YIELD: 10 servings.**

simplicity and variety are key cooking elements for Ruth Lee. "Nutrition is also a big factor when I'm planning a meal," she shares from Troy, Ontario. "I like to cook with lots of vegetables and other produce.

"I also like to save money, so I plan menus around whatever items are on sale at the grocery store," she says. "I avoid convenience products and buy most of my produce at the local outdoor market whenever I can."

The supper Ruth shares here is an all-time favorite with her family, and is true comfort food at it's best. In addition, it's a perfect lineup for busy weeknights.

Her Chicken a la King has a thick and creamy sauce that's terrific over biscuits or rice. "I've been making this for years," says Ruth. "It's a wonderful way to create a quick dinner or lunch from leftover chicken and veggies."

For an easy and colorful salad, Ruth serves Tomatoes with Feta Cheese. "I make this simple dish at least once a month," she writes. "It puts fresh summer tomatoes to great use and adds zip to winter tomatoes as well."

Black Forest Sundaes make a sweet ending to the meal, and best of all, they take just 5 minutes to prepare since they call for only a few ingredients. "My husband, children and grandchildren just love them," Ruth says.

chicken a la king

4	individually frozen biscuits
1-3/4	cups sliced fresh mushrooms
1/4	cup chopped onion
1/4	cup chopped celery
1/3	cup butter, cubed
1/4	cup all-purpose flour
1/8	to 1/4 teaspoon salt
1	cup chicken broth
1	cup milk
2	cups cubed cooked chicken
2	tablespoons diced pimientos

Bake biscuits according to package directions. Meanwhile, in a large skillet, saute the mushrooms, onion and celery in butter until crisp-tender. Stir in flour and salt until blended. Gradually stir in broth and milk. Bring to a boil; cook and stir for 2 minutes or until thickened.

Add chicken and pimientos. Bring to a boil. Reduce heat; simmer, uncovered, for 4-6 minutes or until heated through. Serve with the baked biscuits. YIELD: 4 servings.

tomatoes with feta cheese

8	slices tomato
2	tablespoons crumbled feta cheese
1	tablespoon balsamic vinegar
2	tablespoons minced fresh basil

Pepper to taste

Arrange tomato slices on a serving plate. Sprinkle with feta cheese. Drizzle with vinegar; sprinkle with basil and pepper. YIELD: 4 servings.

black forest sundaes

1/2	cup crushed cream-filled chocolate sandwich cookies
4	scoops vanilla ice cream
1	can (21 ounces) cherry pie filling

Whipped cream in a can

Chopped walnuts

Divide cookie crumbs among four dessert dishes; top each with ice cream and pie filling. Garnish with whipped cream and walnuts. Freeze until serving. YIELD: 4 servings.

mom's best made easy

family suppers

have always been extremely important to Dona Hoffman of Addison, Illinois. To keep kitchen time to a minimum, though, Dona plans ahead, relying on stress-free but satisfying menus.

The Italian-inspired menu she shares here makes supper time a breeze any night of the week. And, since it serves six, Dona is guaranteed to have a few extra lunches for work the next day.

To start the meal on a healthy note, she serves Tomato Olive Salad. "My daughters love salad," Dona says. "Each night, I try to have a different version for them. This amazingly simple dish features a sweet three-ingredient dressing that's ready in moments. I often top the salad with fresh mozzarella, feta or Parmesan cheese," Dona adds. "To add color, I use some red lettuce with a smaller amount of the leaf lettuce."

Speedy Minestrone makes a hearty entree on cold winter nights. Filled with veggies, sausage and beans, the flavorful soup counts on several convenience products, so it's a snap to assemble. As Dona explains, "Everything is precooked, so you're just chopping, combining and heating. To trim fat from the soup, use a reduced-fat sausage."

Ending the meal on a sweet note isn't a problem with Mini Rum Cakes. "A good recipe for rum cake is hard to find," Dona says. "Many of them turn out dry, but these individual cakes are so moist. Plus, they use basic ingredients that are usually in your pantry. I like to serve them slightly warm with vanilla ice cream and a dollop of whipped cream."

speedy minestrone

- 2   cans (14-1/2 ounces *each*) beef broth
- 1   package (24 ounces) frozen vegetable and pasta medley in garlic sauce
- 1   pound smoked sausage, cut into 1/2-inch slices
- 1   can (16 ounces) kidney beans, rinsed and drained
- 1/4 cup chopped onion
- 1   teaspoon dried basil
- 1   teaspoon dried parsley flakes

Shredded Parmesan cheese

In a large saucepan, combine the first seven ingredients. Bring to a boil. Reduce heat; simmer, uncovered, for 10-15 minutes or until heated through. Sprinkle with Parmesan cheese. **YIELD: 6 servings.**

tomato olive salad

- 4   cups torn leaf lettuce
- 1/2 cup cherry tomatoes
- 1/3 cup sliced red onion
- 1   can (2-1/4 ounces) sliced ripe olives, drained

DRESSING:

- 2   tablespoons vegetable oil
- 1   tablespoon red wine vinegar
- 1   tablespoon brown sugar

In a large bowl, combine the lettuce, tomatoes, onion and olives. In a small bowl, whisk the dressing ingredients. Drizzle over salad and toss to coat. Serve immediately. **YIELD: 6 servings.**

mini rum cakes

- 2   cups cold milk
- 1   package (3.4 ounces) instant vanilla pudding mix
- 1   teaspoon rum extract
- 6   individual round sponge cakes
- 1-1/2 cups whipped topping

Fresh *or* frozen raspberries

In a small bowl, whisk milk and pudding mix for 2 minutes; stir in extract. Let stand for 2 minutes or until soft-set. Set cakes on plates; top with pudding. Garnish with whipped topping and berries. **YIELD: 6 servings.**

creativity in the kitchen isn't anything new for Betty Jean Nichols. "I enjoy cooking and have been working up recipes for years," she says from her home in Eugene, Oregon.

Betty Jean garnered a lot of recognition for her culinary talents by winning several state and national recipe contests. But when she fixes dinner, she prefers to serve dishes that are simple but special. Such is the case with the three recipes featured in this mouthwatering meal for four.

Moist Cider Pork Chops are flavored with a sensational combination of garlic, green onions, celery, dried thyme and apple cider. "If you have fresh thyme from your garden, use that," Betty Jean recommends. "And boneless chops cook even faster." You can even try Betty Jean's terrific seasoning blend on poultry, too.

To complement the pork, she serves Asparagus with Mushrooms. "This side dish is not fussy, but looks and tastes very impressive," she notes. "People say it's delicious."

With just three items, Broiled Blueberry Dessert makes an easy, yummy ending to any meal. "My daughter and her husband grow blueberries, so we like to try new ways to prepare them," she relates. "This recipe is a keeper!"

In a large resealable plastic bag, combine the flour, salt and pepper. Add pork chops and toss to coat. In a large skillet, brown chops in oil over medium heat for 3-4 minutes. Remove and keep warm.

In the same skillet, saute the celery, onions, garlic and thyme for 2-3 minutes or until crisp-tender. Return pork to the pan. Add cider. Bring to a boil. Reduce heat; cover and simmer for 7-8 minutes or until the meat juices run clear. Serve with a slotted spoon. **YIELD: 4 servings.**

asparagus with mushrooms

1	pound fresh asparagus, trimmed and cut into 2-inch pieces
2	teaspoons ground ginger
2	tablespoons canola oil
3	cups sliced fresh mushrooms
1	teaspoon salt
1/8	teaspoon sugar
1/8	teaspoon pepper

In a large skillet, saute asparagus and ginger in oil for 2-3 minutes or until asparagus is crisp-tender. Add the mushrooms, salt, sugar and pepper. Cook and stir 2-3 minutes longer or until mushrooms are tender. **YIELD: 4 servings.**

cider pork chops

2	tablespoons all-purpose flour
1/2	teaspoon salt
1/4	teaspoon pepper
4	bone-in pork loin chops (1/2 inch thick)
1	tablespoon canola oil
1	cup sliced celery
1/2	cup sliced green onions
2	teaspoons minced garlic
1/4	teaspoon dried thyme
1	cup apple cider *or* unsweetened apple juice

broiled blueberry dessert

3	cups fresh blueberries
1/2	cup sour cream
2	tablespoons brown sugar

Divide blueberries among four ovenproof 8-oz. custard cups. Spread with sour cream; sprinkle with brown sugar. Place on a baking sheet. Broil 4-6 in. from the heat for 3-4 minutes or until bubbly and sugar is melted. **YIELD: 4 servings.**

Tabitha spends 15 to 20 minutes preparing dinner in her Meriden, Connecticut kitchen. Her favorite meal starts with Portobello Roast Beef Hoagies. "Meals don't get easier than this," she notes.

For a side dish, Tabitha fixes Pepperoncini Arugula Salad and completes the menu with Chocolate Cake with Coconut Sauce. "It's guaranteed to make your sweet tooth happy," Tabitha assures.

pepperoncini arugula salad

2	cups fresh arugula *or* baby spinach
2	cups torn romaine
1/4	cup chopped red onion
2	pepperoncinis, sliced
1	medium tomato, sliced
1/4	cup balsamic vinaigrette

In a large bowl, combine the arugula, romaine, onion, pepperoncinis and tomato. Drizzle with vinaigrette; gently toss to coat. **YIELD: 4 servings.**

editor's note: Look for pepperoncinis (pickled peppers) in the pickle and olive section of your grocery store.

portobello roast beef hoagies

4	whole wheat hoagie buns, split
4	tablespoons butter, softened, *divided*
1	teaspoon Italian seasoning
1/4	teaspoon garlic salt
3/4	pound sliced deli roast beef, julienned
1/2	pound sliced baby portobello mushrooms
1	teaspoon dried rosemary, crushed
1/4	teaspoon pepper
1/2	pound sliced provolone cheese
1/2	cup sour cream
1	tablespoon prepared horseradish

Spread cut sides of buns with 2 tablespoons butter; sprinkle with Italian seasoning and garlic salt. Set aside.

In a large skillet, saute the beef, mushrooms, rosemary and pepper in remaining butter until the mushrooms are tender. Spoon onto buns; top with the cheese.

Place on a baking sheet. Broil 2-3 in. from the heat for 2-4 minutes or until cheese is melted. In a small bowl, combine sour cream and horseradish; serve with sandwiches. **YIELD: 4 servings.**

chocolate cake with coconut sauce

1	package (19.6 ounces) frozen chocolate fudge layer cake
1/2	cup flaked coconut
1/2	cup sweetened condensed milk
1/2	teaspoon vanilla extract
1/4	cup red raspberry preserves
4	scoops vanilla ice cream

Cut cake in half. Return half to the freezer. Let remaining cake stand at room temperature to thaw.

Meanwhile, in a small saucepan, combine the coconut, milk and vanilla. Cook and stir over medium heat for 2-3 minutes or until heated through.

Cut cake into four slices; place on dessert plates. Spread with preserves. Top with coconut mixture and ice cream. **YIELD: 4 servings.**

editor's note: This recipe was tested with Pepperidge Farm frozen three-layer cake.

a speedy, well-rounded meal is important to Linda Coleman of Cedar Rapids, Iowa. "When you have three young, extremely active children who need to be in three different places at once, there's no time for fancy meals," she writes.

Although Linda usually can't do fussy dinners, she provides her family with quality meals such as the one she offers here.

Regular chicken becomes a savory specialty with barbecue sauce, crisp bacon and melted cheese. Her Monterey Barbecued Chicken gets even better with a sprinkling of fresh tomato and green onions.

Barbecue flavor keeps going with Linda's In-a-Flash Beans. No one will guess this recipe begins with a can. Chopped onion and green pepper lend a little crunch and lots of home-cooked flavor.

Strawberry Pound Cake Dessert adds a pretty and refreshing finish to Linda's meal. This all-time classic dessert comes together in moments and lends a pop of color to the table. You can use fresh strawberries if you have the time to slice 3 cups of them—just add 2 to 3 tablespoons of sugar and let the berries sit for 15 minutes.

"I like to prepare this menu even if I'm not in a hurry," Linda notes. "That way, I can fix it and enjoy the remainder of the night."

monterey barbecued chicken

4	bacon strips
4	boneless skinless chicken breast halves (4 ounces *each*)
1	tablespoon butter
1/2	cup barbecue sauce
3	green onions, chopped
1	medium tomato, chopped
1	cup (4 ounces) shredded cheddar cheese

Cut the bacon strips in half widthwise. In a large skillet, cook the bacon over medium heat until cooked but not crisp. Remove the bacon to paper towels to drain; keep warm.

Drain the bacon drippings from the skillet; cook the chicken breasts in butter over medium heat for 5-6 minutes on each side or until the chicken juices run clear.

Top each chicken breast half with barbecue sauce, green onions, tomato and two reserved bacon pieces; sprinkle with the cheddar cheese. Cover and cook for 5 minutes or until cheese is melted. **YIELD: 4 servings.**

in-a-flash beans

1	can (15-3/4 ounces) pork and beans
1/2	cup barbecue sauce
1/2	cup chopped onion
1/4	cup chopped green pepper, optional

In a large saucepan, combine the beans, barbecue sauce, onion and green pepper if desired. Cook and stir bean mixture over medium heat until heated through. **YIELD: 4 servings.**

strawberry pound cake dessert

1	loaf (10-3/4 ounces) frozen pound cake, thawed
2	containers (16 ounces *each*) frozen sweetened sliced strawberries, thawed and drained
1-1/2	cups whipped topping

Slice the pound cake loaf into eight pieces. Place one cake slice on each of four dessert plates. Top each cake slice with 1/2 cup strawberries, 3 tablespoons whipped topping and another cake slice. Serve the desserts with the remaining strawberries and whipped topping. **YIELD: 4 servings.**

effortless
thanksgiving
feast,
page 240

holiday menus

mom's best
holiday menus

Whether Thanksgiving or Christmas, St. Patrick's or the Fourth of July, Mom always turns holidays into special celebrations filled with many wonderful foods. Creating those heartfelt occasions for your family is easy with the impressive menus that follow.

yuletide extravaganza, page 244

halloween treats, page 239

summer salute, page 231

the wonderful aroma of baked ham inevitably calls Easter guests to the table.

Raspberry-Chipotle Glazed Ham is an irresistible main dish for this special spring celebration. And instead of an ordinary salad, serve Caramelized Onion-Tortellini Spinach Salad.

...an't beat Peppery Parmesan Bread. The dough ...antly made in your bread machine.

raspberry-chipotle glazed ham

1	bone-in fully cooked spiral-sliced ham (9 to 10 pounds)
2-1/4	cups seedless raspberry jam
3	tablespoons white vinegar
3	chipotle peppers in adobo sauce, drained, seeded and minced
3	to 4 garlic cloves, minced
1	tablespoon coarsely ground pepper

Place ham on a rack in a shallow roasting pan. Bake, uncovered, at 325° for 2 to 2-1/2 hours or until a meat thermometer reads 130°.

In a small saucepan, combine the jam, vinegar, peppers and garlic. Bring to a boil. Reduce heat; simmer, uncovered, for 5 minutes.

Brush some of the sauce over ham. Bake 20 minutes longer or until meat thermometer reads 140°, brushing twice with sauce. Sprinkle pepper over ham. Serve ham with the remaining sauce. **YIELD: 16-20 servings.**

caramelized onion-tortellini spinach salad

- 4 **cups thinly sliced sweet onions**
- 3 **tablespoons butter**
- 3 **tablespoons olive oil**
- 2 **teaspoons brown sugar**
- 1 **package (19 ounces) frozen cheese tortellini**
- 3 **tablespoons balsamic vinegar**
- 1/4 **teaspoon salt**
- 1/4 **teaspoon pepper**
- 1 **package (10 ounces) fresh spinach, stems removed and torn**
- 1/3 **cup shredded Parmesan cheese**

In a large skillet over medium-low heat, cook onions in butter and oil for 5 minutes or until tender. Add brown sugar; cook over low heat for 20 minutes or until onions are golden brown, stirring frequently. Meanwhile, cook tortellini according to package directions.

Add the vinegar, salt and pepper to onion mixture. Bring to a boil. Reduce heat; cook 1-2 minutes longer or until syrupy.

Drain tortellini and rinse in cold water. In a large serving bowl, combine the tortellini, spinach and Parmesan cheese. Add onion mixture and toss to coat. **YIELD: 12 servings.**

peppery parmesan bread

- 3/4 **cup plus 2 tablespoons warm water (70° to 80°)**
- 1 **tablespoon olive oil**
- 1/2 **teaspoon hot pepper sauce**
- 1/2 **cup freshly grated Parmesan cheese**
- 1 **tablespoon sugar**
- 1 **teaspoon pepper**
- 1/2 **teaspoon dried basil**
- 1/2 **teaspoon dried oregano**
- 1/2 **teaspoon salt**
- 2-1/2 **cups bread flour**
- 2-1/4 **teaspoons active dry yeast**
- 1 **tablespoon cold water**

In bread machine pan, place the first 11 ingredients in order suggested by manufacturer. Select dough setting (check dough after 5 minutes of mixing; add 1 to 2 tablespoons of water or flour if needed).

When the cycle is complete, turn dough onto a lightly floured surface. Punch down; knead until smooth and elastic, about 5 minutes. Shape into an 8-in. round loaf. Place on a greased baking sheet. Cover and let rise in a warm place until doubled, about 30 minutes.

Slash top of loaf with a sharp knife; brush with cold water. Bake at 400° for 25-30 minutes or until golden brown. Remove to a wire rack to cool. **YIELD: 1 loaf (12 slices).**

peppery parmesan bread

a brunch fit for a queen is a brain-child that Janice Hose of Hagerstown, Maryland created. Her meal includes a variety of dainty yet easy foods she knows her guests enjoy.

Her fruit dish relies on canned goods and comes together quickly. Best of all, the casserole, pecan cups and coffee cake can be made in advance.

sausage egg casserole

10	eggs
2-1/4	cups milk
1-1/2	teaspoons ground mustard
1/2	teaspoon salt
1	pound bulk pork sausage, cooked and drained
2	cups cubed white bread
1-1/2	cups (6 ounces) shredded cheddar cheese

In a large bowl, whisk the eggs, milk, mustard and salt. Stir in the sausage, bread cubes and cheese. Pour into a greased 13-in. x 9-in. baking dish. Cover and refrigerate overnight.

Remove from the refrigerator 30 minutes before baking. Bake, uncovered, at 350° for 30-40 minutes or until a knife inserted near the center comes out clean. Let stand for 10 minutes before serving. **YIELD: 12 servings.**

mary's baked fruit

1	can (16 ounces) apricot halves, drained
1	can (16 ounces) pear halves, drained
2	cans (15 ounces *each*) plums, drained and halved
1	can (29 ounces) peach halves, drained
1	can (8 ounces) pineapple slices, undrained
1/3	cup packed brown sugar

1	tablespoon butter
1/2	teaspoon ground cinnamon
1/4	teaspoon ground cloves

In a greased 13-in. x 9-in. baking pan, starting at the 9-in. end, arrange rows of fruit in the following order: half of the apricots, pears and plums, all of the peaches, then add the remaining apricots, pears and plums.

Drain pineapple, reserving 1/2 cup of juice. Lay pineapple over fruit in pan. In a saucepan, combine the pineapple juice, brown sugar, butter, cinnamon and cloves. Cook and stir until sugar is dissolved and butter is melted. Pour over fruit.

Bake, uncovered, at 350° for 20-25 minutes or until heated through. **YIELD: 12-16 servings.**

pecan goody cups

3/4	cup butter, softened
2	packages (3 ounces *each*) cream cheese, softened
2	cups all-purpose flour

FILLING:

1-1/2	cups packed brown sugar
2	eggs
1	tablespoon butter, melted
48	pecan halves

In a large bowl, cream butter and cream cheese until light and fluffy. Gradually add flour, beating until mixture forms a ball. Cover and refrigerate for 15 minutes.

For filling, in a small bowl, combine the brown sugar, eggs and butter; set aside. Roll dough into 48 balls. Press onto the bottom and up the sides of greased miniature muffin cups. Spoon a scant teaspoon of filling into each cup. Top each with a pecan half.

Bake at 350° for 20-25 minutes or until golden brown. Cool for 2-3 minutes before removing from pans to wire racks. **YIELD: 4 dozen.**

crumble-top coffee cake

1/3 cup butter, softened
1/3 cup shortening
2 cups sugar
2 eggs
3 cups all-purpose flour
2 teaspoons baking powder
1 teaspoon ground cinnamon
1/2 teaspoon baking soda
1/4 teaspoon salt
1-3/4 cups buttermilk
2 medium apples, peeled and sliced

TOPPING:

1/2 cup all-purpose flour
1/2 cup packed brown sugar
1-1/2 teaspoons ground cinnamon

3 tablespoons cold butter
1/2 cup chopped walnuts

In a large bowl, cream the butter, shortening and sugar until light and fluffy. Add eggs one at a time, beating well after each addition. Combine the flour, baking powder, cinnamon, baking soda and salt; add to creamed mixture alternately with buttermilk, beating well after each addition.

Spoon half of the batter into a greased 13-in. x 9-in. baking dish. Top with apple slices; spread with remaining batter.

In a small bowl, combine the flour, brown sugar and cinnamon; cut in butter until crumbly. Stir in walnuts. Sprinkle over batter.

Bake at 350° for 55-60 minutes or until a toothpick inserted near the center comes out clean. **YIELD:** 12 servings.

spring luncheons, baby

and wedding showers, a surprise for Mom—these are just as few of the occasions for which refreshing food is called for.

When you want a meal that's fast yet looks like you fussed, turn to this light-and-lovely meal from our Test Kitchen home economists. Each of the three delicious dishes is eye-appealing and palate-pleasing. Best of all, they're easy to assemble.

To begin, you'll need just three ingredients to make Broccoli Roll-Ups. Broccoli spears and American cheese are wrapped in convenient crescent roll dough to create the savory baked bites.

The tender crescents are a tasty complement to Tuna-Stuffed Tomatoes. Fresh tomatoes are hollowed out, then filled with a flavorful tuna salad mixture that gets crunch from celery and cashews.

If you like, round out each plate with a simple salad of mixed greens with julienned yellow pepper, sliced fresh mushrooms and croutons.

For dessert, serve slices of Mousse-Topped Pound Cake. A smooth creamy filling with a mild cocoa flavor is spread on layers of pound cake, then topped with sliced kiwifruit for a pretty presentation that looks extra special.

Whether celebrating Mother's Day or just enjoying the spring weather, this menu surely satisfies.

broccoli roll-ups

- 1 tube (4 ounces) refrigerated crescent rolls
- 1 slice process American cheese, quartered
- 4 frozen broccoli spears, thawed and patted dry

Separate the crescent dough into four triangles. Place a piece of cheese and a broccoli spear along the wide edge of each triangle; roll up the dough. Place point side down on an ungreased baking sheet. Bake at 375° for 12-15 minutes or until golden brown. **YIELD: 4 servings.**

tuna-stuffed tomatoes

- 4 large tomatoes
- 1/2 cup mayonnaise
- 1/2 teaspoon celery salt
- 1/2 teaspoon dill weed
- 1/4 teaspoon pepper
- 2 cans (6 ounces *each*) tuna, drained and flaked
- 2 celery ribs, chopped
- 1/2 cup chopped cashews, optional

Cut a thin slice off the top of each tomato. Scoop out pulp, leaving a 1/2-in. shell for each. Invert tomatoes onto paper towels to drain.

In a bowl, combine mayonnaise, celery salt, dill and pepper. Stir in tuna, celery and cashews if desired. Spoon into tomato shells. **YIELD: 4 servings.**

mousse-topped pound cake

- 1 cup heavy whipping cream
- 1/4 cup confectioners' sugar
- 2 teaspoons baking cocoa
- 1/2 teaspoon vanilla extract
- 1 frozen pound cake (10-3/4 ounces), thawed
- 1 medium kiwifruit, peeled, halved and sliced, optional

In a small bowl, beat cream until it begins to thicken. Add the confectioners' sugar, cocoa and vanilla; beat until stiff peaks form.

Split cake into three horizontal layers. Spread about 1/2 cup mousse on bottom layer; repeat layers twice.

Garnish with kiwi if desired. Refrigerate leftovers. **YIELD: 6-8 servings.**

irish eyes will surely be smiling with these fast and fun recipes that mark St. Patty's Day.

Whether you're proud to be Irish or just Irish for the day, you'll enjoy this minute-saving menu that offers a taste of the Emerald Isle. While we can't promise it will give you the luck of the Irish, it certainly will make the holiday more festive.

Start out this themed meal by assembling swift corned beef sandwiches from Toni Keyworth of Yale, Michigan. She got the recipe from her mother-in-law, and it remains a staple in her home year-round.

From Canandaigua, New York, Naomi Kay Smith shares her Irish Spud Strips. Tossed with seasonings and Parmesan cheese, they can't be beat!

Then, finish things off with cute shamrock-shaped snacks that will leave the whole family doing a joyful jig. Our Test Kitchen staff created the clever crisps that are sure to keep Irish hearts happy. Best of all, this meal won't have you in the kitchen for hours—and that's no blarney!

hot corned beef buns

- 1 pound deli corned beef, chopped
- 1 cup (4 ounces) shredded cheddar cheese
- 2/3 cup mayonnaise
- 2 tablespoons dried minced onion
- 1 tablespoon dill *or* sweet pickle relish
- 2 tablespoons butter, softened
- 6 hamburger buns, split

In a bowl, combine the corned beef, cheese, mayonnaise, onion and relish. Spread butter over cut side of buns. Spoon corned beef mixture over bottom halves; replace tops. Place in an ungreased 13-in. x 9-in. baking pan. Cover with foil. Bake at 425° for 15-20 minutes or until heated through. **YIELD: 6 servings.**

irish spud strips

- 3 tablespoons grated Parmesan cheese
- 4-1/2 teaspoons Cajun seasoning
- 2-1/2 cups vegetable oil
- 3 medium potatoes, peeled and sliced lengthwise into 1/4-inch strips

Additional Parmesan cheese, optional

In a large resealable plastic bag, combine the Parmesan cheese and Cajun seasoning. In an electric skillet, heat oil to 375°. Pat potatoes dry with paper towels; place a third of the strips in bag and shake to coat. Cook in hot oil for 3-4 minutes or until golden brown, turning occasionally. Drain on paper towels. Repeat with remaining potato strips. Sprinkle with additional Parmesan cheese if desired. **YIELD: 4-6 servings.**

clover crispies

- 3 tablespoons butter
- 4 cups large marshmallows (about 40)
- 1/4 teaspoon peppermint extract
- 6 cups crisp rice cereal
- 6 ounces white candy coating, chopped
- 4 drops green food coloring, optional

Green sprinkles

In a large saucepan, melt the butter. Add marshmallows; cook and stir over low heat until melted. Remove from the the heat; stir in extract and cereal; mix well. With buttered hands, press mixture into a greased foil-lined 13-in. x 9-in. pan. Cool completely on a wire rack.

Turn onto a cutting board; remove foil. Cut with a 3-in. shamrock cookie cutter; reshape shamrock stem if needed (save scraps for another use). In a microwave, melt candy coating. Stir in food coloring if desired. Spoon over cutouts and spread evenly. Decorate with sprinkles. Let stand until set. **YIELD: 15 servings.**

Summer

salute summer with this Memorial Day menu that spotlights Mary Jo Hopkins' grilled chicken entree. The Hobart, Indiana cook says it turns out perfect every time.

From Geneva, Illinois, Cathleen Bushman's tomato salad rounds out the menu nicely, as does a fruit pie from Nancy Barker of Silverton, Oregon.

grilled lemon-basil chicken

- 1   cup minced fresh basil
- 1   cup canola oil
- 1/2 cup lemon juice
- 1/4 cup white wine vinegar
- 2   teaspoons grated lemon peel
- 3   to 4 garlic cloves, minced
- 1   teaspoon salt
- 1/2 teaspoon pepper
- 8   boneless skinless chicken breast halves (6 ounces *each*)

In a small bowl, combine the first eight ingredients. Pour 1-1/2 cups into a large resealable plastic bag; add chicken. Seal bag and turn to coat; refrigerate for 4 hours or overnight, turning occasionally. Cover and refrigerate the remaining marinade for basting the next day.

Drain and discard marinade. Grill chicken, covered, over medium heat for 6-8 minutes on each side or a meat thermometer reads 170°, basting occasionally with reserved marinade. **YIELD:** 8 servings.

chilled tomato salad

- 3   large tomatoes, peeled and sliced
- 2   medium cucumbers, sliced
- 2   medium sweet red peppers, sliced into rings
- 2   medium green peppers, sliced into rings

DRESSING:
- 1/4 cup canola oil
- 1/4 cup minced fresh parsley
- 2   tablespoons white vinegar
- 2   teaspoons prepared mustard
- 1   teaspoon sugar
- 1   garlic clove, minced
- 1/4 teaspoon pepper

In a large serving bowl, combine the tomatoes, cucumbers and peppers. In a jar with a tight-fitting lid, combine the dressing ingredients; shake well. Pour over vegetables; toss gently to coat. Cover and refrigerate for at least 3 hours. Serve with a slotted spoon. **YIELD:** 8 servings.

star-studded blueberry pie

- 4   cups fresh *or* frozen blueberries
- 1   cup sugar
- 1/4 cup quick-cooking tapioca
- 1   tablespoon lemon juice
- 1/4 teaspoon salt

Pastry for double-crust pie (9 inches)
- 2   tablespoons butter

In a large bowl, combine the blueberries, sugar, tapioca, lemon juice and salt; toss gently. Let stand for 15 minutes. Line a 9-in. pie plate with bottom pastry; add filling. Dot with butter; flute edges.

Cover edges loosely with foil. Bake at 400° for 25 minutes. Remove foil; bake 20-25 minutes longer or until set. Cool on a wire rack.

From remaining pastry, cut out 15 large stars with a 2-in. cookie cutter and 15 small stars with a 1/2-in. cookie cutter. Place on an ungreased baking sheet. Bake at 350° for 5-10 minutes or until golden brown. Remove to wire racks to cool. Randomly place the stars over the cooled pie. **YIELD:** 8 servings.

dad's day

meals should be as fun as the man himself, so why not whet his appetite with this menu from our Test Kitchen? It's quick, easy and sure to lure dear old Dad to the table.

Share the bounty of the deep with flaky fish fillets that get a spicy twist from a handful of seasonings. Next, reel in compliments with a summery salad, corn muffins and a delectable chocolate dessert.

angler's delight

- 6 frozen haddock *or* cod fillets (6 ounces *each*), thawed
- 1/2 cup lime juice
- 1/2 cup all-purpose flour
- 2 tablespoons taco seasoning
- 1/2 teaspoon ground cumin
- 1/4 teaspoon cayenne pepper
- 3 tablespoons canola oil

In a large resealable plastic bag, combine fish and lime juice; seal bag and turn to coat. Let stand for 15 minutes. In a shallow dish, combine the flour, taco seasoning, cumin and cayenne. Drain fillets; coat with flour mixture.

In a large skillet, cook fillets in oil over medium-high heat for 6-8 minutes on each side or until fish flakes easily with a fork. **YIELD: 6 servings.**

bait and tackle salad

- 2 cups grape *or* cherry tomatoes
- 2 small zucchini, coarsely chopped
- 2 small yellow summer squash, coarsely chopped
- 2 tablespoons minced fresh cilantro
- 5 tablespoons white wine vinegar
- 3 tablespoons sugar

- 1 teaspoon Dijon mustard
- 1/4 teaspoon salt
- 1/8 teaspoon pepper
- 2 tablespoons olive oil

In a large bowl, combine tomatoes, zucchini, yellow squash and cilantro. In a blender, combine vinegar, sugar, mustard, salt and pepper. While processing, gradually add oil. Drizzle over vegetables; toss to coat. Cover and refrigerate for at least 20 minutes. **YIELD: 6 servings.**

cane pole corn muffins

- 1 package (8-1/2 ounces) corn bread/muffin mix
- 1/2 cup shredded cheddar cheese
- 1 jalapeno pepper, seeded and chopped
- 1 tablespoon minced chives
- 6 pieces fresh chives
- 6 pretzel sticks
- 3/4 cup miniature fish-shaped crackers
- 1/3 cup spreadable chive and onion cream cheese

Prepare corn bread batter according to package directions for muffins; stir in the cheddar cheese, jalapeno and minced chives. Fill greased muffin cups three-fourths full. Bake at 400° for 14-16 minutes or until golden brown. Cool for 5 minutes before removing from pan to a wire rack to cool completely.

For fishing poles, tie one end of a piece of chive to each pretzel stick and the other end to a fish cracker. Spread muffin tops with cream cheese. Insert a fishing pole into each muffin. Place on a serving platter. Sprinkle remaining fish crackers on platter. **YIELD: 6 muffins.**

editor's note: When cutting or seeding hot peppers, use rubber or plastic gloves to protect your hands. Avoid touching your face.

gone fishing mocha pie

- 1   **package (3 ounces) cream cheese, softened**
- 1/3 **cup hot fudge ice cream topping**
- 1   **chocolate crumb crust (9 inches)**
- 2   **packages (2.8 ounces** *each***) mocha mousse mix**
- 1-1/2 **cups whipped topping,** *divided*
- 1   **piece black shoestring licorice (about 8 inches)**
- 1   **gummy worm**

In a small bowl, beat cream cheese and hot fudge topping; drop by tablespoonfuls over crust and carefully spread. Prepare mousse mix according to package directions; fold in 1 cup whipped topping. Spread over cream cheese mixture. Chill for 20 minutes.

Place remaining whipped topping in a resealable plastic bag; cut a small hole in a corner of bag. Pipe "Gone Fishing" on pie. Insert a medium star pastry tip into bag; pipe topping around edges of pie. Position licorice on pie in the shape of a fishhook; add gummy worm. **YIELD: 6-8 servings.**

when warm weather rolls around it means eating meals outdoors...and that's a sunny change of pace. Whether it's a backyard barbecue with friends or a large family reunion, picnics are a great way to celebrate. And with the fuss-free recipes you'll find here, planning a pleasing summer menu is always a snap.

See the Kitchen Tip below for handy hints regarding this menu. You'll spend less time in the kitchen and have more time enjoying fun in the sun.

italian submarine

- 1   loaf (1 pound) unsliced Italian bread
- 2   to 3 tablespoons olive oil
- 2   to 4 tablespoons shredded Parmesan cheese
- 1   to 1-1/2 teaspoons dried oregano
- 1   medium tomato, thinly sliced
- 1/2   pound thinly sliced deli ham
- 1/4   pound sliced provolone cheese
- 1/4   pound thinly sliced hard salami

Cut loaf of bread in half lengthwise. Hollow out the bottom half, leaving a 1/4-in. shell (discard removed the bread or save for another use). Brush olive oil over the cut sides of bread.

Combine the Parmesan cheese and oregano; sprinkle over bread. On the bottom half, layer the tomato, ham, provolone and salami. Replace bread top. Slice before serving. **YIELD: 4 servings.**

lime fruit slushies

- 3/4   cup sugar
- 1   package (3 ounces) lime gelatin
- 1   cup boiling water
- 3   cups cold water
- 3   cups unsweetened pineapple juice
- 1   can (6 ounces) frozen orange juice concentrate, thawed
- 1   liter ginger ale, chilled

In a large container, dissolve sugar and gelatin in boiling water. Stir in the cold water, pineapple juice and orange juice concentrate. Freeze. Remove from the freezer 1-2 hours before serving. Stir in the ginger ale just before serving. **YIELD: 12 servings.**

grape melon medley

- 2   cups cubed cantaloupe
- 1-1/2   cups green grapes, halved
- 1-1/2   cups seedless red grapes, halved
- 1   can (11 ounces) mandarin oranges, drained
- 1/2   cup pineapple preserves

In a large bowl, combine the cantaloupe, grapes and oranges. Whisk the preserves; pour over the fruit mixture and toss to coat. Chill until serving. **YIELD: 8 servings.**

Kitchen Tip

"My husband's mother made Italian Submarines for him when he was kid. I like the recipe since it can be made a few hours in advance and kept in the refrigerator until you're ready to serve." —Christine Lupella, Fifty Lakes, MN

"A container of my lime slushies keeps items in a cooler cold." —Linda Horst, Newville, PA

"Feel free to add whatever fruits you have on hand to my Grape Melon Medley." —Doris Russell, Fallsont, MD

celebrate Independence Day—or most
any backyard occasion—with this mouthwatering three-course menu shared by our Test Kitchen home economists.

The all-American meal is a snap to prepare, so it's perfect for the lazy days of summer. And since both the main course and side dish cook on the grill, you don't need to spend hours over a hot stove.

To begin, fire up the coals for Teriyaki Turkey Burgers. Basted with a finger-licking teriyaki sauce, the pineapple-topped burgers are moist, tender and ready in minutes.

At the same time the burgers are sizzling, you can cook Grilled Honey-Ginger Corn, too. The perfect accompaniment to the tasty burgers, the corn has a sweet flavor that gets a no-fuss makeover with a little bit of honey, ground ginger and zippy cayenne pepper.

End the meal with a bang when you bring out cute and oh-so-easy Dipped Ice Cream Sandwiches. With just a few ingredients, these sweet frozen treats are sure to make your family ooh and aah on Independence Day and all summer long.

teriyaki turkey burgers

1	egg
1/2	cup dry bread crumbs
3	green onions, chopped
4	tablespoons teriyaki sauce, *divided*
1/4	teaspoon onion powder
1	pound ground turkey
1	can (8 ounces) sliced pineapple, drained
4	hamburger buns, split and toasted

In a large bowl, combine the egg, bread crumbs, onions, 2 tablespoons teriyaki sauce and onion powder. Crumble turkey over mixture and mix well. Shape into four 3/4-in.-thick patties.

Coat grill rack with nonstick cooking spray before starting the grill. Grill the patties, covered, over medium heat for 6-8 minutes on each side or until a meat thermometer reads 165°; brush with remaining teriyaki sauce during the last 5 minutes.

Grill pineapple slices for 3-4 minutes on each side or until heated through. Serve burgers and pineapple on buns. **YIELD: 4 servings.**

grilled honey-ginger corn

1/3	cup butter, softened
1	tablespoon minced chives
1	tablespoon honey
1/4	to 1/2 teaspoon ground ginger
1/8	teaspoon cayenne pepper
4	medium ears sweet corn

In a small bowl, combine the first five ingredients; spread over corn. Place each ear of corn on a double thickness of heavy-duty foil. Fold foil around corn and seal tightly. Grill, covered, over medium heat for 15-20 minutes or until tender, turning every 5 minutes. **YIELD: 4 servings.**

dipped ice cream sandwiches

6	squares (1 ounce *each*) semisweet chocolate, chopped
1	tablespoon shortening
4	ice cream sandwiches

Red, white and blue sprinkles

Line a baking sheet with waxed paper; set aside. In a microwave or heavy saucepan, melt chocolate and shortening; stir until smooth. Quickly dip ice cream sandwiches partway in melted chocolate; coat chocolate with sprinkles. Place on prepared baking sheet and freeze. **YIELD: 4 servings.**

Fall

halloween

halloween is tops with kids of all ages. So why not surprise your gang of goblins with this spooky spread?

Start with Rebecca Eremich's cute appetizer. The Barberton, Ohio cook uses cheese logs and cream cheese to create a mummified masterpiece.

For a quick and easy Halloween entree, Julianna Tazzia turns to her stuffed pepper jack-o'-lanterns. "I have time to get the little ones ready to go out trick-or-treating, yet they still get a hot meal," she writes from West Bloomfield, Michigan.

From Huntington Beach, California, Amy McCoy shares her cute Trick-or-Treat Cake. It couldn't be easier with a boxed cake mix and canned frosting.

trick-or-treat cake

- 1 package (18-1/4 ounces) chocolate cake mix
- 2 cans (16 ounces each) vanilla frosting
- 1 tube *each* black, orange and green decorating gel

Assorted candies

Prepare and bake cake according to package directions, using a greased and floured 13-in. x 9-in. baking pan. Cool for 10 minutes before removing from pan to a wire rack to cool completely.

Transfer the cake to a 20-in. x 17-in. covered board. Create a zigzag pattern on one short end of cake to resemble the top of a treat bag. Spread top and sides of cake with frosting; decorate, as desired, with gels and candies. **YIELD: 12 servings.**

worms for brains

- 8 to 10 medium sweet orange peppers
- 1 package (16 ounces) spaghetti
- 1 pound ground beef
- 1 jar (26 ounces) spaghetti sauce

Cut tops off peppers and set aside; remove seeds and membranes. Cut a jack-o'-lantern face on one side of each pepper; set aside.

Cook spaghetti according to package directions. Meanwhile, in a Dutch oven, cook beef over medium heat until no longer pink; drain.

Drain spaghetti and add to beef. Stir in spaghetti sauce; heat through. Spoon into peppers; replace tops. **YIELD: 8-10 servings.**

yummy mummy cheese spread

yummy mummy cheese spread

- 2 port wine cheese logs (12 ounces *each*)
- 1 package (8 ounces) cream cheese, softened
- 1 tablespoon milk
- 2 whole peppercorns
- 1 pimiento strip

Cut cheese logs into pieces for mummy's head, body, arms and legs; arrange on a serving plate.

In small bowl, beat cream cheese and milk. Cut a small hole in the corner of a pastry or plastic bag; insert basket weave tip #47. Pipe rows across the mummy, creating bandages. Add peppercorns for eyes and pimiento strip for mouth. Chill until serving. **YIELD: 1 cheese log.**

golden turkey is the hallmark of Thanksgiving. Our Test Kitchen shares this recipe along with a side from Tina McFarland of Elko, Nevada and a pie from Betty Milligan of Bedford, Indiana.

maple-butter turkey with gravy

2	cups apple cider *or* juice
1/3	cup maple syrup
3/4	cup butter, cubed
2	teaspoons dried thyme
1	teaspoon dried sage leaves
2	teaspoons dried marjoram
1	teaspoon *each* salt and pepper
1	turkey (14 to 16 pounds)
2	to 2-1/2 cups chicken broth
3	tablespoons all-purpose flour

For maple butter, in a small heavy saucepan, bring cider and syrup to a boil. Cook until reduced to 1/2 cup, about 20 minutes. Remove from the heat; stir in the next six ingredients. Transfer to a bowl; cover and refrigerate until set.

Carefully loosen the skin from both sides of turkey breast. Rub 1/2 cup maple butter under turkey skin. Refrigerate remaining maple butter. Skewer turkey openings; tie drumsticks together. Place on a rack in a roasting pan. Cover with foil and bake at 325° for 2 hours.

Brush top with 1/3 cup maple butter. Bake, uncovered, 1 to 1-1/2 hours longer or until a meat thermometer reads 180°, basting occasionally with pan drippings. (Cover loosely with foil if turkey browns too quickly.) Remove turkey to a serving platter and keep warm. Cover and let stand for 20 minutes before carving.

Pour drippings and loosened brown bits into a 4-cup measuring cup. Skim and discard fat. Add enough broth to drippings to measure 3 cups. In a large saucepan, combine flour and broth mixture until smooth. Stir in remaining maple butter. Bring to a boil; cook and stir for 2 minutes or until thickened. Serve with the turkey. **YIELD: 14-16 servings (3-1/3 cups gravy).**

mushrooms au gratin

2	pounds sliced fresh mushrooms
1/4	cup butter, cubed
1/2	cup white wine *or* chicken broth
2	tablespoons all-purpose flour
2/3	cup sour cream
1	teaspoon pepper
1/4	teaspoon ground nutmeg
1	cup (4 ounces) shredded Gruyere *or* Swiss cheese
2	tablespoons minced fresh parsley

In a large skillet, saute mushrooms in butter until tender. Add wine. Bring to a boil. Reduce heat; simmer, uncovered, for 4 minutes.

Combine the flour, sour cream, pepper and nutmeg until smooth; stir into mushrooms. Cook and stir for 1-2 minutes or until bubbly. Transfer to a shallow serving dish. Sprinkle with cheese and parsley. **YIELD: 8 servings.**

persimmon squash pie

1	unbaked pastry shell (9 inches)
1/4	cup buttermilk
1/2	cup mashed cooked butternut squash
1/2	cup mashed ripe persimmon pulp
3/4	cup sugar
1/4	cup packed brown sugar
3	tablespoons all-purpose flour
1/2	teaspoon ground cinnamon
1/4	teaspoon baking powder

1/4	teaspoon baking soda
1/4	teaspoon salt
2	eggs
1/4	cup heavy whipping cream
1/4	cup butter, melted
1	teaspoon vanilla extract

CARAMEL TOPPING:

30	caramels
2	tablespoons milk
1/3	cup chopped pecans
1/3	cup English toffee bits *or* almond brickle chips

Bake unpricked pastry shell at 450° for 5-6 minutes or until lightly browned; cool on a wire rack. Reduce heat to 350°.

In a blender, combine the buttermilk, squash and persimmon pulp; cover and process until smooth. In a large bowl, combine the sugars, flour, cinnamon, baking powder, baking soda and salt. In a small bowl, combine the eggs, cream, butter, vanilla and squash mixture; stir into dry ingredients just until moistened.

Pour into pastry shell. Bake for 40-45 minutes or until a knife inserted in the center of the pie comes out clean.

In a small saucepan, combine caramels and milk. Cook and stir over medium heat until melted and smooth. Pour over hot pie. Sprinkle with pecans and toffee bits. Cool completely on a wire rack. Store in the refrigerator. **YIELD: 8 servings.**

simple dinners

don't mean you have to sacrifice flavor. This year, make holiday meals a snap with this effortless menu. Each of the following dishes requires a handful of items.

From Ingleside, Texas, Cindy Carlson shares Moist Turkey Breast. A few seasonings and a bottle of Italian dressing make this the tastiest, and easiest, bird you've ever prepared. Serve it with the wonderful garlic-flavored gravy from Hannah Thompson of Scotts Valley, California.

Holiday meals just wouldn't be complete without mashed potatoes and stuffing. You'll adore these versions from Caroline Sperry, Shelby Township, Michigan and Taryn Kuebelbeck, Plymouth, Minnesota respectively.

moist turkey breast

- 1   bone-in turkey breast (about 7 pounds)
- 1   teaspoon garlic powder
- 1/2 teaspoon onion powder
- 1/2 teaspoon salt
- 1/4 teaspoon pepper
- 1-1/2 cups Italian dressing

Place turkey breast in a greased 13-in. x 9-in. baking dish. Combine the seasonings; sprinkle over turkey. Pour dressing over the top.

Cover and bake at 325° for 2 to 2-1/2 hours or until a meat thermometer reads 170°, basting occasionally with pan drippings. Let stand for 10 minutes before slicing. **YIELD: 12-14 servings.**

seasoned garlic gravy

- 1   teaspoon minced garlic
- 3   tablespoons butter
- 1/4 cup all-purpose flour
- 1/2 teaspoon poultry seasoning
- 1/8 teaspoon pepper
- 2   cups chicken broth

In a small saucepan, saute garlic in butter until tender. Stir in the flour, poultry seasoning and pepper; gradually add broth. Bring to a boil; cook and stir for 1-2 minutes or until thickened. **YIELD: 2 cups.**

sour cream mashed potatoes

- 2   pounds red potatoes, quartered
- 1   cup (8 ounces) sour cream
- 2   tablespoons minced fresh parsley
- 1   teaspoon salt
- 1/2 teaspoon garlic powder
- 1/2 teaspoon pepper

Place potatoes in a large saucepan and cover with water. Bring to a boil. Reduce heat; cover and simmer for 15-20 minutes or until tender.

Drain and transfer to a large bowl. Add all of the remaining ingredients and beat mixture until blended. **YIELD: 5 servings.**

dried fruit stuffing

- 1   package (6 ounces) stuffing mix
- 1/2 cup dried cranberries
- 1/2 cup chopped pitted dried plums
- 1/2 cup chopped dried apricots
- 1/3 cup slivered almonds, toasted

Prepare stuffing mix according to package directions, adding dried fruits when adding contents of stuffing mix. Just before serving, stir in almonds. **YIELD: 4 cups.**

Winter

magical
memories are sure to abound this holiday season with a Christmas dinner that friends and family won't soon forget.

Guests will realize this is no ordinary event when you set Carol Stevens' rib roast on the table. It's a highlight at her Basye, Virginia home.

A simple salad gets a wonderful treatment with poached pears from Park Hills, Missouri's Barbara Hahn. In addition, Jamie Milligan of Kimberley, British Columbia gives the Yuletide a tasty twist by adding sun-dried tomatoes to her potato side dish.

herbed standing rib roast

3	tablespoons grated onion
2	tablespoons olive oil
4	garlic cloves, minced
2	teaspoons celery seed
1	teaspoon coarsely ground pepper
1	teaspoon paprika
1/4	teaspoon dried thyme
1	bone-in beef rib roast (6 to 7 pounds)
2	large onions, cut into wedges
2	large carrots, cut into 2-inch pieces

2 celery ribs, cut into 2-inch pieces
1/4 cup red wine *or* beef broth
Assorted herbs and fruit, optional

In a bowl, combine the first seven ingredients; rub over roast. Place the onions, carrots and celery in a large roasting pan; place roast over vegetables.

Bake, uncovered, at 325° for 1-3/4 to 2-1/2 hours or until meat reaches desired doneness (for medium-rare, a meat thermometer should read 145°; medium, 160°; well-done, 170°).

Remove roast to a serving platter and keep warm; let stand for 15 minutes before slicing.

Meanwhile, for au jus, strain and discard vegetables. Pour drippings into a measuring cup; skim fat. Add wine to roasting pan, stirring to remove any browned bits. Stir in drippings; heat through. Serve with roast. Garnish platter with herbs and fruit if desired. **YIELD: 10-12 servings.**

sun-dried tomato scalloped potatoes

1 jar (7 ounces) oil-packed sun-dried tomatoes, drained and patted dry
1/2 cup grated Parmesan cheese
2 tablespoons chopped fresh basil
2 tablespoons chopped fresh parsley
1 garlic clove, peeled
1/4 teaspoon salt
7 cups sliced peeled potatoes
2 cups (8 ounces) shredded cheddar cheese
1 cup chicken broth

Place the first six ingredients in a food processor; cover and process until blended. In a greased 3-qt. baking dish, layer half of the potatoes, tomato mixture and cheese. Repeat layers. Pour broth over top.

Cover and bake at 325° for 1-1/2 hours. Uncover; bake 15 minutes longer or until potatoes are tender. Let stand for 10 minutes before serving. **YIELD: 10 servings.**

poached pears with mixed greens

2 medium ripe Bartlett pears
1/2 cup dry red wine *or* grape juice
1 tablespoon red wine vinegar
1 teaspoon sugar
1 teaspoon olive oil
1/4 teaspoon salt
1/8 teaspoon cayenne pepper
1/8 teaspoon pepper
8 cups fresh arugula *or* baby spinach
2 cups torn curly *or* Belgian endive
1/4 cup crumbled blue cheese
3 tablespoons chopped walnuts

Peel, core and quarter the pears. Place cut side down in an 11-in. x 7-in. baking dish. Add the wine. Bake, uncovered, at 350° for 15-20 minutes or until crisp-tender. Drain, reserving 1 tablespoon liquid. Cool pears to room temperature.

For dressing, in a small bowl, whisk the vinegar, sugar, oil, salt, cayenne, pepper and the reserved poaching liquid. Thinly slice the pears. In a large salad bowl, combine the arugula, endive and pears. Drizzle with dressing; toss to coat. Sprinkle with blue cheese and walnuts. **YIELD: 10 servings.**

poached pears with mixed greens

warm up holiday gatherings with a quick cheese ball from Susan Seymour, Valatie, New York and open-faced sandwiches from Margaret Pache of Mesa, Arizona. Need a New Year's nibble? Try Peggy Allen's Shrimp Cocktail. She shares the recipe from Pasadena, California.

garlic-parmesan cheese ball

    2   packages (one 8 ounces, one 3 ounces)
        cream cheese, softened
  1/3   cup grated Parmesan cheese
  1/4   cup mayonnaise
  1/2   teaspoon dried oregano
  1/4   teaspoon garlic powder *or* 1/2 to 1
        teaspoon minced garlic
  3/4   cup chopped walnuts, optional
Assorted fresh vegetables *and/or* crackers

In a large bowl, combine the first five ingredients. Shape into a ball. Roll in walnuts if desired. Chill for 2 hours. Serve with vegetables and/or crackers. **YIELD: about 2 cups.**

beef 'n' pepper bread slices

    2   cups shredded cooked roast beef
  1/2   cup mayonnaise
  1/4   cup plain yogurt
    2   green onions, chopped
    1   jalapeno pepper, seeded and chopped
    2   tablespoons prepared horseradish
    2   teaspoons lemon juice
  1/2   teaspoon grated lemon peel
    1   loaf (1 pound) French bread, halved
        lengthwise
    1   jar (7-1/4 ounces) roasted sweet red
        peppers, drained and chopped

1-1/2   cups (6 ounces) shredded pepper Jack
        cheese
  1/4   cup minced fresh parsley

In a small bowl, combine the first eight ingredients. Spread the mixture over the cut sides of the French bread. Place on an ungreased baking sheet. Top with roasted red peppers; sprinkle with the pepper Jack cheese and parsley.

Bake at 450° for 8-10 minutes or until bread is golden and cheese is melted. Cut into slices. Serve warm. **YIELD: 10-12 servings.**

shrimp cocktail

    3   quarts water
    1   small onion, sliced
  1/2   medium lemon, sliced
    2   sprigs fresh parsley
    1   tablespoon salt
    5   whole peppercorns
  1/4   teaspoon dried thyme
    1   bay leaf
    3   pounds uncooked large shrimp, peeled
        and deveined (tails on)
SAUCE:
    1   cup chili sauce
    2   tablespoons lemon juice
    2   tablespoons prepared horseradish
    4   teaspoons Worcestershire sauce
  1/2   teaspoon salt
Dash cayenne pepper

In a Dutch oven, combine the water, onion, lemon, parsley, salt, peppercorns, thyme and bay leaf. Bring to a boil. Add the shrimp. Reduce heat; simmer, uncovered, for 4-5 minutes or until the shrimp turn pink.

Drain shrimp and immediately rinse in cold water. Refrigerate for 2-3 hours. In a small bowl, combine the sauce ingredients. Refrigerate until serving.

Arrange shrimp on a serving platter; serve with sauce. **YIELD: about 6 dozen (1-1/4 cups sauce).**

mom's best made easy

show some heartfelt affection for your loved one on Valentine's Day by setting a pretty table for two and serving an enchanted dinner.

Skip an expensive meal at a restaurant and head to your own kitchen to prepare impressive Coq au Vin from our home economists. With chicken, mushrooms and onions cooked in wine, this fancy French stew is sure to capture the attention of your one and only.

You'll fall for our simple Sweetheart Salad as well. It calls for just four ingredients and tosses together in moments.

Then don't forget to dote on your dear with Chocolate Cream Dip and sliced fruit. Lois Zigarac of Rochester Hills, Michigan sent the delightful topping that's sure to be a hit in your home.

towels. Sprinkle chicken with salt and pepper. Brown chicken in the drippings; remove and keep warm. Add onions to drippings; saute until crisp-tender. Add mushrooms and garlic; saute 3-4 minutes longer or until almost tender.

Combine flour and broth; stir into onion mixture. Add wine or additional broth, bay leaf and thyme; bring to a boil. Return chicken and bacon to the pan. Reduce heat; cover and simmer for 25-30 minutes or until a meat thermometer reads 170°.

Remove chicken and keep warm. Cook sauce over medium heat until slightly thickened. Discard bay leaf. Serve chicken and sauce with noodles. **YIELD: 2 servings.**

coq au vin

4	cups water
1	cup pearl onions
4	bacon strips, cut into 1-inch pieces
2	bone-in chicken breast halves (8 ounces *each*)
1/4	teaspoon salt
1/8	teaspoon pepper
3/4	cup sliced fresh mushrooms
2	garlic cloves, minced
4-1/2	teaspoons all-purpose flour
3/4	cup chicken broth
3/4	cup white wine *or* additional chicken broth
1	bay leaf
1/2	teaspoon dried thyme

Hot cooked noodles

In a large saucepan, bring water to a boil. Add onions; boil for 3 minutes. Drain and rinse in cold water; peel and set aside.

In a large skillet, cook bacon over medium heat until crisp. Using a slotted spoon, remove to paper

chocolate cream dip

4	ounces cream cheese, softened
1-1/2	cups whipped topping
1/2	cup caramel ice cream topping
1/4	cup chocolate ice cream topping

Sliced apples and graham cracker sticks

In a small bowl, beat cream cheese until smooth. Beat in the whipped topping and ice cream toppings until blended. Transfer to a serving bowl. Serve with apples and graham cracker sticks. **YIELD: 2 cups.**

sweetheart salad

3	cups spring mix salad greens
1/4	cup dried cranberries
1/4	cup balsamic vinaigrette
2	tablespoons honey-roasted sliced almonds

Divide salad greens and cranberries between two salad plates. Drizzle with vinaigrette and sprinkle with almonds. **YIELD: 2 servings.**

alphabetical recipe index

Refer to this index for a complete alphabetical listing of all recipes in this book.

general recipe index

This handy index lists every recipe by its food category, major ingredient and/or cooking method.